ABSOLUTE BEGINNER'S GUIDE

Microsoft® Office
OneNote™ 2003

Patricia Cardoza

800 East 96th Street,
Indianapolis, Indiana 46240

Absolute Beginner's Guide to Microsoft® Office OneNote™ 2003

International Standard Book Number: 0-7897-3148-7

Library of Congress Catalog Card Number: 2004100881

Printed in the United States of America

First Printing: April 2004

09   08   07   4   3   2

Trademarks

Warning and Disclaimer

Bulk Sales

Que Publishing offers excellent discounts on this book when ordered in quantity for bulk purchases or special sales. For more information, please contact

U.S. Corporate and Government Sales
1-800-382-3419
corpsales@pearsontechgroup.com

For sales outside of the U.S., please contact

International Sales
international@pearsoned.com

Publisher
Paul Boger

Associate Publisher
Greg Wiegand

Acquisitions Editor
Stephanie J. McComb

Development Editor
Laura Norman

Managing Editor
Charlotte Clapp

Project Editor
Tricia Liebig

Production Editor
Benjamin Berg

Indexer
Mandie Frank

Proofreader
Katie Robinson

Technical Editor
Ben Schorr

Publishing Coordinator
Sharry Lee Gregory

Interior Designer
Anne Jones

Cover Designer
Anne Jones

Contents at a Glance

Table of Contents

About the Author

Patricia Cardoza is an Exchange and Outlook applications developer, writer, avid OneNote user, and Microsoft Outlook MVP. Patricia currently serves as Exchange administrator and lead developer for Pacific Southwest Container, a large manufacturing company. She has authored two other books, *Special Edition Using Microsoft Office Outlook 2003* and *Access 2003 VBA Programmer's Reference*. She has also written numerous articles about Outlook, Exchange, and wireless devices for a variety of journals including *.NET Magazine* and *Tech Republic*. In her spare time, she loves to cook, read, watch movies with her husband, and spoil her cats.

Dedication

This book is dedicated to my wonderful husband, Rob, for his patience during the long hours I spent at the computer every night. To my parents, I love you both. And to my very spoiled cats, thanks for not biting me when I ignored you for nights on end.

Acknowledgments

There's a lot that goes into writing a book. Before I wrote my first book, I had no idea there were so many people involved in the process. But each person who works on a book such as this is vital to the book's success. I would like to thank Senior Acquisitions Editor Stephanie McComb for giving me the opportunity to write this book. I love OneNote, and I jumped at this opportunity. This is the second time I've worked with Laura Norman, the best development editor any author could ask for. She's always responded to any of my questions quickly and completely. I'd also like to thank Ben Berg, the copy editor, for making sure all of my sentences actually made sense. Tricia Liebig, the project editor, helped keep me true to my deadlines and ensured the entire production process ran smoothly. I'd also like to thank my technical editor, Ben Schorr, a OneNote MVP and a friend.

Lastly, I need to thank the entire group of Outlook MVPs. I've known these people for several years now, and I learn from them every day. Thanks to Sue, Diane, Ken, Jessie Louise, Russ, Vince, Robert, Jay, Hollis, Jocelyn, Bill, Milly, Steve, Dmitry, Nikki, Thomas, Peter, Randy, and Patrick.

We Want to Hear from You!

As the reader of this book, *you* are our most important critic and commentator. We value your opinion and want to know what we're doing right, what we could do better, what areas you'd like to see us publish in, and any other words of wisdom you're willing to pass our way.

As an associate publisher for Que Publishing, I welcome your comments. You can email or write me directly to let me know what you did or didn't like about this book—as well as what we can do to make our books better.

Please note that I cannot help you with technical problems related to the topic of this book. We do have a User Services group, however, where I will forward specific technical questions related to the book.

When you write, please be sure to include this book's title and author as well as your name, email address, and phone number. I will carefully review your comments and share them with the author and editors who worked on the book.

Email: feedback@quepublishing.com

Mail: Greg Wiegand
Associate Publisher
Que Publishing
800 East 96th Street
Indianapolis, IN 46240 USA

For more information about this book or another Que Publishing title, visit our Web site at www.quepublishing.com. Type the ISBN (excluding hyphens) or the title of a book in the Search field to find the page you're looking for.

INTRODUCTION

OneNote, the focus of this book, is a powerful note-taking program. OneNote allows you to type your notes or use your Tablet PC's pen to write your notes. Through features such as Note Flags, highlighting, and collaboration with other applications, OneNote can help you with organizing your notes for business, school, or home.

I've been using OneNote since it was first introduced in the Office beta program. I don't just use it to write about it; I use it in my everyday work. This book was written as my company was going through a major software upgrade project. Throughout the project I used OneNote to keep myself organized. After reading this book, I hope you'll find OneNote as valuable as I do.

How This Book Helps You Learn OneNote

All this power doesn't do you much good if you don't know how to use it. *The Absolute Beginner's Guide to Microsoft Office OneNote 2003* is truly designed for the OneNote novice. If you've never even installed the program, or if you've fiddled around with it a little and want to learn more, this book can help. Even though you don't need any previous OneNote experience, this book does assume that you have some basic computer knowledge. You should be familiar with opening and closing files, using the mouse, and have some basic experience browsing the Internet.

You begin by learning the basic building blocks of OneNote. You'll learn the difference between pages, sections, and folders, as well as learn how to create detailed outlines and to-do lists. Finally, I'll give you some detailed examples of how to use OneNote in the real world.

How This Book Is Organized

This book is organized into five parts. Each part builds on the previous part. *The Absolute Beginner's Guide to Microsoft Office OneNote 2003* can be used in two different ways. You can use it as a total learning tool and read each chapter in order, or you can use it as a reference book, jumping directly to the chapter you need. While some chapters might need more review than others, each chapter provides information you can use in later chapters. Chapter 5 is the one exception. It's designed for Tablet PC users and covers how to use the Tablet PC's pen within OneNote. If you don't have a Tablet PC, you can skip that chapter.

Part 1, "Learning to Take Notes"

Before you can work with OneNote, you must understand the various components of the application. You'll learn how to take your first note, and just a little about organizing the information within your notes.

Part 2, "Taking Your First Notes"

If you're using OneNote on a Tablet PC, you can take advantage of the special features of the pen to make your note taking easier. From changing ink colors and highlighting to drawing diagrams and other objects within your notes, your tablet's pen can enhance your note-taking experience.

Part 3, "Managing and Printing Your OneNote Files"

Like any notebook or filing system, when you compile more than a page or two of information, you're bound to need some way of organizing that information. The chapters within this part are designed to help you open, save, move, and organize the various pages, sections, and folders within OneNote.

Part 4, "Organizing Information Within Pages"

Each OneNote page has several components of its own. This part will help you manipulate the notes you take by adding bulleted lists, numbers, Note Flags, and highlighting. You'll also learn how to add sound and pictures to your notes.

Part 5, "Going Further with OneNote"

This part explores the integration between OneNote and other applications. You'll learn how to share information with others through email and SharePoint Team Services, as well as see examples of OneNote in action in a variety of situations.

Appendixes

This book contains several appendixes that cover topics such as installing OneNote, getting help with OneNote, and the various keyboard shortcuts you can use in OneNote.

Conventions Used in This Book

Each chapter in the book begins with a bulleted list of "In This Chapter" highlights that outline what you're about to learn. At the end of each chapter, you'll find a summary of key concepts that were covered within the chapter in "The Absolute Minimum."

In addition, there are three different types of special information that appear throughout the book. Notes provide more in-depth information about a particular topic, tips help you perform a process more efficiently, and cautions identify potential problems.

note

A note provides some in-depth information about a topic. You can safely skip the information in notes while you're learning OneNote.

tip

Tips provide helpful information that can save you time while you work.

caution

Cautions identify potential problems you want to avoid while working with OneNote.

Final Thoughts

I hope you find this book helpful and enjoyable. If you have any suggestions, comments, or questions, email me at patricia@mvps.org. I will do my best to respond to all emails I receive.

PART I

LEARNING TO TAKE NOTES

1

JOIN THE DIGITAL NOTE TAKING REVOLUTION

Microsoft Office Systems OneNote 2003, a new member of the extended Office product family, might seem at first glance like little more than a digital notepad—a place to scribble notes and draw pictures. That's not entirely incorrect. OneNote can function just like a yellow legal pad. You can take notes, draw pictures, highlight, and scratch out text. However, OneNote is much more.

OneNote allows you to flag important items within your notes and search for them later. You can paste information from Internet Explorer, insert images, move notes around between pages and sections, and create Outlook tasks directly from your notes. In this chapter you'll get a brief glimpse at all of these features.

OneNote: More Than Just a Digital Notepad

In order to understand what OneNote can do for you, this chapter starts by breaking down OneNote's features into several different categories.

Capture a Wide Variety of Information

With OneNote, you can capture a wide variety of information in multiple ways. You can begin by typing or using a Tablet PC pen to write anywhere on the screen. Recording audio notes is also easy with OneNote. Besides simply recording audio, OneNote keeps track of what you were typing or writing at the time the note was recorded. When you replay your audio recording, OneNote highlights the text you were typing or writing at the time the audio was recorded.

You can draw diagrams and pictures directly on your notes using your mouse, Tablet PC's pen, or other external input device such as a graphire. You can also insert graphics and other information directly from the Internet. Whenever you insert information from a Web page, OneNote also inserts the Web address so you can refer back to the source Web page at a later date. For a preview of the types of information OneNote can capture, see Figure 1.1.

FIGURE 1.1

A OneNote note page can contain figures, text, graphics, and pasted Internet Information.

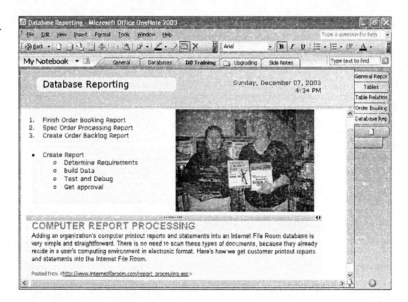

Organize Your Information

One of the biggest drawbacks to those yellow legal pads is that if you need to add information within a list you created, it's almost impossible to insert information between items already present in the list. With OneNote, you can easily move lines, paragraphs, or whole pages of information anywhere within the application.

Figure 1.2 shows a list taken during an application training class. If your instructor suddenly remembers that he forgot to tell you about "Step 5: Test Your Code," you can easily position your cursor after Step 4, click Enter, and add that missing step. The subsequent steps renumber themselves automatically so your notes are always up-to-date.

FIGURE 1.2

Create detailed lists in OneNote that are easily modified.

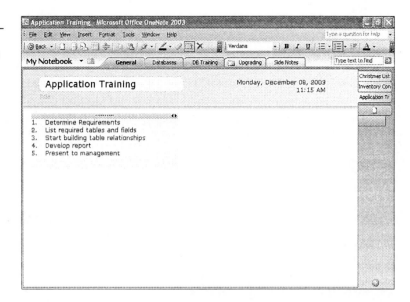

OneNote has a variety of structural components such as pages, folders, sections, and note containers. You can easily add or rearrange any of these components to suit your needs.

Another drawback of a paper notepad is that it's quite difficult to scan through multiple pages of notes to find a specific word or phrase. OneNote can search text and ink (*ink* is the name for information written with a Tablet PC's pen) for a specific term and can display the search results for you.

Note flags are used to highlight important information within a note. There are nine customizable note flags you can use to categorize information within your notes.

Share Your Notes with Others

OneNote stores information in files with a .one extension. You can manipulate those files much like any other type of file. You can open, close, and share those files with others. If you have Outlook 2003, you can email your OneNote files to other users directly within OneNote, as shown in Figure 1.3. Even if you don't have Outlook 2003, you can still email the .one files just like any other type of file attachment.

FIGURE 1.3

Use Outlook 2003 to email OneNote files to others.

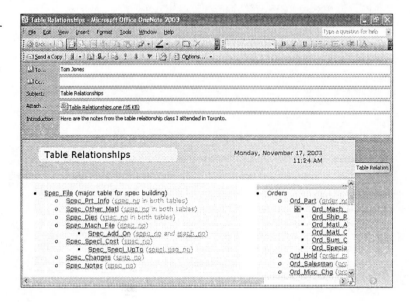

You can convert your OneNote pages to a Web page format as well.

I Don't Have a Tablet—Can I Use OneNote?

If you listen to all of the marketing information on OneNote, you might wonder if it's beneficial for a laptop or desktop user. The short answer is yes, you can still benefit from OneNote. While certain features are only easily usable on a Tablet PC, there are very few capabilities of OneNote you can't use on a desktop or a laptop.

In order to demonstrate the differences between using OneNote on a desktop and on a Tablet PC, I'll demonstrate the process of taking the same notes on two different computers using OneNote. You'll see that both a Tablet and a non-Tablet (desktop or laptop) can take effective notes.

tip

If you have access to a Windows SharePoint Server, you can even place your OneNote files on that server and allow multiple people to access them. While two people can't work on the same OneNote page at the same time, it's possible for one person to change a page and another user to see those changes within just a few minutes.

As you can see from Figure 1.4, the desktop computer takes very legible notes. Several bulleted lists are visible, and you can use highlighting and underlining for emphasis.

FIGURE 1.4

Using OneNote on a laptop or desktop can provide very detailed, legible notes.

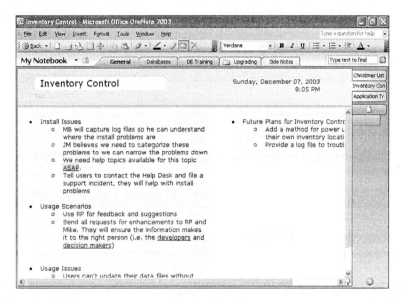

If you had been in that same meeting using a Tablet PC, your notes might look something like Figure 1.5. The first difference you'll notice is that fewer notes are visible on the screen at any one time. (Unless you write really small, typed notes will almost always take up less space than written notes.)

If you have poor handwriting, you'll probably like taking notes on a laptop or desktop instead of on a Tablet. There are a few words in Figure 1.5 that aren't completely legible. If you're trying to write as fast as the speaker is talking, you might have a hard time reading those notes later.

It can be slightly easier to highlight or emphasize items within your note while using a Tablet. It's quite simple to quickly change the pen from the thin black pen to a colored highlighter for emphasis.

The last main difference between using OneNote on a Tablet PC and a desktop or laptop PC is that you can draw on a Tablet PC as shown in Figure 1.6. You might want to draw a flow chart or diagram while taking notes. Doing that on a laptop or desktop can be cumbersome at best. While you can change the mouse pointer to a pen even on a laptop computer, drawing with a mouse or touch pad isn't as accurate as using the Tablet's pen.

FIGURE 1.5

Taking notes on a Tablet produces different results than a laptop or desktop.

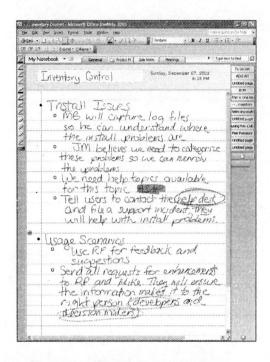

FIGURE 1.6

Using a Tablet makes it easy to draw inside your notes.

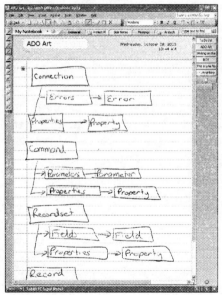

What's the Difference Between OneNote and the Tablet PC's Journal?

If you have a Tablet PC, you've probably played around with the Tablet's Windows Journal program. The Journal is a good program and has some of the same features as OneNote. You can write anywhere on the screen, draw pictures, highlight, and even insert flags for important information. Figure 1.7 shows the same information in Figure 1.5 duplicated in the Journal. You'll notice a few key differences.

FIGURE 1.7

The Tablet PC's Windows Journal has some of the same features as OneNote.

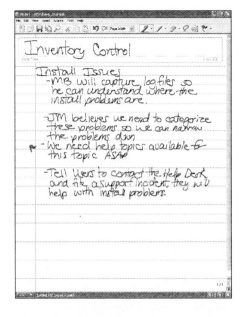

First, there are no bullets in the Journal. You can draw them in, as shown in the figure, but they won't automatically indent themselves like they will in OneNote.

Second, all you can see on the screen is the note you're currently working on. With OneNote, if you have other pages in the same section, you're able to see their names easily no matter what page you're currently viewing.

Even with the few differences noted previously, the two programs are definitely similar. If you were to liken OneNote and the Windows Journal to Word and WordPad, you might say that OneNote is to Journal as Word is to WordPad. Both programs are powerful. Both have the ability to take notes and store drawings. However, in much the same ways as WordPad doesn't have all the features of Microsoft Word, the Windows Journal doesn't have all the sophisticated searching and organizational features that OneNote does.

Starting OneNote and Taking Your First Note

To launch OneNote for the first time and start taking notes, you have two options. To launch OneNote from the Start menu, select Start, All Programs, Microsoft Office, and choose Microsoft Office OneNote 2003. OneNote opens to the General section and displays a blank page. You can click anywhere on the page and start typing.

You can also launch OneNote from the system tray. OneNote places an icon in the system tray with a purple *N*. You can click that icon with your right mouse button to display the OneNote Quick Launch menu, shown in Figure 1.8. Select Open OneNote to launch OneNote. Click anywhere on the page and start typing your first note.

FIGURE 1.8

You can launch OneNote from the system tray.

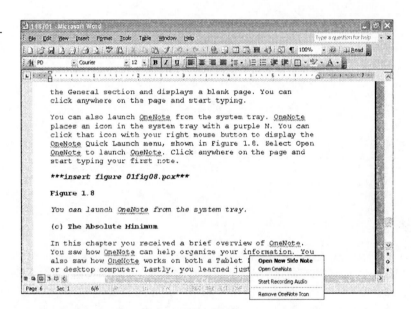

You can use OneNote to store a wide variety of information. As shown in Figure 1.9, you can insert notes, pictures, hyperlinks, and audio recordings.

OneNote is made up of a variety of structures. The tabs at the top of Figure 1.9 represent sections. Each section is its own file within Windows with an extension of .one. The tabs along the side of the screen represent pages. You can have multiple pages within each section. Each of the groups of notes on the page is a note container. You can create multiple note containers on every page.

We'll cover each of these structures in detail in later chapters.

FIGURE 1.9

You can store a variety of information in OneNote.

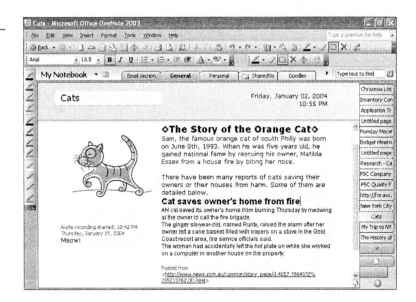

THE ABSOLUTE MINIMUM

In this chapter you received a brief overview of OneNote. You learned

▓ How OneNote can help organize your information.

▓ How OneNote works on both a Tablet PC and a laptop or desktop computer.

▓ A few of the differences between OneNote and the Windows Journal.

Now you're ready to learn some of the basic components of OneNote. The next chapter covers examples of OneNote in action.

IN THIS CHAPTER

- Using OneNote for college classes
- Using OneNote for business meetings
- Using OneNote for personal use
- Using OneNote in journalism
- Using OneNote for collaboration and project planning

2

EXAMPLES OF ONENOTE IN ACTION

OneNote is a very flexible program. There are no rules for the type of information you can record in OneNote. From text to handwriting, links to pictures, you can capture many forms of information in a variety of different ways.

This chapter focuses on a wide variety of examples of how to use OneNote. We'll cover a few potential types of OneNote uses in this chapter, college classes, business meetings, journalism, and project planning. The examples in this chapter utilize both the Tablet PC and a conventional laptop or desktop.

Using OneNote to Take Notes in Class

OneNote is quite popular with college students. You can create a section for each class and keep an entire semester's worth of notes in the section. When you're done with the class, close and back up the section. Figure 2.1 shows a typical OneNote window for a college biology class. As you can see from the figure, Sally has a section for each of her five classes.

FIGURE 2.1

You can create a section for each class and multiple pages for each class.

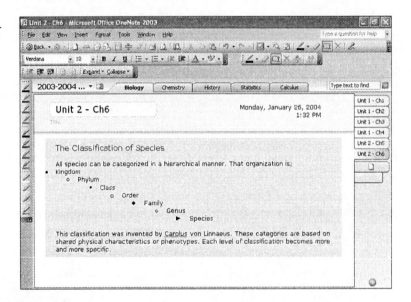

As you can see from the figure, there are a large number of pages within the Biology section. Every lecture receives its own page in the section. When it comes time for a test, all Sally needs to do is review the appropriate pages.

With OneNote's search capabilities, Sally can search all the pages within her biology notes for the relevant topics. To search for cell membrane, Sally can type `cell membrane` in the search box directly above the page tabs and press Enter on the keyboard. Sally's search results are shown in Figure 2.2.

note

For more information about creating multiple sections, opening, and closing sections, see "Working with Note Files," Chapter 6.

FIGURE 2.2

Students can easily search through multiple pages of notes.

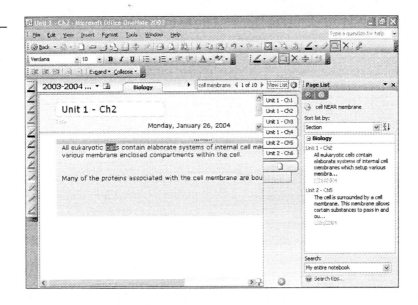

Using a Tablet PC can be quite helpful for several types of classes. Chemistry and calculus classes in particular don't lend themselves to only typewritten notes. Chemical reactions and calculus equations often need handwritten structures for clarity. Figure 2.3 illustrates how well OneNote captures handwritten chemistry notes.

You can search through handwritten notes in the same manner as typewritten notes. The only limitation you'll encounter when searching for handwritten notes is that unless OneNote recognizes your writing as text (as opposed to recognizing it as a drawing), you won't be able to search for that text. In Figure 2.3, you cannot search for the chemical symbols displayed in the figure, only the text surrounding them.

OneNote includes many templates you can use, including several designed for taking notes in class. The History Class template is shown in Figure 2.4.

note

For more information about using OneNote to capture more than just text, see "A Picture Is Worth a Thousand Words," Chapter 12.

FIGURE 2.3

Using a Tablet PC can capture handwritten equations and structures.

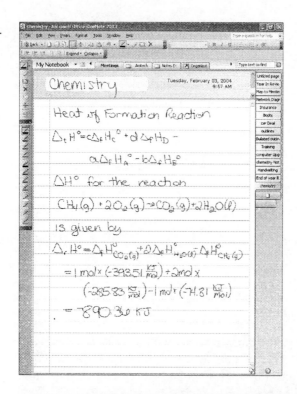

FIGURE 2.4

OneNote includes a variety of templates.

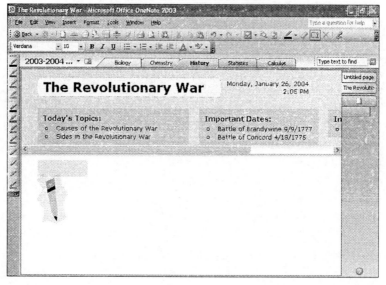

Using OneNote for Meetings

It's rare to attend a meeting these days and not take notes. If you know you'll have tasks to complete from the meeting, it's definitely a good idea to take notes. Figure 2.5 shows a typical page of meeting notes. As you can see, there are a variety of structures utilized within the note page.

There are several types of structures utilized in Figure 2.5. To-Do lists can help you keep track of the action items from the meeting. You can flag notes as Important, Remember for Later, Definitions, and even customize your own Note

For more information about creating templates, see "Creating Your Own OneNote Templates," in Chapter 4.

Flags. Later, you can use OneNote's Note Flags Summary task pane, shown in Figure 2.6, to display all of your flagged items. This Task pane makes it easy for you to find all the notes you flagged over a variety of pages.

FIGURE 2.5

A page of meeting notes can contain a variety of OneNote structures.

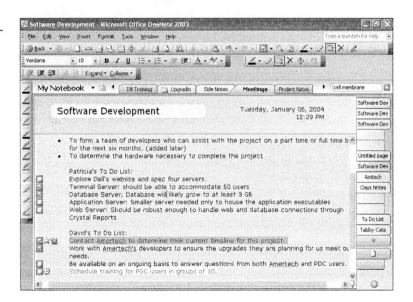

In addition to Note Flags, if you have Outlook 2003 along with OneNote, you can create Outlook tasks directly from OneNote. As shown in Figure 2.7, creating an Outlook task from OneNote allows you to insert portions of your note page into your Outlook task. Creating a task allows you to set a reminder, assign the task to others, or create a recurring task.

After a long session of note-taking, you might want to read over your notes and make some subtle changes. For example, you can turn some of your notes into an outline. While you're in a meeting, you might not have time to carefully format an outline. OneNote makes it easy to turn existing text into an outline by selecting lines of text and clicking the bullet or numbering buttons on the toolbar.

OneNote also allows you to share information with other users. If your colleague missed the meeting, you can forward him a copy of the meeting notes through Outlook 2003. By choosing E-mail from the File menu, you can send the current OneNote page through Outlook 2003, as shown in Figure 2.8.

As you can see from the figure, the OneNote page is preserved in its original format. You can add an introduction and send the note to any other OneNote 2003 user. They can open the email and view the OneNote page, or double-click the attached .one file and open the note in a special section of OneNote, Notes E-mailed to Me, as shown in Figure 2.9.

For more information about creating to-do lists and Note Flags, see "Using Note Flags," in Chapter 10.

For more information about creating Outlook tasks from your notes, see "Creating Outlook Tasks from OneNote," in Chapter 20.

FIGURE 2.6

The Note Flags Summary task pane can display a clickable list of all your Note Flags.

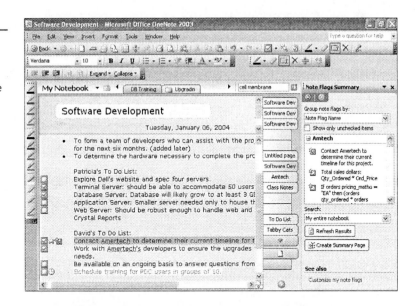

FIGURE 2.7

An Outlook task allows you to set a reminder or assign the task to another person.

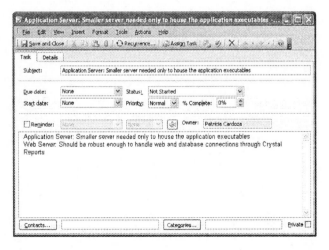

FIGURE 2.8

OneNote pages
can be emailed
to other
OneNote users.

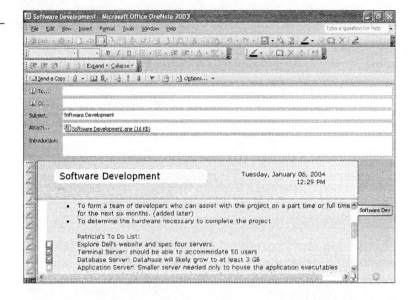

FIGURE 2.9

OneNote stores
all the notes you
receive via
email in their
own section.

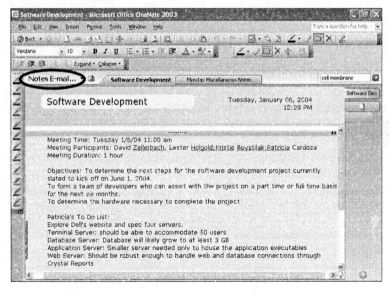

Using OneNote in Project Planning

In addition to its use in meetings, OneNote can also be helpful for another business use—project planning. For example, in Figure 2.10, OneNote is used to store information about an upcoming software upgrade project.

There's a section for each component of the project: hardware, software, and training. Each section has multiple pages. The training section, for example, has a page for each department. The training notes for the Customer Service Department are shown in Figure 2.11.

None of this information does any good in a vacuum. If the project organizer creates these training schedules and doesn't share them with the various department heads, nothing will ever get done. The solution is to store these sections on a SharePoint site or network file share. Doing this allows multiple users to access the information at the same time. Only one user at a time can make changes to the OneNote page, but any number of users can access the page.

If the customer service manager attempts to access his training page while the project organizer is editing it, he'll see the words "read only" displayed after the name of the page. As long as the project organizer has the page locked, the customer service manger can't make any changes. However, once the file lock is released (typically five minutes after OneNote has become idle on the project organizer's machine), the customer service manager can make his changes.

A SharePoint site is an excellent repository for OneNote pages that need to be accessed by multiple individuals. As shown in Figure 2.12, users can browse the Document Library for the project's SharePoint site and upload, download, or open a OneNote section file stored in the library.

tip

Creating Outlook tasks with reminders from OneNote ensures that you won't forget the various action items you received in the meeting. Assigning the task to others allows even those who weren't in the meeting to receive a portion of the notes with the task.

note

For more information about creating outlines from existing text, see "Creating Outlines from Existing Text," Chapter 15.

FIGURE 2.10

Users can store information about entire projects in OneNote.

FIGURE 2.11

Storing training information in OneNote can enable multiple departments to share information.

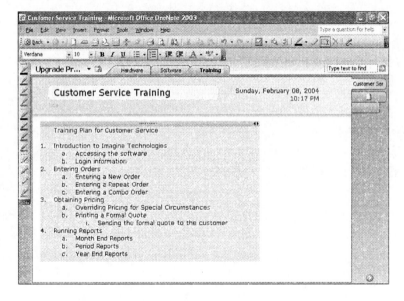

FIGURE 2.12
A SharePoint site provides advanced collaboration features.

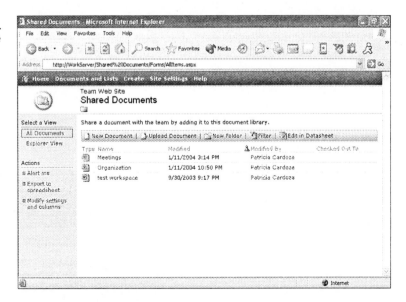

When the project has been completed, you can remove the .one files from the SharePoint installation for archival.

Using OneNote for Personal Use

OneNote's abilities to create lists and organize information can also be helpful for personal uses. Figures 2.13 and 2.14 show moving information stored in OneNote. As you can see, there are numerous lists for packing, moving checklists, and research about a new area of the country.

note

SharePoint Team Services and SharePoint Portal server are products that run on a shared server to allow users to access a variety of information. SharePoint includes support for real-time collaboration along with shared tasks, contacts, and documents. For more information about sharing notes, see "Collaborating with Others," in Chapter 23.

Since there's really no limit to the type of information you can store in OneNote, you can include any type of information you'll need for your new home. This could include a map to some local take-out restaurants and a grocery store (since there's always something you can't find when you move).

In addition to moving, OneNote is a helpful place to store gift lists and recipes, as shown in Figure 2.15.

You can store virtually any type of information within OneNote. You'll need to experiment a bit to see how OneNote can work best for you.

For more information about emailing your notes to others, see "Emailing Notes," in Chapter 23.

FIGURE 2.13

You can store checklists for packing and moving in OneNote.

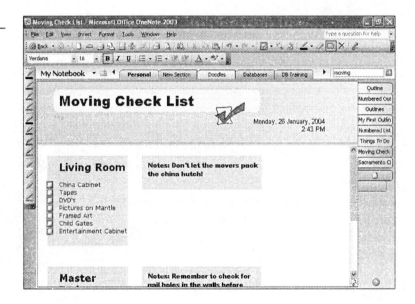

FIGURE 2.14

Storing information about the area you're moving to can be helpful, especially locations of restaurants and stores.

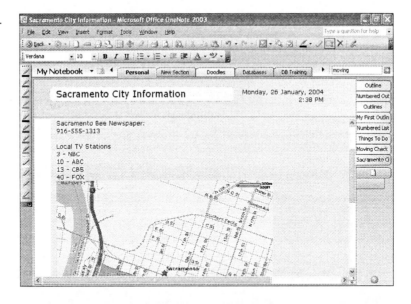

FIGURE 2.15

OneNote includes a template for storing recipes.

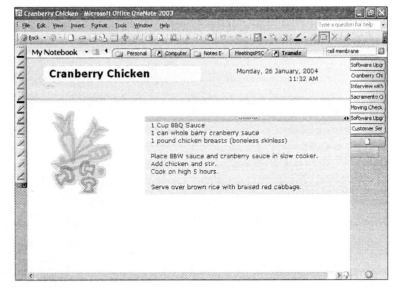

Recording Audio in OneNote

OneNote has the ability to record audio as you type (or use the Tablet PC to write your notes). If you're a reporter, this can sometimes be an effective method of capturing information in an interview. Simply record the interview as you're taking notes. Doing this can ensure you don't miss any information. The audio files are stored in the same folder as your OneNote section files and can be accessed through a link within the OneNote page, as shown in Figure 2.16.

FIGURE 2.16
You can record audio while you're taking notes.

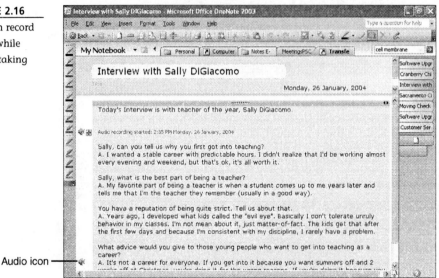

Audio icon

When the interview is complete, you can go back and have OneNote replay your audio. As the audio plays, OneNote can highlight the particular line you were typing or writing at the time the audio was recorded. Every few seconds, as the audio plays, OneNote will advance to the next line you wrote, as shown in Figure 2.17.

note

For more information about recording audio in OneNote, see "It's Too Quiet in Here—Let's Add Some Sound," Chapter 17.

Audio toolbar

FIGURE 2.17

OneNote can replay your audio recording and highlight lines you were typing at the time.

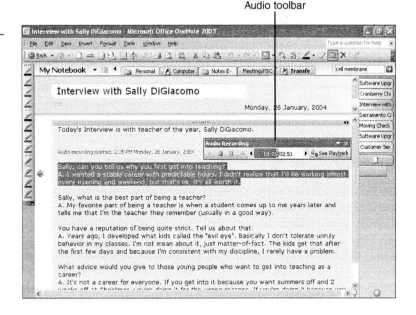

When you're done summarizing the interview, you can publish the page in OneNote (by publishing it as an HTML page) or use the copy and paste functionality common to all Office programs and transfer your interview into Microsoft Word.

tip

The ability to record audio can be useful in many situations. A student can record a lecture to add context to their written notes. An employee can record a meeting in order to provide accurate feedback at a later time. The possibilities are pretty limitless.

The Absolute Minimum

As you've seen in this chapter, OneNote can help you with a variety of note-taking tasks. Whether you're using OneNote for business, school, or pleasure, you can organize, search, and print your notes. You've seen

- How OneNote can help you take notes for school
- How OneNote can help you organize your meeting notes
- How OneNote can be helpful for collaboration
- How OneNote can be useful in organizing tasks and other information in your personal life
- How OneNote's audio recording features can be helpful

The next chapter introduces you to the various components of OneNote. You'll get an in-depth look at OneNote's sections, pages, folders, and note containers.

PART

TAKING YOUR FIRST NOTES

3

USING ONENOTE'S STRUCTURE TO ORGANIZE YOUR NOTES

Just like this book is made up of parts, chapters, sections, and pages, OneNote is made up of sections as well. You can have multiple folders within your OneNote notebook. There are folders that contain sections, sections that contain pages, and pages that contain note containers.

Understanding OneNote's Structure

Microsoft OneNote contains a variety of different structures to help you organize your note-taking experience. Much like one of those spiral-bound divided notebooks you might have purchased in high school or college, each OneNote notebook contains folders, sections, and pages. Within those pages, you can have an almost infinite number of note containers that contain the text or Tablet PC ink you've stored within the program.

Much like the other programs in Microsoft Office, OneNote stores information in distinct files. These files are stored in the Windows File System as files with the extension .one. Each .one file represents a distinct section within one of your notebooks. Before we go any further discussing OneNote's structure, refer to Figure 3.1 to get a feel for what sorts of information the different types of OneNote objects can hold. A typical OneNote window is shown with two folders, some sections, pages, and note containers.

FIGURE 3.1

A typical OneNote window has tabs for each notebook section and folder across the top.

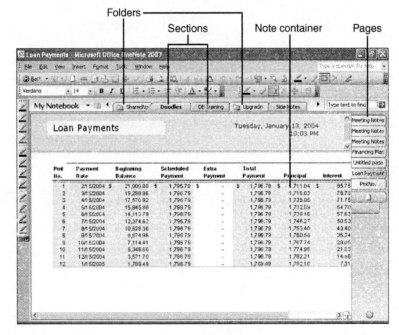

Using Sections to Store Related Information

Each of the tabs without a file folder icon (such as Doodles, DB Training, and Side Notes) represents a notebook section that's currently open in OneNote. You can have as many notebook sections as you want within OneNote, however, as you add note-book sections, you could end up with so many that the section names are com-pressed across the top of the screen. In that case, it might be helpful to close some sections for ease of navigation. You can close any open section at any time to remove it from display. When you open OneNote, it remembers which sections were open when the application was closed and only opens those sections (see Chapter 6, "Working with Note Files," for more information on opening and closing notebook sections).

In Figure 3.1, General, Databases, Training, Side Notes, and Meetings are all note-book sections. The tab for Upgrading actually represents an additional folder. You can tell it represents a new folder rather than a new section because it has an icon of a file folder. When you click on the tab for the additional folder, OneNote makes that the active folder and displays that folder's sections across the top of the page. The sections available in the previous folder are hidden.

In order to view them again, click the icon of the File Folder with the green arrow on it to display OneNote's structure as shown in Figure 3.2.

FIGURE 3.2

Use this naviga-tion window to switch between folders and sec-tions.

From OneNote's navigation window, you can select any currently open folder or sec-tion. You cannot use this dialog to switch to a closed section or folder.

Creating and Using Multiple Folders

You can have multiple folders within OneNote to help you organize information. For example, if you use OneNote for both business and personal projects, you can create a different folder for each. That way you're not distracted by the Christmas shopping checklist you stored in OneNote while trying to manage the database implementa-tion project at the office.

Of course there's no strict rule that says you should always create different folders for different types of projects. You can certainly use OneNote for years and only use the default folder created during installation. However, as indicated in the following list, there are several key advantages to separating certain types of information into a new folder.

▓ Keeping Information Separate—If you use OneNote for both business and personal projects, creating a separate folder for each can help keep your personal life personal. For example, if you're using OneNote in a business presentation, you probably don't want to show your surprise-party planning checklist to your colleagues.

▓ Archiving Information—If you use OneNote extensively for all of your projects, you can compile a vast amount of information very quickly. Once a particular project is completed, simply archive the entire folder to a CD and remove it from your computer. In this case, creating a separate folder for each project can save you from hunting through all existing .one files to find the ones particular to the closed project.

▓ Sharing Information—In any business setting, there are probably certain projects you share with others in your organization. If you create a separate folder for these projects, you can copy entire folders from your computer to a colleague's computer or create a new folder in a shared network location. While two users can't edit the same section at the same time, one can view a static version of the page while another edits the page.

Working with Pages

Within each section (such as the Database section shown in Figure 3.1), you can have multiple OneNote pages. Each page can contain graphics, text, ink, and other pasted content such as Web site content and content from other Microsoft Office programs. In Figure 3.3, you'll notice that within the Database section, there are seven distinct pages, each corresponding to a particular type of database application. To switch from one page to another, simply click the page name.

You might think from looking at the figure that there are actually nine pages. In addition to the named pages shown in the figure are two other tabs displayed on the screen. The first, with the icon of a piece of paper, allows you to create a new page. Just click the tab and OneNote inserts a blank page immediately following the last named page, as shown in Figure 3.4.

FIGURE 3.3

Each tab along the right side of the page is a notebook page.

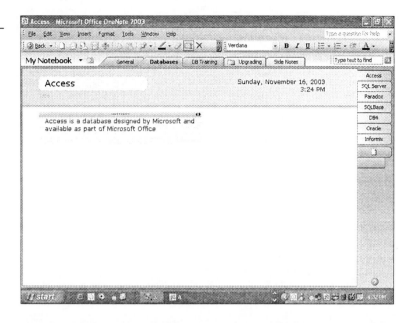

FIGURE 3.4

A new page is always inserted following the last existing page.

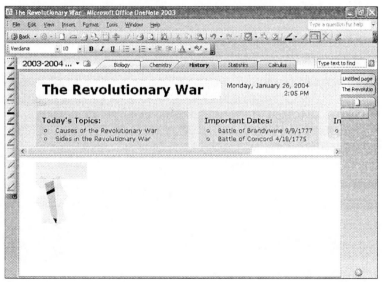

The last tab seen in Figure 3.3 is a subpage. You can use subpages to further segregate and categorize information. For example, if you were comparing the different types of databases available today, you might have a page on SQL Server listing its features and benefits. However, there are several different types of SQL Server

(Enterprise, Standard, and Desktop Version). You could create a subpage for each type of SQL Server and store information about each type on that subpage.

To create a new subpage, click the new subpage tab, as shown in Figure 3.5.

New Subpage

FIGURE 3.5

You can click the new sub-page tab to cre-ate a subpage.

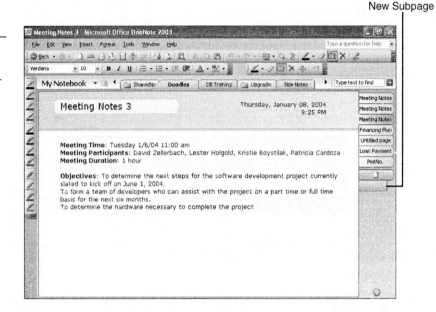

The subpage is created under whatever page you were viewing at the time you created the subpage. You can think of a subpage as a page 2 for the ini-tial page. So, in order to create a subpage to the SQL Server page, make sure you click the SQL Server tab along the right side of the page first, then click the new subpage tab.

Anatomy of a OneNote Page

Pages and subpages have a variety of structures you can use to organize your notes. All of the structures we'll discuss in this section can be seen in Figure 3.6. Each of these structures are covered in detail in later chapters.

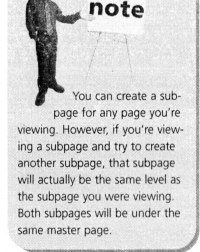

note

You can create a sub-page for any page you're viewing. However, if you're view-ing a subpage and try to create another subpage, that subpage will actually be the same level as the subpage you were viewing. Both subpages will be under the same master page.

Numbered list   Page title   Page header   Graphic

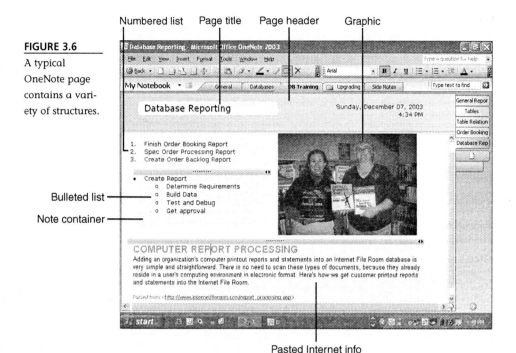

FIGURE 3.6

A typical
OneNote page
contains a vari-
ety of structures.

Bulleted list ——

Note container ——

Pasted Internet info

The Page Header

At the top of every page is a page header. The page
header contains a date stamp that lists the date and
time the page was created. No matter how many
times you edit the page, this date and time stamp
will never change on its own. You can delete it and
type your own date and time.

In addition, the page header contains the page
title, the light oval area on the left hand side of the
page header. Your page title is always displayed
even if you scroll down the page. It's also displayed
on the page tab on the right side of the OneNote
window. To enter a title, click your mouse or tap
your pen in the title area and just start typing or
writing. If you ever want to change the page title,
position your mouse in the light oval window and
click to place your cursor in the title area. You can
also highlight the entire page title and type over it.

note

If you don't see the
page titles on the right
side of the page, you might have
them hidden. Choose Titles in
Page Tabs from the View menu to
display them.

You can enter other information in the page header besides the title and date stamp. Just click in the header and start typing. Later in this chapter you'll learn about the note containers that hold your writing or typing on a page. Those same note containers can exist on the page header or on the page itself. By positioning your mouse or pen on the gray border between the page header and the page, you can even drag up or down to change the size of the page header.

The Note Container

All notes, whether typed or written, are stored in note containers. These containers can be easily deleted or moved by using the container's handle. Figure 3.7 shows a typical note container.

FIGURE 3.7

A note container's note handle helps you move the container on the page.

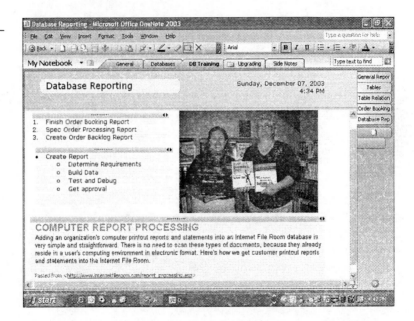

When you first install OneNote, all note containers have a faint gray shading to them. This helps you identify the different note containers on the screen. Figure 3.6 showed several different note containers on the page. As soon as you start typing or writing, a note container is created. If you press Enter on the keyboard, you start a new line of type, but remain in the same note container. As you can see in Figure 3.7, a note container can contain multiple lines. If you click somewhere else on the page, you'll start a new note container.

Clicking on the top border of a note container selects the entire container. You can then move the container anywhere on the page or even up to the page header. To change the width of the note container, move your mouse over the container to display the header. You'll notice two arrows on the right side of the container header. Click on those arrows to widen or narrow your note container. You can even combine two note containers by dragging one note container on top of another (for more on working with note containers, see Chapter 16, "Working with Your Note Page").

tip

If you don't like seeing the note containers highlighted on the page, select Tools, Options and click the Display category. Uncheck the box marked Show note containers on pages.

Formatting Within Note Containers

Figure 3.6 shows both a bulleted list and a numbered list. You can create highly formatted information within a note container, including hyperlinks, graphics, and even information pasted from Internet Explorer or other programs.

Advanced Note-taking Preview

In addition to typing, writing, and creating various lists in OneNote, you can perform a variety of advanced organization and note-taking operations. Figure 3.8 shows a note with a variety of advanced features.

note

For detailed information on creating bulleted and numbered lists in OneNote, check out Chapter 14, "Creating Outlines in OneNote."

Recording Audio in OneNote

If you have a laptop or Tablet with a built in microphone (or a microphone attached to your desktop computer), you can record audio from a meeting or conversation as you take notes. OneNote is smart enough to add markers to the audio recording to record what you're typing during the recording. So if you record a two-minute conversation and type five separate sentences during those two minutes, OneNote can highlight the sentences you were typing during each segment of the recording. Recording audio is covered in depth in Chapter 17, "It's Too Quiet in Here, Let's Add Some Sound."

Note flags   Audio marker   Audio Recording

FIGURE 3.8

You can record audio, add note flags, and create lists in OneNote.

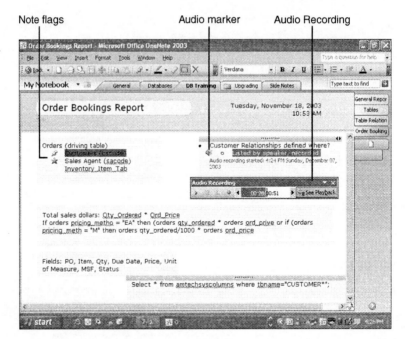

Adding Flags to Your Notes

You can type pages and pages of notes while in meetings or working on projects, but if all you do is type, your notes might look rather boring. It's not easy to find information on a huge page of notes without some flags and highlighting. Figure 3.8 shows three of the nine types of note flags. You can flag lines of text or writing as questions, to do's, important, a definition, or to remember for later. Five of the note flags are predefined. Four note flags are undefined by default. You can customize any of the nine note flags to meet your needs. You might create a note flag for further discussion or one for each major project you're working on. Later, you can use the Note Flag Summary task pane, shown in Figure 3.9, to display all note flags in the current section, current page, or your entire notebook.

FIGURE 3.9

The Note Flag Summary task pane helps you keep on top of your note flags.

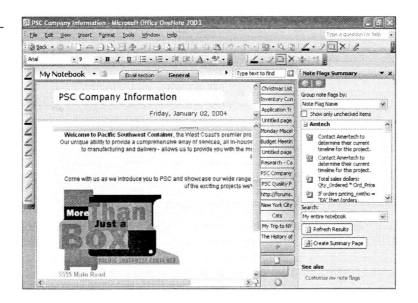

THE ABSOLUTE MINIMUM

In this chapter, you saw a preview of a wide variety of OneNote's features. You learned a little about

- How you can use the various components of OneNote's structure to organize your notes
- Using Note Flags to create to-do lists and flag important items
- Recording audio in OneNote to further enhance your notes

Now that you've seen what OneNote can do, the next chapters will show you how to use these features in your everyday use of OneNote.

IN THIS CHAPTER

- Work with and understand the parts of a OneNote page
- Configure the writing surface
- Create templates to make note taking more efficient and fun
- Write your first note

4

NOTE TAKING 101: ONENOTE BASICS

In the first three chapters, you learned a little about OneNote and how it's structured. You also saw a number of examples of OneNote in action. You've even probably taken a few simple notes by now. By this point, you might be wondering how you can best configure your individual pages to suit your particular needs.

This chapter will introduce you to all aspects of a OneNote page. You'll learn about the different parts of the page, and how each can be used to help structure your notes. You'll learn about creating and using page groups, as well as how to configure your writing surface. Lastly, we'll cover creating templates to save you time and help customize your note-taking experience.

Working with Pages

Let's review the structure of your OneNote window. A typical OneNote window is shown in Figure 4.1. Within this window you can see sections, pages, and subpages.

FIGURE 4.1

Your OneNote window can contain sections, pages, and subpages.

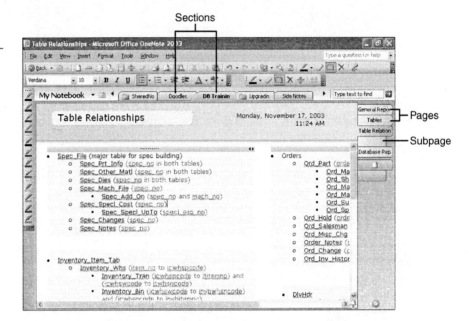

Each of these structures serves a different purpose. A *section* is a container for a group of pages. You can think of a section as a file folder or a section in a spiral-bound notebook. You can use sections to store multiple pages and subpages for a specific topic. For example, if you use OneNote for class notes in school, you can create a section for each class. If you use OneNote for business, you can create a section for each project or department you deal with.

Within sections, you can have multiple pages. Each *page* is displayed as a tab down the right side of the OneNote window. You can display the title of the page on the page tab or choose to view only the page numbers, as shown in Figure 4.2.

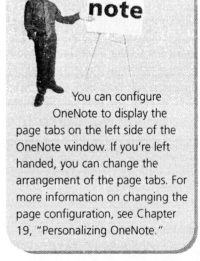

note

You can configure OneNote to display the page tabs on the left side of the OneNote window. If you're left handed, you can change the arrangement of the page tabs. For more information on changing the page configuration, see Chapter 19, "Personalizing OneNote."

FIGURE 4.2

You can display
page names or
page numbers
on the page
tabs.

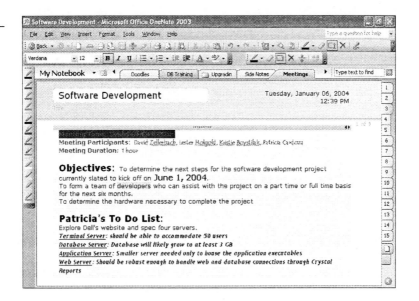

As shown, OneNote displays the page name in the page tab. While this can be help-ful in navigation between pages, it does take up a significant amount of screen space. If you don't need the page titles and would rather have the extra screen space, you can toggle the display of page titles. Simply choose Titles in Page Tabs from the View menu. You can change this option at any time.

If you display page numbers instead of page names in the page tabs, you'll notice an interesting occurrence when you add new pages. Unlike a spiral notebook, when you add new pages, the existing pages renumber themselves. So, in Figure 4.2, if you added a new page between pages 6 and 7, the new page would be page 7, and all following pages would increment their number by one.

Using The Page Header

The page header is visible at the top of every page and subpage. The page header contains two default features, the page title and the time and date stamp. A page header is shown in Figure 4.3.

Adding or Changing the Page Title

To add a page title to a page, position your cursor or pen in the Title box and just start typing. The size of the page title will grow with the amount of information you add to it. After the page title box grows to approximately half way across the OneNote page, it will expand to a second line.

FIGURE 4.3

The page header contains the title field and date stamp.

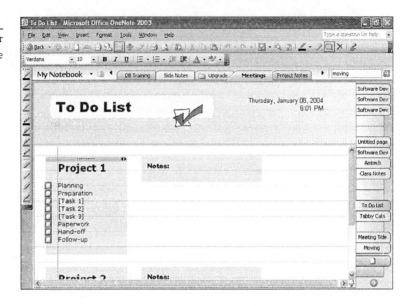

If you type too many characters in the page title, you won't be able to see the entire page title in the page tab on the right side of the screen. This can cause multiple pages to look identical. For example, in Figure 4.4, the first three pages look like they have the same name. However, the pages are actually named Meeting Notes 1, Meeting Notes 2, and Meeting Notes 3.

Font and Font size are adjusted here

FIGURE 4.4

Using long page titles can cause confusion in the page tabs.

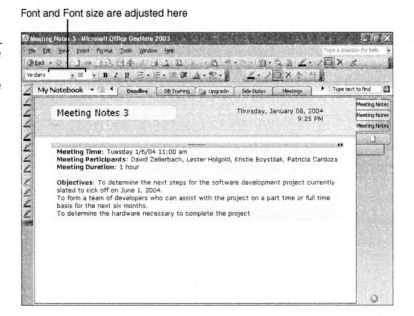

If you need to differentiate between page names in the page tabs, try to keep your page titles to no more than 10 or 12 characters.

Within the page header, you can customize the font of the page title. To change the font of an existing page title, use your mouse to select the text of the page title. You can then use the Font and Font Size drop-downs on the Formatting toolbar to change the title font.

note

Changing the font for the page title won't allow you to display any additional characters in the page tab.

The Page Header's Date and Time Stamp

On the right side of the page header, OneNote inserts the date and time the page was created. By default, OneNote uses the long date format specified in Windows Control Panel. To change the date format, use the following steps.

1. In Windows XP, launch **Control Panel** from the **Start** menu. (If you're using Windows 2000, choose Control Panel from the Settings option of the Start menu.)

2. Double click the **Regional and Language Options** icon in Windows XP or the Regional Options icon in Windows 2000.

3. In Windows XP, click the **Customize** button.

4. In Windows 2000 and XP, choose the **Date** tab. You can modify the default long date format by choosing the appropriate format from the drop-down. Clicking the **Time** tab allows you to modify the time display.

5. Click **OK** until you return to the Control Panel. All future pages created will use the newly modified date and time settings.

An often-requested feature of OneNote is the ability to change an existing date stamp on a page header. Once you create a new page, you cannot change the time and date stamp. If you click either the time or the date, you can highlight the entire line, but you can't change what's there. You can, however, delete the date stamp and replace it with your own custom note container.

To remove the date and time from the page header, click the date or time once to select it. Press the Delete key on the keyboard to delete the selection.

note

There's one drawback to changing the date in the page header: If you search or sort your pages by date, the original date, rather than the changed date, is used.

Once you've deleted the date and time, you can create a new note container in your page header and type the current date and time yourself. However, this date and time will look slightly different. It's contained in a note container and behaves exactly like any other note container on your page or in your page header. This means that you can move, delete, format, flag, highlight, and change the text within the note container.

Storing Information in the Page Header

As the last section alluded to, you can store a variety of information in the page header. Any information that can be stored in a note container on the page can also be stored in the page header. You can create a new note container in the page header by clicking with your mouse (or tapping with your pen) anywhere in the header. Figure 4.5 shows a page header with several different note containers.

FIGURE 4.5

You can add note containers to any page header.

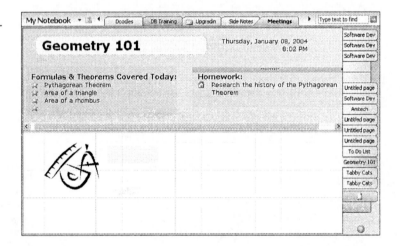

When adding notes to the page header, creating multiple lines in a note container will cause the page header to scroll. You can resize the page header by positioning your mouse or pen on the solid gray line at the bottom of the page header. Your pointer should change to two horizontal lines with two arrows. A ScreenTip message will also appear instructing you to click or drag to change the size of the header. Clicking automatically increases the size of the header by a preset amount (usually about double the original header height). You can also click, hold, and drag the header to make it any size you need.

You can reduce the size of the header using the same method.

Hiding the Page Header

If you don't want the header taking up space on your OneNote screen, you can hide it entirely. Select Page Header from the View menu to remove the orange check mark next to the menu item and hide the page header. You won't be able to see any of the page header on the screen, allowing you more space to display notes, as shown in Figure 4.6.

FIGURE 4.6

Hiding the page header shows you more of the note page at once.

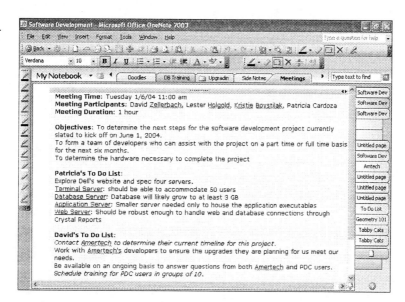

You can restore the page header at any time by selecting Page Header from the View menu to toggle the option on again.

Using Page Tabs

The page tabs, shown along the side of the OneNote window, allow you to quickly navigate to a particular OneNote page. Simply use your mouse or pen and click on the page tab of the page you'd like to display. Earlier in this chapter we covered displaying the page title in the page tab. You can use the page tabs for more than just navigating to a particular page. They can perform a variety of functions.

Quickly Scroll Through Pages

You can use the page tabs to quickly scroll through each of your pages. Much like flipping the pages in a book or notebook, you can flip through each page within a specific section. To flip through pages, click and hold your left mouse button (or pen pointer) over the first page tab and drag down through the remainder of the page tabs. The pages will flip by. Simply release your mouse at any point to stop and activate the currently selected page.

Show Search Results

We'll discuss searching notes in detail in Chapter 18, "Note Taking 301: Finding and Researching Information," but the page tabs play a role here as well. When you search for a specific word or phrase, OneNote highlights the tab for any page that contains the search phrase in yellow, as shown in Figure 4.7. You can then quickly navigate to the particular page.

FIGURE 4.7

OneNote high-lights pages in yellow that contain search results.

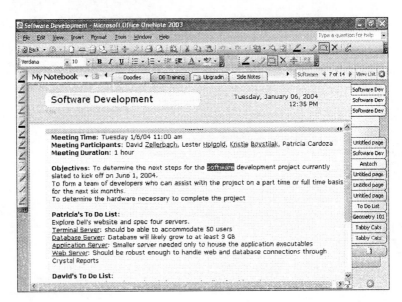

Moving Pages

You can perform several operations on pages by right-clicking on the page tab. Some of the operations are

- Cut, Copy, and Paste—You can cut a page to the clipboard, copy and paste to the clipboard, or paste a page from the clipboard. If you right-click an existing page tab and select Paste, the content you copied is pasted into a new page created directly under the page you right-clicked.

- Delete—The easiest way to delete a page is to choose Delete from the right-click context menu.

- New Page—You can create a new page immediately following the current page.

- New Subpage—You can create a new subpage under the existing page. Subpages are discussed in the next section.

- Page Setup—You can launch the Page Setup task pane from the right-click context menu to control how the page displays on the screen and prints.

- Convert Handwriting to Text—If the page contains any handwriting elements, you can convert the last handwriting element created to text.

- Move Page To—You can move pages between sections using the right-click context menu.

> **note**
>
> For more information about creating pages and page groups, see "Creating Page Groups, Sections, and Folders," in Chapter 9.

- Group and Ungroup Pages—Creating and modifying page groups is discussed in a later section.

Creating New Pages

The last two visible page tabs in OneNote have special functions. The first, with an icon of a piece of paper, allows you to create a new, untitled page. The second narrower tab allows you to create a new subpage.

Working with Page Groups

A page group is a collection of pages that are related. For example, if you think of a section as a hanging file folder and a page as a piece of paper that is stored in that folder, you can think of a page group as a manila folder you can store within the hanging file folder. You can have multiple page groups within a section. Figure 4.8 shows several page groups.

Creating a Page Group

You can create a page group by simply creating a subpage. When you create a subpage, it becomes part of a page group with the currently selected page. So from Figure 4.8, if you wanted to create a subpage to Meetings, you would first select the Meetings page. Then click the New Subpage tab. A new page is created with a tab that's narrower than the master page.

FIGURE 4.8

A page group is
a collection of
related pages.

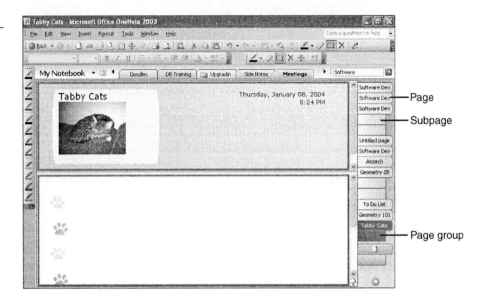

By default, the page title for the subpage is the same as the page title for the main
page. So when you create that subpage to the Meetings page, it will have a title of
Meetings. You can change the title by highlighting the title using your mouse or pen
and typing or writing over it. You can't display a page name on a subpage's page
tab. The subpage will always have a blank page tab.

When viewing a subpage, as shown in Figure 4.9, you'll notice two features. First,
the subpage contains the same date and time stamp as the main page. If the main
page was created on January 6, 2004 and the subpage was created on February 15,
2004, both pages will have the January 6, 2004 date stamp.

The other noteworthy feature of the subpage is a small indicator in the upper-right
corner of the page. In Figure 4.9, it's 2 of 3. This indicates the total number of pages
in the page group and which page you're currently viewing. The main page is
always Page 1. The first subpage is Page 2, and so on.

Ungrouping Pages

If you create a subpage and then change your mind and want to make it a standard page, you can easily accomplish this in two ways. First, you can right-click on
the master page or the subpage and click Ungroup Pages. This takes all subpages of
that group and makes them master pages. When a subpage becomes a master page,
its title is once again displayed in the page tab.

FIGURE 4.9

The subpage contains the same time and date as the main page.

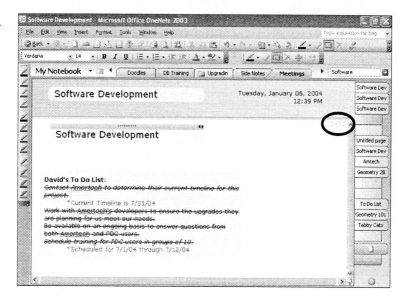

In addition to right-clicking on a page tab, you can also ungroup pages from the Edit menu. Simply select Ungroup pages from the Edit menu. As with the previous method, there is no way to ungroup just one subpage and leave another subpage grouped.

Other Grouping Options

If you want to group two adjacent pages and turn the second one into a subpage, you can accomplish that fairly easily.

1. Select the first page by clicking its **page tab**.

2. Hold down the **Shift** key and click the second page.

3. Now that both are selected, you can select **Edit**, **Group Pages**, or you can right-click one of the selected page tabs and choose **Group Pages**.

In order to group two pages that are not adjacent to one another, you can use the Ctrl key while clicking two non-adjacent pages. However, the master

note

When you ungroup pages, you ungroup all subpages at once. There is no way to ungroup a single subpage and leave other subpages.

page will always be the page higher in the page list. If you want to take a lower page and make it a master page, you'll need to move one of the pages. To move a page, do the following:

1. Click the **page tab** once to select it.
2. Click the page tab again to turn the tab a darker orange and place a blue border around the page header and the page.
3. Click a third time and hold the left mouse button down as you drag the page to its new position. You'll see a small blue arrow move between pages that indicates where the page will appear.
4. Release the mouse button to drop the page.

Now that the two pages are adjacent, you can use the Shift key and the mouse or pen to select them and group them as described previously.

You can group more than just two pages at once. In fact, you can select as many pages as you have and group all of them at once. The process for grouping multiple pages is the same as for grouping two pages.

Viewing All Pages in the Task Pane

If you have multiple sections in OneNote, it can be difficult to remember which pages were in which sections. You can use the Page List task pane to view all of your pages in all sections in an easy-to-navigate list. To display the Page List task pane, choose Page List from the View menu to display the screen shown in Figure 4.10.

By default, your pages are sorted and grouped by section. All pages in your entire notebook are displayed. At the top of the Task pane is a count of the total number of pages found.

You can sort the pages by selecting either Section, Title, or Date from the Sort list by drop-down. By default, the results are sorted by section in descending order. If you want to change the sort order, click the Sort button next to the Sort list by drop-down.

note

By default, subpages are not displayed in the Page List task pane. You cannot change this behavior.

FIGURE 4.10

You can view all pages in all sections in the Task pane.

To change the search scope, click the Search drop-down at the bottom of the Task pane. You can choose to search the Current section, Current folder, Current folder and its subfolders, or My entire notebook (the default). When you change the search scope, the search results will change automatically.

The Page List Task pane allows you to click any of the listed pages to jump directly to the page. Simply click the blue page title and OneNote will switch to that page.

Configuring the Page Background

Now that you know a bit about working with pages, you can make some changes to your writing surface to better meet your needs. These changes include using one of OneNote's built-in preformatted stationery options or creating your own stationery.

Customizing Your Page with Stationery

To create a new page using stationery, you'll need to use the Task pane. You can't use the New Page tab to create a new page with customized stationery. You can create a page based on specified stationery using the following steps.

tip

If you already have a Task pane open, you can switch Task panes by clicking the title of the Task pane to display a drop down list.

Choose New from the list to switch to the New Task pane.

1. Launch the New task pane by selecting **File**, **New** to display the screen shown in Figure 4.11.

The lower third of the New task pane as shown in Figure 4.12 allows you to choose a variety of different types of stationery. The types of stationery are Tablet PCs, Business, Academic, Planners, Decorative, and blank.

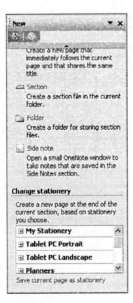

2. Click the **plus sign** next to a stationery group to display the various types of stationery available. Each time you choose a type of stationery, you create a new page. Figure 4.13 shows a OneNote page with Formal Meeting Stationery.

3. When you're satisfied with the type of stationery, you can close the New task pane by clicking the **X** in the upper-right corner of the Task pane. Figure 4.14 shows a decorative stationery.

You'll probably need to choose a number of different stationery types before you find the one you need.

Adding or Changing Rule Lines

In addition to configuring stationery, you can add rule lines to your OneNote pages. *Rule lines* can serve as writing guides on a Tablet PC. They can also be decorative. You can add several different types and sizes of rule lines and grids. To configure rule lines on a OneNote page, choose Rule Lines from the View menu. You can choose from three different widths of rule lines: College, Standard, and Wide. Figure 4.15 shows a OneNote page with custom stationery and College rule lines.

note

Depending on your screen resolution, you might have to scroll down in the New task pane in order to see the Change stationary portion.

caution

When choosing stationery, you might need to select a number of different types before you find one you're happy with. Each time you select a stationery, you're creating a new page. You might not need all these pages. You can easily delete unused pages by right-clicking the page tab and choosing Delete.

FIGURE 4.13

OneNote includes a variety of business templates, such as meeting note templates.

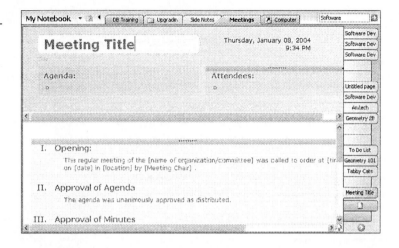

FIGURE 4.14

Decorative stationery can be used for personal tasks in OneNote.

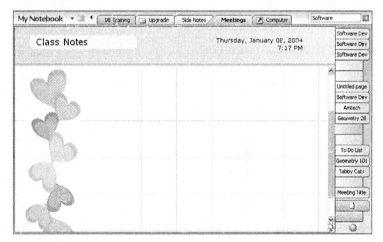

FIGURE 4.15

Rule lines can serve as writing guides.

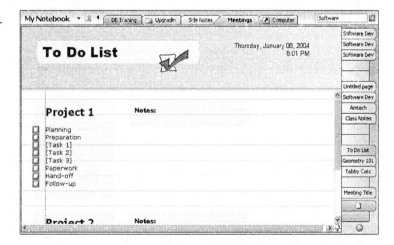

You can use rule lines with a blank OneNote page or with a stationery page. If the three rule line choices don't meet your needs, you can choose from three different types of grids instead. Small, medium, and wide grids are available.

You can use a grid with certain types of stationery to create a unique OneNote page look, as seen in Figure 4.16.

note

Rule and grid lines appear on the screen, but you cannot print them.

FIGURE 4.16

A medium grid and the Math/Science Notes stationery offer a unique look.

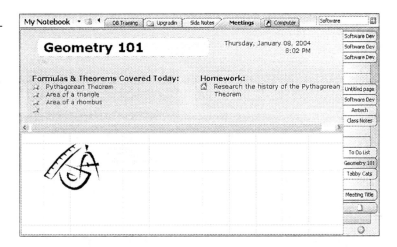

Creating Your Own OneNote Templates

You can create your own custom OneNote templates and add them to the My Stationery section of the New task pane. You can create a template from scratch by adding rule lines, images, and configuring the page setup, or you can start from an existing stationery and apply your customizations from there.

Create a New Template from an Existing Template

You can customize existing stationery and save it as your own stationery. To do this, choose <u>N</u>ew from the <u>F</u>ile menu to display the New task pane. Choose the type of stationery you need and a new page is automatically created.

You can add rule lines, grid lines, images, and text to your page. When you're done, your custom page might look something like Figure 4.17.

FIGURE 4.17

You can customize your page by adding text, images, and stationery.

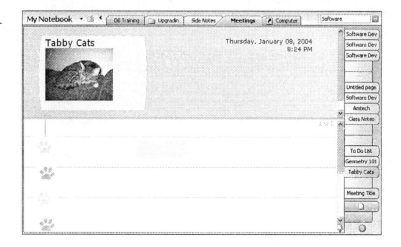

To save your custom page as stationery, click Save current page as stationery on the bottom of the New task pane. Enter a name for your stationery and click Save. When you're done, your custom stationery will be visible under the My Stationery group, as shown in Figure 4.18.

FIGURE 4.18

You can save a page as custom stationery.

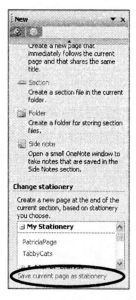

Create a New Template from Scratch

You can also create your own stationery from a blank OneNote page. Simply add titles, images, rule lines, or even a note container with text. Custom stationery can be created for any number of reasons, including

- Meeting note templates
- Shopping lists
- Daily task lists
- Shift responsibility worksheet
- Gift list
- Moving checklist (as shown in Figure 4.19)
- Party planning worksheet

FIGURE 4.19

You can use OneNote to create a moving checklist.

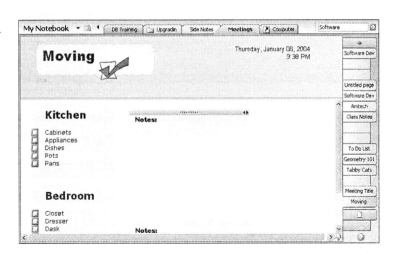

Stationery is stored on your local hard drive in the C:\Program Files\Microsoft Office\Templates\1033\ONENOTE\Stationery directory.

Writing Your Note

Now that you've learned all about OneNote pages and how to customize them, you can write your notes. Whether you use the Tablet PC pen or your keyboard, it's best to just jump in there and start taking notes.

After you've taken some notes, you might start to run out of room. When you reach the bottom of the page, you'll see a scroll bar along the right of the page. At the bottom of that scroll bar, is a small icon of a piece of paper with an arrow as shown in Figure 4.20. If you click that icon, you'll add another half a page of space to the page.

FIGURE 4.20

You can add more space to your page at any time.

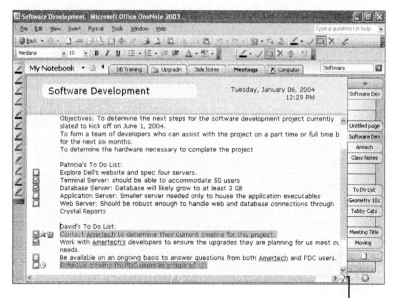

Add more space

You can add space as many times as you'd like, however if you add space to a page and then don't use it, the space will disappear if you scroll around on the page. It will also disappear if you close OneNote and reopen it. OneNote reclaims the extra space to keep your note files small. If you need to add the space back again, simply click the Add More Space icon again.

THE ABSOLUTE MINIMUM

In this chapter, you learned all about working with and customizing OneNote pages. You learned

- How to work with the page header, including how to change the date/time stamp
- How you can use the page tabs, such as how to create subpages and how to move pages
- How to use stationery to enhance the look of your notes
- How to create custom stationery that shows your personal style
- How to add more space to notes

In the next chapter, you'll learn how to use the Tablet PC pen to write notes, as well as other options that are available only to the Tablet PC user.

5

THE BASICS OF USING THE TABLET PC'S PEN

You can use OneNote on a desktop, laptop, or a Tablet PC. Both desktop and laptop computers work with OneNote in a similar manner. You must use the keyboard to enter all of your text in OneNote. If you have a Tablet PC, however, you can use the Tablet's pen to enter information in OneNote. There are two different ways you can do this: through the Tablet PC's Input Panel and directly on the Tablet PC's screen. We'll cover both methods in this chapter.

If you don't have a Tablet PC, but are thinking about getting one, this chapter will show you some of the features you'll be able to take full advantage of within OneNote 2003.

Use the Pen to Take Notes

OneNote is your digital notebook. You can use it much like you would use a yellow legal pad or spiral bound notebook. You can enter text, handwriting, graphics, external content, and diagrams on your OneNote page. Figure 5.1 shows a diagram in OneNote with some highlighting and text mixed in.

FIGURE 5.1

Using the Tablet PC's pen, you can add diagrams and handwriting.

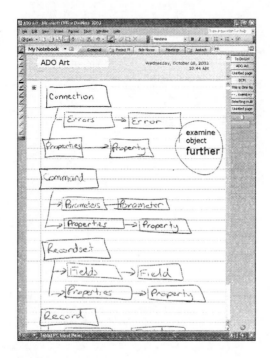

As you can see, it can be helpful to mix different objects on your OneNote page. It would be difficult to convey the appropriate relationships in that diagram if you had to do it via text, and attempting to draw the diagram with the mouse could be quite time consuming.

When used with a Tablet PC, you can take notes directly on the screen in OneNote. Simply place your pen on the screen, and you should see a small dot appear on the screen. The dot will be the same color as your ink color. As you move your pen over the screen, OneNote transcribes exactly what you write onto the screen.

note

All Tablet PCs are different. While the instructions in this chapter should work well for any Tablet PC, refer to the manufacturer's instructions for further information on writing on the screen.

Comparing Writing to Typing

There are definite advantages and disadvantages to using handwritten ink in OneNote instead of typed text. Handwritten ink can be more flexible and functional. You can draw diagrams, arrows, and pictures that you couldn't with a keyboard and mouse. However, as Figures 5.2 and 5.3 illustrate, you can't capture as much information on the screen when writing unless you have exceptionally small handwriting. Figure 5.2 shows meeting notes captured on a Tablet PC using handwritten ink.

FIGURE 5.2

Handwritten meeting notes often take up a large amount of space.

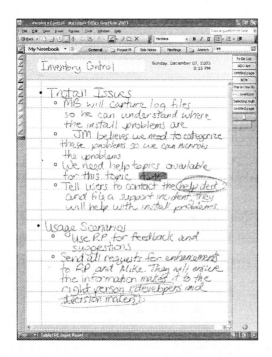

Figure 5.3 shows those same notes as typed text. As you can see, you can fit significantly more information on the screen when typing.

You'll need to try taking notes with the pen and the keyboard to determine which method works best for you. In many cases, the situation can dictate which method works best. For example, if you need to take notes quickly, and you're a fast typist, the keyboard might be the input method of choice. If speed isn't an issue, or you need to draw diagrams, the pen might be the more appropriate choice.

FIGURE 5.3

The same notes, typed, take up significantly less space.

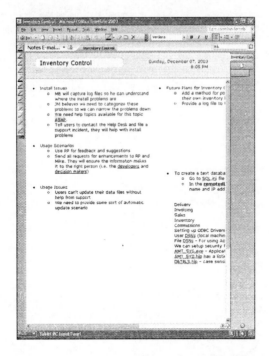

Change the Ink Color and Width

When using the pen to take notes directly on your OneNote page, it's very simple to change your ink color and style. You can choose from four different ink colors (black, red, blue, and green) and two different ink widths (narrow and wide). You can also change your pen to function as a highlighter. There are four colors available when highlighting (yellow, blue, pink, and green).

If you have a Tablet PC, the Pens toolbar is probably displayed by default, but if it isn't, you can easily add it. Choose View, Toolbars and select Pens from the fly-out menu to display the toolbar shown in Figure 5.4.

FIGURE 5.4

You can use the Pens toolbar to change ink color and width.

All you have to do to change ink colors is tap the appropriate button on the Pens toolbar with your Tablet's pen. You can choose from the four available ink colors and two available ink widths. Using multiple pen colors and widths (along with highlighting) can help you organize your notes, as shown in Figure 5.5.

FIGURE 5.5

Using multiple widths, pen colors, and highlighting can create visually appealing notes.

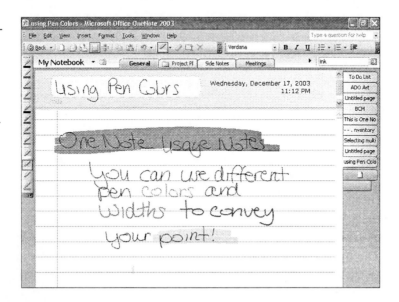

Using the Highlighter

In addition to the two pen widths and four pen colors, you can convert the pen to a highlighter. To select a highlighter color, tap any of the bottom four buttons on the Pens toolbar. Once you have selected a highlighter, you can drag the pen across the text or ink you want to highlight. Every time you drag the pen across the text, you can add another line of highlighting. It might take several strokes of the highlighter to highlight a single line of text, as shown in Figure 5.6.

You cannot change the width of the highlighter in OneNote. To switch back from the highlighter to a narrow or wide pen, just tap the appropriate button on the Pens toolbar.

FIGURE 5.6

If you're trying to highlight handwriting, it might take several strokes to completely highlight the line.

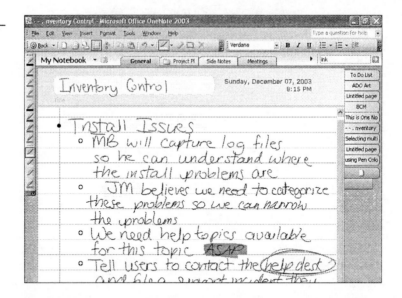

Using the Tablet PC Input Panel with OneNote

If you don't want to write directly on the screen, you can use the Tablet PC's Input Panel with OneNote. Once you have the Input Panel displayed, your OneNote window will look similar to Figure 5.7.

You can use the Input Panel in two modes, Keyboard and Writing Pad. If you use the keyboard, you can tap each individual letter on the keyboard with your pen. If you use the Writing Pad, you can write directly in the Writing Pad and have your writing converted automatically to text.

When you create a new page in OneNote, the cursor is placed in the Page Title area of the page header. Anything you enter in the Input Panel at this point will appear in the Page Title. In order to start inputting text in OneNote using the Input Panel, first, take your pen and tap once within the OneNote page. This will move the cursor location to the note area rather than the page header. Then continue to enter text in the Tablet PC's Input Panel.

note

Typically, you can display the Tablet PC's Input Panel by clicking the small keyboard icon on the Windows Taskbar. If you don't see this icon, click or tap Start to open the Start menu and look for the Input Panel there.

FIGURE 5.7

The Tablet PC's Input Panel appears at the bottom of your OneNote screen.

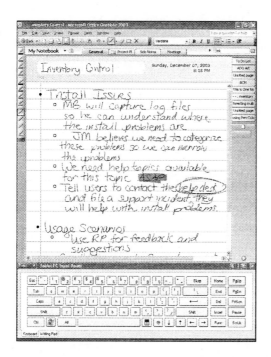

Anything you write in the Input Panel is converted to text in OneNote. You can use the Input Panel for letters, numbers, and most punctuation marks. In order to enter symbols in the Input Panel, you'll need to tap the & symbol on the Input Panel to display the symbol panel, as shown in Figure 5.8, or switch to keyboard view. Otherwise the Input Panel assumes you're entering text and will try to convert the symbol to text.

FIGURE 5.8

You can use the Symbol Panel to enter symbols.

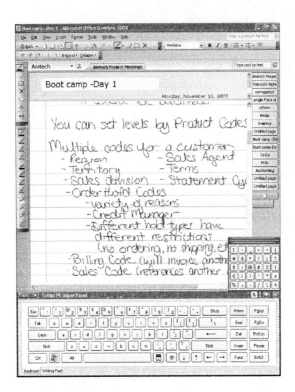

Fixing Mistakes

Even though we might like to think we're all perfect, we all make mistakes while either typing or writing. It might be that the Input Panel misinterpreted what you attempted to tap or write, or you might just need to change what you previously wrote. You can correct mistakes in several ways, but probably the easiest way to correct a mistake is with your Tablet PC's pen.

If you haven't already done so within OneNote, flip your Tablet PC's pen over and place the top of the pen (where the eraser would be if you were holding a pencil) on the Tablet's screen. Instead of the dot that appears on the screen when you use the tip of the pen, you'll see a little eraser appear on the screen. You can actually erase text or ink using this eraser.

Erasing Ink

In order to erase ink that's on the OneNote screen, you will have to press harder on the screen than you do for simply writing. You'll need to experiment with how hard you need to press to erase your ink. Every Tablet PC has a different pen. Your pen might have a small button on the top of the pen. If so, you'll probably need to press hard enough to slightly depress this button.

To erase ink, you can either drag your eraser over the ink while pressing on the screen, or press down directly on a line of ink. For example, if you have a large W on the screen, you can position your eraser on one line of the W and press down. The entire W is deleted.

You cannot delete just one short segment of the W. You can delete one pen stroke at a time. So if you're writing in cursive, you might not be able to delete just one letter of a word. You might only be able to delete the entire word or several letters at a time.

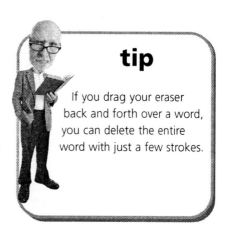

tip

If you drag your eraser back and forth over a word, you can delete the entire word with just a few strokes.

Erasing Typed Text

You can't use the pen eraser to erase typed text. You'll have to use the cursor to select the text and delete it. You can use the pen to select a block of typed or written text and then delete the selected text. We'll cover using the pen as a selection tool later in this chapter.

Recognizing Pen Sensitivity

All Tablet PCs have the capability to recognize how hard you're pressing the pen on the screen. Much like using a felt-tip pen on a piece of paper, the pressure you exert on the Tablet PC screen can affect the width and darkness of your ink. Figure 5.9 illustrates the effect pen sensitivity can have on a note. The first few lines of the note were taken with a light touch of the pen to the screen. The last few lines of the note were taken with a harder pen impression. You can see that even though the text and the handwriting are the same, there is a definite difference in the handwriting.

By default, OneNote doesn't measure pen sensitivity. To change this option, select Options from the Tools menu. From the left side of the Options window, click Handwriting to display Figure 5.10.

tip

Be careful not to push too hard on your Tablet PC's screen. Although the screen is quite durable, it is possible to damage the screen. As a general rule, don't push any harder than you would with a pen on paper.

FIGURE 5.9

You can alter your ink by pressing harder on the screen.

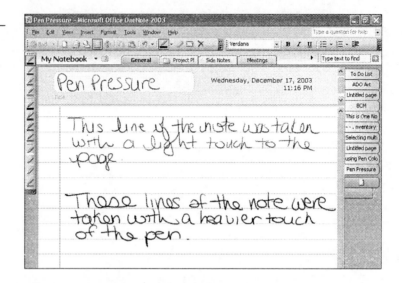

FIGURE 5.10

You can configure OneNote to record pen sensitivity.

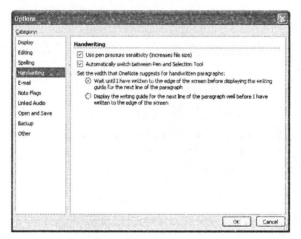

Check the box marked Use pen pressure sensitivity (increases file size). This option will cause your OneNote files to increase in size. For example, a note with pen sensitivity will be X kilobytes larger than the same note taken without pen sensitivity.

Converting Ink to Text

Sometimes you want to take handwritten notes but you want to convert some or all of that handwriting to text for easier readability. You might not have a Tablet PC with a keyboard or you might just find it easier to use the Tablet PC in portrait mode (holding the Tablet like a pad of paper). You can have OneNote convert the last line of handwriting to text, or you can select an entire section of handwriting to convert to text.

To convert the last handwritten line to text, select the <u>T</u>ools menu and choose Con<u>v</u>ert Handwriting to Text. Unless you have near perfect handwriting (and few of us do), it's possible OneNote will misinterpret your handwriting. For example, the word "more" can often be interpreted as "move." After OneNote converts handwriting to text, you can hover your pen over the first converted word. A small green symbol will appear that looks like the corner of a square. If you press with your pen over that symbol, a drop-down list appears, as seen in Figure 5.11.

FIGURE 5.11

If OneNote misinterprets your handwriting, you can choose the appropriate word.

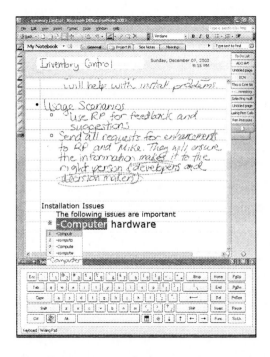

This drop-down list shows you four options for other text you can choose. At the bottom of the drop-down you'll see the original handwritten word OneNote used to convert. To choose another word, click the appropriate line. Unfortunately, if you have five words on a line and you want to alter the third word, you can only use this method to correct the first word on the line. If you need to correct the third word on the line, you'll need to select the text and delete it using the keyboard or selection tool. We'll cover the selection tool later in this chapter.

Using the Pen to Select Ink or Text

You can use the pen to select multiple lines of text to either move the text or convert multiple lines of ink to text all at once. If you want to select multiple lines of ink and convert them all to text or convert a line other than the last line you wrote, you can use two different methods. First, you can switch from the pen to the Selection tool. To do this, click the Selection tool on the toolbar. It looks like a box with a dotted border, immediately to the left of the Delete toolbar button. You can then hold the pen down on the screen and drag to select multiple note containers on the screen. As you select the note containers, a dark blue box appears around the selected note containers. Once all the necessary note containers are selected, choose Convert Handwriting to Text from the Tools menu. You'll see results similar to Figure 5.12.

Selection tool

FIGURE 5.12

You can convert multiple note containers to text using the Selection tool.

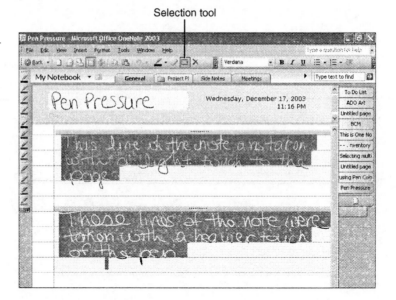

If you remember from earlier in this chapter, you cannot use the pen's eraser to delete typed text. In order to delete typed text on the OneNote screen with your pen, change the pen to the selection tool by clicking the Selection tool button on the toolbar. You can now drag your pen across one or many note containers to select them. To delete the selected note containers, click the Delete button on the toolbar. You can select both handwritten and typed note containers with the Selection tool.

To switch from the Selection tool back to the pen, just click the Pen button on the toolbar.

The second method you can use to convert a line of handwriting to text involves selecting the entire note container using the pen. Hover your pen over the line of text you're interested in. The cursor changes to a symbol that looks like a plus sign with arrows. Tap that icon once to select your note container. The icon and the selected note container are shown in Figure 5.13.

FIGURE 5.13

You can use the note container selector to choose your note container.

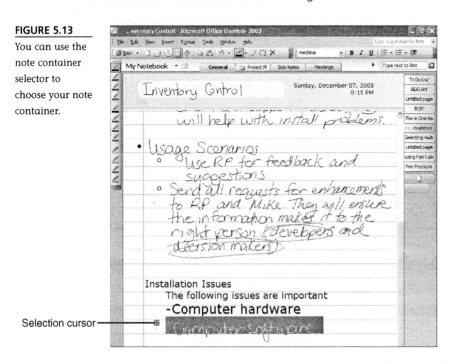

Selection cursor

Once the note container is selected, choose Convert Handwriting to Text from the Tools menu.

Drawing Versus Writing

You can use the pen for both writing and drawing. Most of the time you don't even need to distinguish between the two, OneNote will distinguish for you. If you draw a cube on the screen and then try to choose Convert Handwriting to Text from the Tools menu, you'll find that it's unavailable. However, what if you're drawing something more ambiguous? By default, OneNote allows you to use the pen to create both handwriting and drawings. If you attempt to draw something that looks like a letter (for instance drawing a corner that looks like the letter L), OneNote might not treat it as you would expect. OneNote could treat it as a letter even though you intended it as a drawing.

In addition to the default behavior (allowing both handwriting and drawings) you can configure OneNote to accept only handwriting or only drawings.

Changing the Pen from Handwriting to Drawing

To change the pen behavior in OneNote, select Tools, Pen Mode to display a fly-out menu. From this menu choose Create Both Handwriting and Drawings, Create Handwriting Only, or Create Drawings Only. The following examples will illustrate the differences between these modes.

Trying to Draw in Handwriting Mode

If you choose handwriting mode and then attempt to draw on the screen, you can certainly still draw on the screen. However, if you select the note container that contains the drawing, you'll be able to convert the selected handwriting to text, but you might get some unexpected results. For example, Figure 5.14 shows a cube drawn on the screen. Believe it or not, after drawing that cube, choosing Convert Handwriting to Text turns the cube into the word TEA. Your results might differ based on the quality of your cube and your handwriting style, but you definitely will end up with something other than your original cube.

FIGURE 5.14

If the pen is in handwriting mode, you can convert your drawings to text.

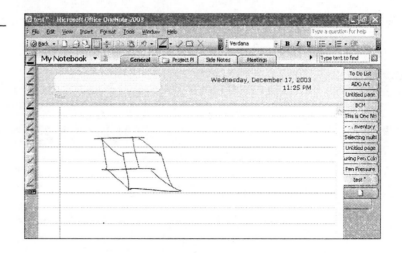

Writing in Drawing Mode

Attempting to write in drawing mode can be a little trickier. For example, in Figure 5.15, the word Supervisor is written on the screen. It's quite legible and should easily be recognizable as text. However, Convert Handwriting to Text isn't available from the Tools menu and if you select the note container, you'll notice that the selected note container looks a little different. That's because you're not selecting text; you're selecting a drawing.

FIGURE 5.15

You cannot convert handwriting to text in drawing mode.

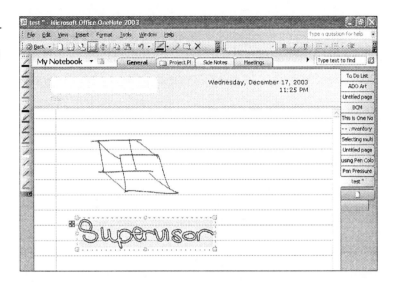

As a general rule, it's probably best to leave the Pen mode set to Create Both Handwriting and Drawing. This gives you the greatest flexibility within your notes.

Changing How Selected Ink Is Treated

If you've configured your pen to accept both handwriting and drawing, there might be occasions when OneNote believes you're drawing when you're actually writing. In this case, you can tell OneNote specifically how to treat the selected ink. Just choose the note container and then select Tools, Treat Selected Ink As to display the fly-out menu. You can choose either Handwriting or Drawing. For example, in Figure 5.14, the selected text was treated as a drawing. To change the text to handwriting so you can convert the handwriting to text, choose Handwriting from the Treat Selected Ink As fly-out menu. You can then choose Convert Handwriting to Text from the Tools menu.

THE ABSOLUTE MINIMUM

Using OneNote with a Tablet PC enables you to create diagrams and drawings, and to take notes in your own handwriting. Taking handwritten notes allows you to have complete control and flexibility over your note taking.

In this chapter, you learned how to use the Tablet PC's pen to take notes in OneNote. You learned about

- Displaying the pen toolbar
- Writing notes using the pen
- Erasing handwritten notes

- Converting handwriting to text

- Using the different modes of the pen

In the next chapter, you'll learn how to work with the various files OneNote creates. You'll learn where they are stored, how to open and close them, and how to back them up.

PART III

MANAGING AND PRINTING YOUR ONENOTE FILES

6

WORKING WITH NOTE FILES

Now that you know a little about pages, sections, and folders, you might be wondering where all these structures are located and how to access them. This chapter will provide information on opening, closing, saving, and deleting OneNote files.

Where Does OneNote Save Files?

As mentioned in Chapter 3, "Using OneNote's Structure to Organize Your Notes," OneNote is made up of folders, sections, pages, and note containers. Figure 6.1 illustrates the various components of OneNote.

FIGURE 6.1

OneNote contains a variety of structures to hold your notes.

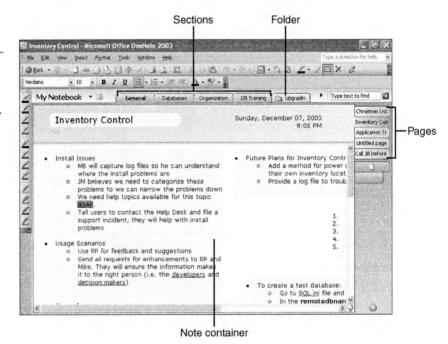

By default, all OneNote files are stored in a folder called My Notebook. You can find this folder inside your My Documents folder on your local hard drive. If you open the My Notebook folder, you'll see a structure similar to Figure 6.2.

Each folder in your My Notebook folder represents a folder within OneNote. As you can see from comparing Figures 6.1 and 6.2, folders within OneNote have their own folder within the My Notebook folder. Each section (such as the Databases section in Figure 6.1) has its own OneNote file. The extension for a OneNote file is .one. Within each section file, you'll find individual pages. For example, in Figure 6.2, the files DB Training.one and General.one represent the DB Training and General sections, respectively. However, within the General section (shown in Figure 6.1) there are five pages. None of these pages have their own files. The pages are stored within the file for the section.

FIGURE 6.2

Your My Notebook folder might contain a variety of files and folders.

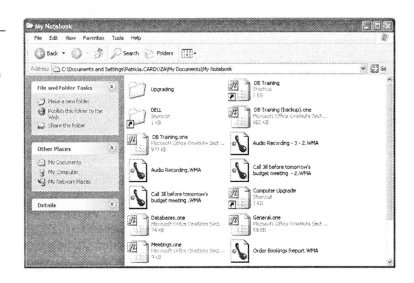

You can also view the structure of your OneNote files by clicking the My Notebook heading in the upper left of the OneNote window, as shown in Figure 6.3. As you can see, there's a folder for each folder you've created and a smaller icon for each section. Individual pages don't have their own icon.

FIGURE 6.3

You can view OneNote's structure from the main OneNote window.

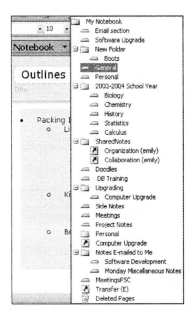

OneNote's Default Files and Folders

There are several built-in files and folders you'll see in the My Notebook folder. If you've ever used OneNote's Side Note feature (discussed in Chapter 8, "Creating Side Notes"), you'll have a file named Side Notes.one. This represents the Side Note section. All the Side Notes you create are stored within this section. This section is created the first time you activate and enter data in a Side Note.

If you've received a note in Outlook 2003, you'll have a folder called Notes E-mailed To Me. This folder contains a .one file for every note you've received through email. You can change where any of these files and folders are located, as shown in the next section.

Changing OneNote's Default Save Location

You can change the location OneNote uses to save your files using the following steps.

1. Choose **Options** from the **Tools** menu.

2. Click **Open and Save** from the Categories pane of the Options window to view the Open and Save options shown in Figure 6.4.

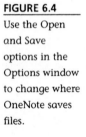

FIGURE 6.4

Use the Open and Save options in the Options window to change where OneNote saves files.

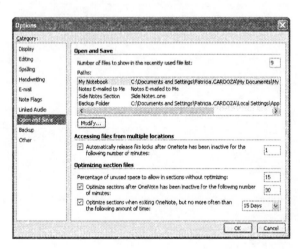

3. You can change the default save location of four different types of OneNote files and folders. To change the location of the My Notebook folder (for example, to move it to a network location), click the first line in the Paths box and then click **Modify** to display the Select Folder dialog box shown in Figure 6.5.

4. Navigate to where you want the My Notebook folder to be located and then click **Select**.

FIGURE 6.5

You can choose any location on your computer or network to store your My Notebook folder.

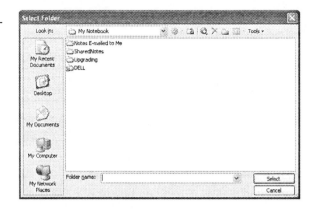

You can change the location of any item in the list using these steps.

Changing the location of your My Notebook folder can have unexpected results. The next time you open OneNote, you'll be presented with a blank section in the folder you selected in step 4. All of your previously created files remain in the original location (the My Notebook folder inside My Documents), but there's no easy way to access them from within OneNote. This method is an easy way to start over within OneNote. All your original files remain in their original location, and you can always use Windows Explorer to double-click them and open them in OneNote.

Sharing OneNote Files

The next section in the Options dialog box (Open and Save) allows you to configure OneNote to be used by more than one person. When you open a OneNote file, a lock is placed on that file, which prevents it from being edited by another user. By default, 5 minutes after OneNote detects inactivity (the absence of typing, writing, or working with the menus), the lock is released and another user can edit the file, even if the first user still has the file open. When the second user edits the file, the first user is locked out until the second user has been inactive for 5 minutes. You can change this default locking interval to any number of minutes between 1 and 99,999. You cannot set the lock interval to 0 minutes. We'll cover sharing files later in Chapter 23, "Sharing and Collaboration."

tip

Changing the location of your My Notebook folder can be a good way to clean the slate with OneNote. You'll start with a blank OneNote notebook. You can then back up your previous My Notebook folder to a CD for archival.

Optimizing Sections to Save Space and Improve Performance

Given the freeform nature of OneNote, sometimes you can end up with a large amount of empty space. For example, if you're writing or typing to the edge of a page, you can click the Page Extension button at the bottom right corner of the OneNote page to add another page of space. Once you do that, however, your OneNote file size grows. If you change your mind and don't end up using that space, you've just added unneeded size to your OneNote .one file. OneNote can reclaim that space through a process called optimization.

By default, OneNote optimizes your files when there is 15% of the total section space unused. This might be an entire new page you created but never modified, or a page you extended but never used. You can change this percentage threshold through the Options dialog previously shown in Figure 6.3. Increasing the percentage to 25% or 50% will prevent OneNote from optimizing as frequently. Generally, unless you find OneNote is optimizing all the time and eating battery life on your laptop or Tablet PC, it's best to leave the default percentage of 15%.

Optimizing does cause your computer's processor to work a little harder, so it might cause a very slight drain on your battery if your computer is running on battery power.

In addition to controlling how much unused space OneNote allows in your sections before it optimizes the file, you can also tell OneNote how often you want to optimize. The two scheduling options shown in Figure 6.6 can be a little confusing. By default, OneNote will start to optimize its sections when the program has been inactive for 30 minutes. You can change this interval to any number between 1 and 99,999 minutes. This doesn't mean your computer needs to be inactive. You can be happily working away in any other program as long as OneNote is running but isn't currently being used. OneNote can be minimized or hidden behind other applications. When the optimizing process starts, you might notice your hard drive working just a little harder. Unless there is an extreme amount of unused space in your sections, the optimization process shouldn't take more than 5 or 10 minutes. If you don't want OneNote to optimize when inactive, you can uncheck this box.

note

Optimizing can sometimes cause unexpected results. For example, if you have a large amount of blank space between two note containers on a page, OneNote will occasionally try to remove that space. While that can be helpful if you created the space by accident, it can be annoying if you created the space on purpose for later use. If you find OneNote's optimizing annoying, you can easily turn it off by unchecking the two optimize check boxes.

FIGURE 6.6

Use this section of the Open and Save options to configure when your OneNote page sections are optimized.

Optimizing section files

Percentage of unused space to allow in sections without optimizing: `15`

☑ Optimize sections after OneNote has been inactive for the following number of minutes: `30`

☑ Optimize sections when exiting OneNote, but no more often than the following amount of time: `15 Days ▾`

The second optimization option allows you to have OneNote optimize when you exit the program. By default, OneNote optimizes when you exit the program every 15 days. You can change this value by clicking the drop-down box. You can choose values from 5 minutes to 4 weeks. If you never want OneNote to optimize when you exit, uncheck this box.

To save your changes to the Open and Save options dialog, click OK. Click Cancel to discard all of your changes.

Opening and Closing Sections

After you've used OneNote for a while, you might find that you have too many sections open at once. As you can see in Figure 6.7, once you get a large number of sections open at once, you can't view the entire section name for each section. Sometimes you can't even view all available sections. When this occurs you'll need to click the black right arrow to display hidden section names.

Having a large number of sections open at once can also slow OneNote's loading time. If you're having problems with OneNote taking too long to load or you can't see the names of your open sections, you can close sections you don't need. Closing a section doesn't delete it. You can reopen the section at any time. It merely removes it from the current OneNote view and gives you more space for the remaining sections.

You can close an open OneNote section in two ways. You can right click on the section tab and

note

The changes you make in OneNote's optimization behavior won't take effect until after you close and then reopen OneNote.

note

You cannot close pages within a section. If you want to remove a page from a section, you'll need to either delete the page or move it to another section.

choose <u>C</u>lose, or choose <u>C</u>lose from the <u>F</u>ile menu. Both methods close only the currently active section.

Click to scroll to the next section

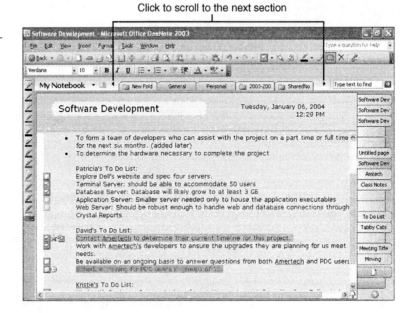

If you need to reopen a closed section, you can do that at any time. Choose <u>F</u>ile, <u>O</u>pen to display the File Open dialog box shown in Figure 6.8.

All sections are represented by individual files. Those files contain all pages within that section. To reopen the DB Training section, choose the DB Training.one file from Figure 6.6 and click <u>O</u>pen. This reopens the section.

OneNote Section Order

You'll notice that when you close and reopen a section, it opens in the same position within the section tabs. When you create a new section, OneNote places it in a specific position depending on how you created it. We'll cover creating sections further in Chapter 9, "Organizing Your Note Pages," but if you create a new section by right-clicking on an existing section and choosing New Section, your section will appear immediately after the existing section. To rearrange the sections, right-click the section tab you want to move and choose Mo_v_e to display Figure 6.9.

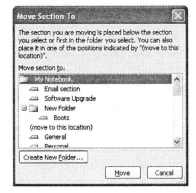

In Figure 6.9, if you want to move the Meetings section after the Project Notes section, choose the Project Notes section from the list. You can move a section immediately following any existing section.

If you want to create a new folder, click the Create New _F_older button. Enter a name for your folder and click OK. You can then move your section into this new folder.

Should You Close Inactive Sections?

Asking if you should close inactive sections is much like asking if you should make the bed every morning. If you're going to need to access the section again soon (like within a few hours or even a day), you might just want to leave the section open. If you know you're not going to use the section again for a while, you can easily close it. For example, if you create a OneNote section for each major project or class, you can close the section when you're completely done with the project or class. If you

note

You cannot move multiple sections at a time. If you need to move more than one section, you'll need to move them individually. You cannot move sections by dragging and dropping them within OneNote.

ever needed to access the information at a later date, you could always reopen the section, but the section wouldn't be taking up space or system resources on a regular basis.

Backing Up OneNote Files

You'll probably notice that there's no save button on any of OneNote's toolbars. That's because OneNote automatically saves your pages, sections, and folders when they are open. OneNote acts very much like a notepad; once you've written or typed the information, it's saved almost immediately. This greatly reduces the possibility of losing your OneNote information if your computer crashes. While there's still a possibility you could lose a few minutes of information, the vast majority of your information will be retained. In addition to saving your notes continuously, when you exit OneNote, it performs an additional save of all open sections and pages.

> **tip**
>
> If you're running OneNote on a computer with limited system resources, closing open sections can free up necessary resources. You can always reopen the section later.

Just because OneNote saves your information continuously doesn't mean you shouldn't back up your information. Computers can and do crash, and sometimes hard drives become corrupt and unreadable. Imagine how you'd feel if you lost your spiral-bound notebook that contained all of your class notes or project-planning information. Backing up your OneNote information is a smart idea.

You can back up your files in several ways. Previously, in Figure 6.4, you saw how to modify your OneNote backup location. By default, the backup location is your local hard drive, but you can alter that location to a network drive or removable disk such as a writable CD drive or removable USB drive.

To configure the frequency of your OneNote backup, choose Options from the Tools menu to display the Options dialog box. Then choose Backup from the list of options in the Category pane to display Figure 6.10.

By default, OneNote is set to automatically back up your notebook every day. You can change this interval by using the drop-down box. You can choose a wide variety of backup intervals from 1 minute to 6 weeks.

> **tip**
>
> Unless you're taking copious and highly critical notes, you probably don't want to set your backup interval to less than every hour or so. While OneNote backs up your notebook, you might notice momentary delays in your work.

FIGURE 6.10

You can alter the frequency of your backups or start a backup immediately.

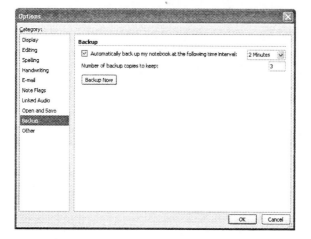

The last backup option you can set is how many copies of your backup you want to keep. If you choose to back up once a week, and also choose to keep three backup copies, you'll actually end up with three week's worth of backups at all times. OneNote will store two previous backups as well as the most current one. When a fourth backup copy is created, the oldest backup will be deleted.

If you want to override OneNote's backup schedule and back up immediately, click Backup Now from the Options dialog box. A new backup copy will be created. You can open .one files directly from your backup file should a note page or section become corrupted or data loss occur. To open a backup copy, navigate to the backup folder and simply double-click on any of the .one files. The section will open in your existing notebook. The backup copy is indicated by the word "backup" next to the section name as shown in Figure 6.11.

You can compare the backup copy with the original copy and even move note containers between the two copies. When you're done, close the backup copy of the section.

Backing up OneNote to another folder on your hard drive won't protect you from a total system crash. If you keep critical data in your OneNote files, you might want to back up to an external device on occasion. To do this, change your Backup location in the Open and Save window of the Options dialog box. Then switch to the Backup options and click Backup Now. For example, if you have a writable CD or DVD drive, change your back up location to the drive, insert a blank disk, and then tell OneNote to back up your files.

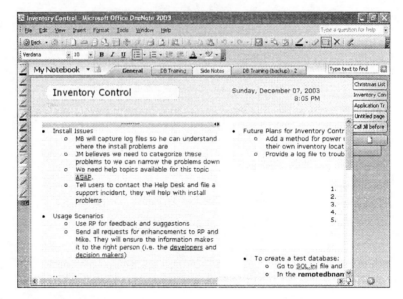

Deleting Notes

Sometimes you realize that you just don't need those notes you took on the future of
telecommuting or Aunt Irma's Christmas list. You can delete notes in several different ways.

Deleting an Individual Note Container

If the note page contains valuable information,
but a particular note container isn't needed any
more, you can delete just the individual container. Move your mouse over the unnecessary
note container until your mouse pointer
changes to a four-pointed arrow. When it does,
your mouse will be directly above the top of the
note container. Click and the entire note container will be selected. Press Delete on the keyboard, click the Delete button on OneNote's
toolbar, or right-click the note container and
choose Delete.

tip

If you want to handle the
backup manually, you can
simply copy the OneNote
files from the My Notebook
folder (and any other folders
you might have created) to
an external location.

Deleting a Page

If you want to delete an entire page, you can accomplish this two ways. First, you can right-click on the page's tab on the right side of the OneNote screen. Choose Delete from the pop-up menu, and your page will be instantly deleted.

You can also delete a page using OneNote's menus. Choose the Edit menu and hover your mouse over the Select option. A pop-out menu will appear as shown in Figure 6.12.

FIGURE 6.12

Use the menus to select an entire page for deletion.

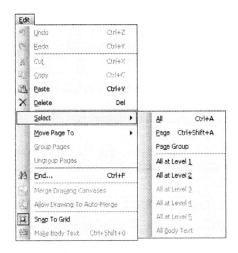

Choose Page from the pop-out menu to select the entire page. You can also select Page Group if you want to select the current page and all of its subpages. Once your page is selected, you can delete the page by using the Delete key on the keyboard or the Delete button on the toolbar. You can also select Delete from the Edit menu.

Deleting a Section

If you want to delete an entire section, you can do that in much the same way as deleting pages. You can always right-click on a section tab at the top of the OneNote screen and choose Delete from the pop-up menu. OneNote will ask if you're sure you want to delete the .one file. If you choose Yes, the section is removed. Choosing No cancels the delete operation.

You can also use the menus to delete a section. Choose the File menu and move your mouse over the Current Section option to display the pop-out menu shown in Figure 6.13.

FIGURE 6.13
You can perform several section operations from the File menu.

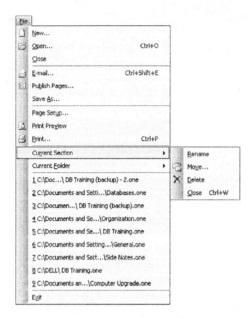

Choose Delete to delete the entire section.

Restoring a Deleted Note Page

If you delete a page from a section inadvertently or simply change your mind about deleting the page, you can restore the page within OneNote. Click on the words My Notebook that appear to the left of the section tabs (see Figure 6.14).

Click the Deleted Pages container to display Figure 6.15. Any deleted pages are shown with the same section structure they had before they were deleted. For example, deleting a page from the Meetings section results in a Meetings section residing in the Deleted Pages folder.

To restore a deleted page, right-click on the page tab and choose Restore, or choose Restore from the Edit menu. The page is returned to its original location.

caution

When you exit OneNote, all pages in the Deleted Pages container are cleared by default. You can change this behavior by unchecking Empty Deleted Pages folder on OneNote exit from the Editing category of the Options dialog box.

You can view
OneNote's file
structure
through this dia-
log.

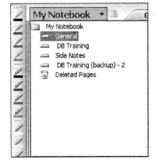

You can view all
of your deleted
pages within
OneNote.

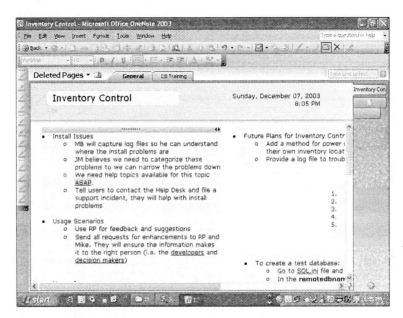

Restoring Deleted Sections

When you delete a section, the entire .one file is also deleted. In order to restore it,
you'll need to find the .one file in the Windows Recycle Bin and restore it to its original location. Once you do that, the section will immediately reappear in OneNote.

THE ABSOLUTE MINIMUM

In this chapter you learned about opening, closing, and deleting sections and a bit about working with pages. You learned about

- Changing the default save locations for your OneNote files
- Opening and closing a section
- Creating a backup of your OneNote files
- Deleting note containers, pages, and entire sections
- Restoring deleted information

In the next chapter you'll learn about printing your notes.

In This Chapter

- Print pages in OneNote
- Modify OneNote's page setup
- Save modified page setups as stationery

7

Printing Notes

As with all other Microsoft programs, once you start using OneNote to store information, you're eventually going to want to print that information. Of course, you can always click the print icon on the toolbar, but there are many customizations you can make to enhance your printed OneNote pages.

As you play around with your print styles, you'll probably find a type of page setup that works best for you. Once you've done this, you can save your print style as stationery so it's always available when creating new pages.

Printing and Sharing Your Notes

Years ago, when computers started to gain popularity in business environments, the buzzword was paperless. Computers promised to eliminate the need for paper in a business situation. After all, if you could just create your document on the computer and fax or email it to the intended recipient, no one would ever need to print anything.

That might have been a noble goal, but the dream of the paperless office quickly faded. No matter how much you might love your computer, you'll still need to print information on a regular basis. Either you need to share the information with someone without a computer, or you just need a paper copy in case of a computer crash.

You might want to print your OneNote notes to share them with colleagues who don't have OneNote. Even if you have a Tablet PC or laptop, you might not want to carry it around with you to every meeting. You could also print all of your OneNote notes and compile a booklet containing the history for an entire project or class.

Regardless of why you need to print your OneNote notes, you'll need to know the basics of printing in OneNote, and how to best layout a OneNote page for printing.

Controlling How OneNote Prints

Like just about all Office programs, OneNote has a Print icon on its standard toolbar. If you want to print a page with the default settings, just click the Print button. The page you're currently viewing is printed to your default printer.

Printing with the Default Page Setup

If you want to print to a printer other than your default printer, or want to print multiple copies at once, click the File menu and choose Print to display Figure 7.1.

You can choose from any printer currently installed on your system in the Select Printer area. In the Page Range box, the page number of the current page is displayed. OneNote fills in the page range for you automatically. If you're currently viewing the second page in a section, for example, the Page Range displays page 2.

If you want to print multiple pages within the same section, you can enter a range of pages in the Page Range section of the Print dialog. For example, to print both pages 2 and 3, enter 2-3 in the Pages box.

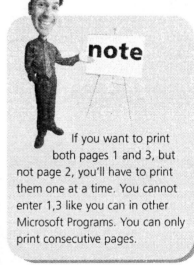

note

If you want to print both pages 1 and 3, but not page 2, you'll have to print them one at a time. You cannot enter 1,3 like you can in other Microsoft Programs. You can only print consecutive pages.

FIGURE 7.1

Use the Print dialog to choose a printer.

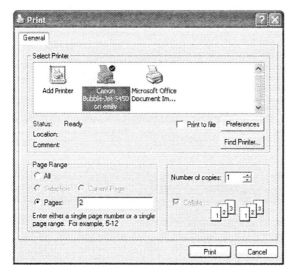

If you want multiple copies of your OneNote page, enter the total number of copies that you want to print in the Number of copies box. If you enter more than one copy, OneNote automatically collates all copies so the pages are in order. Click Print to start printing.

Unless you have pages with relatively little information on them, you probably won't want to use OneNote's default page setup very often. All of the text is printed on one page, even if it takes up multiple screens on your computer. This can produce printed documents that are unreadable without a magnifying glass.

Customizing OneNote's Default Print Setup

In order to print your notes legibly, you'll need to modify OneNote's default page setup or create your own print style to save as stationery.

You can edit OneNote's default page setup through the Print Preview dialog box. To display this dialog, select Print Preview from the File menu or click the Print Preview icon on the toolbar to display Figure 7.2.

The Print range drop-down allows you to print the current page group, the current page, or the current section. You can click the check box marked Print page header on a separate page to print a separate page with the page header and no notes. If you choose this option, your page header won't print on the same page as the notes; it will print on a page by itself.

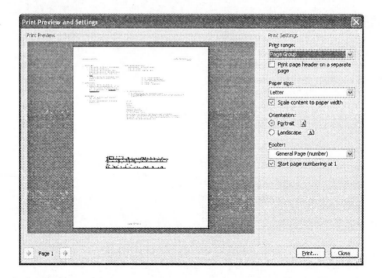

The default page size is the letter size. However, as previously shown, the default page setup scales content to fit page width. This means that no matter how wide your notes appear onscreen, they will always print one page wide. This can lead to very small print. To change this behavior, uncheck the box marked S̲cale content to paper width.

As you make changes to the page setup, the Print Preview dialog updates to show you how many pages the current page occupies when printed. As you can see from Figure 7.3, making just a few changes to your page setup changes the print layout to print the current page on five printed pages instead of one.

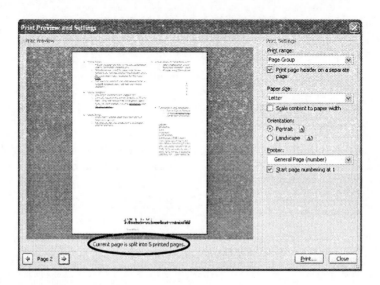

Choose your page orientation by clicking the appropriate box, either Portrait or Landscape. You can configure a page footer by choosing an option from the Footer drop-down. The default selection is the name of the section, followed by the word Page and the page number. You can choose other options, or remove the page footer by selecting (none). If you choose a footer option that displays the page number, the page numbering always starts at 1, even if the page you're printing is page two or three within the current section. If you want to change this, uncheck the box marked Start page numbering at 1.

To print your OneNote pages with the settings you've chosen, click the Print button to display the Print dialog previously shown in Figure 7.1. Make sure the desired printer is selected and the correct number of copies is entered, and then click Print.

Saving a Print Style as Stationery

The changes you make to the page setup in the Print Preview dialog box persist for all pages as long as OneNote is open. As soon as you close OneNote, however, and reopen it, the page setup reverts to the default page setup. If you want to create your own custom setup to use on some or all of your OneNote pages, create a print style and save it as stationery.

The first step in creating a custom print style is to display the Page Setup task pane. Select Page Setup from the File menu to display the task pane shown in Figure 7.4.

FIGURE 7.4

The Page Setup task pane allows you to customize how OneNote prints.

To tell OneNote to print only the amount of information that fits on a standard 8.5 × 11 inch sheet of paper, select Letter from the Page size drop-down. You'll notice that your page changes slightly, as shown in Figure 7.5.

FIGURE 7.5

Changing the page size to letter can prevent the entire page from printing.

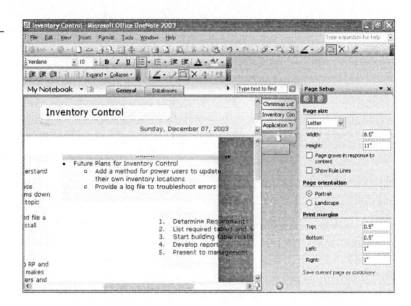

As you can see from the figure (which has been scrolled to the right for illustration purposes), parts of note containers are cut off on the right side of the page (in the gray-shaded area). That information will not print on the same page as the other note containers. If you scroll down, you'll notice the same dark gray area at the bottom of the page. OneNote uses these visual indicators to show you exactly what prints on one page.

You can create a custom page size (for instance, if you're printing on note cards or large-format printers) by changing the width and height of your page. As soon as you alter either value, the Page size option changes to Custom.

If you want a flexible page size (usually only necessary for large-format printers), you can check the box marked Page grows in response to content. This will change your page size automatically as new note containers are added or existing note containers are edited.

To show rule lines on your page (as shown in Figure 7.6), check the box marked Show Rule Lines. This puts the default college-ruled rule lines on your OneNote page. You can use rule lines as writing guides. They can be particularly helpful on a Tablet PC. It's easy to end up writing on a slant on a Tablet PC, as shown in Figure 7.6. Using rule lines can help you take legible notes (see Figure 7.7).

FIGURE 7.6

On a Tablet PC it's easy to start writing illegibly.

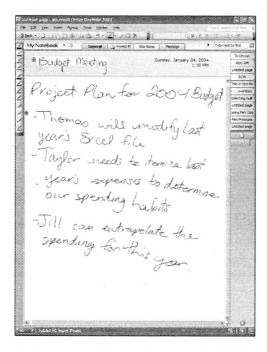

You can change your page orientation by selecting either Portrait or Landscape in the Page orientation section of the task pane. You can also create custom margins by changing the values in the Top, Bottom, Left, and Right boxes.

When you've made all your customizations, click the text at the bottom of the task pane that says Save current page as stationery to display Figure 7.8.

Give your stationery a name you'll easily recognize and then click <u>S</u>ave to save your page setup as stationery. You can now create new pages using this stationery. Saving your page setup as stationery can save the time recreating the page setup at a later date.

note

Even though you can use the Page Setup task pane to display your rule lines, you can't actually print rule lines in OneNote.

FIGURE 7.7

You can display rule lines on your OneNote page.

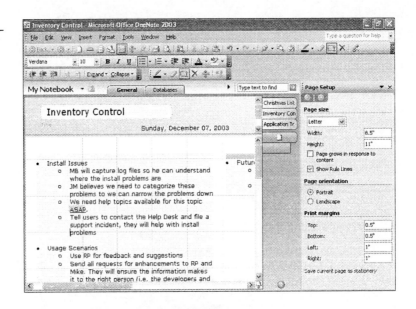

FIGURE 7.8

Type a name for your custom stationery.

THE ABSOLUTE MINIMUM

In this chapter you learned how to customize your page setup to print information the way you want to see it. We covered

- Printing your pages using OneNote's default page layout.

- Printing individual or multiple pages, and how to print multiple copies.

- Creating your own custom page setup using the paper size and layout you choose, and how to save the setup as stationery to make printing your notes a breeze.

Next you'll learn about Side Notes, OneNote's ability to take a quick always-on-top note with a few clicks.

8

CREATING SIDE NOTES

So far you've created your first note and even worked with some of OneNote's structural components such as pages, folders, and sections. You've learned that OneNote can be used just like a legal pad to take notes, create drawings, and organize information. However, many people utilize another type of office supply to take quick notes, the sticky notepad.

This chapter will introduce you to Side Notes, the OneNote equivalent of a paper sticky note. Using Side Notes, you can quickly jot down an idea, take an audio recording, or even launch the full OneNote window.

What Is a Side Note?

A *Side Note* is a miniature OneNote 2003 window that can be launched from the system tray (the area full of icons at the bottom right of your computer screen). When you install OneNote, an icon with a purple *N* is placed in your system tray. You can open a Side Note from the system tray icon, from within OneNote, or from a keyboard shortcut. We'll cover how to start a new Side Note later in this chapter.

The purpose of Side Notes is to allow you to take a quick note while you're working in other applications. You can leave a Side Note up on your screen all day long, and it will float above your other applications, as shown in Figure 8.1.

FIGURE 8.1

A Side Note can float over your other applications without getting in the way.

You can take as many Side Notes as you want from this one window.

Anatomy of a Side Note

The Side Note has several parts as shown in Figure 8.2.

tip

Side Notes can be helpful as you're working in other applications. For example, you can open a Side Note while browsing in Internet Explorer. Then copy and paste text from Internet Explorer into your Side Note as you work.

FIGURE 8.2

A Side Note has its own toolbar and controls.

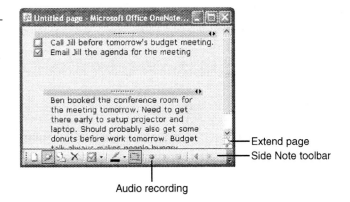

Extend page
Side Note toolbar

Audio recording

The Side Note window has its own toolbar. This toolbar allows you to accomplish a number of functions. If you don't want the Side Note window to remain on top of your other applications, simply click the pushpin button on the toolbar. This "unpins" the Side Note window and allows it to disappear behind other applications. If you want to bring it back to the front so you can type in it, you'll need to activate it by clicking on its icon on the Windows Task bar.

When the pushpin icon is depressed, the Side Note window always remains on top of the other applications you're currently using. Clicking on another application dims the title bar of the Side Note window to show you it's no longer the active window. Clicking on the Side Note window again activates it.

From the Side Note toolbar, you can also move the current Side Note to another section, delete the note, add a new page, change the ink color, select text or images, add a Note Flag, or record an audio note. We'll cover each of these tasks later in this chapter.

Creating Side Notes When OneNote Is Closed

The first way to create a new Side Note is from the OneNote system tray icon. You can right-click this icon to display a context menu, as shown in Figure 8.3.

note

When you close the Side Note window and then use one of the previous methods to open it again, you'll always get a new Side Note. If you need to return to a previous Side Note, you need to use the Previous Page/Next Page buttons on the Side Note window. Later in this chapter we'll cover editing Side Notes in the main OneNote window.

FIGURE 8.3

Choose Open new Side Note to create a new Side Note.

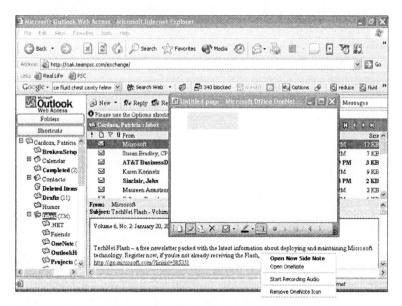

Clicking Open New Side Note will open a blank Side Note. That method of opening a new Side Note takes two mouse clicks. You can actually accomplish the same thing in one mouse click by using your left (or standard) mouse button to single-click on the OneNote system tray icon.

If you rarely use the mouse and prefer a keyboard shortcut, press the Windows key and the letter *N* at the same time.

Accessing Side Notes from Within OneNote

If OneNote is already running, there are two ways you can access Side Notes. If OneNote is the active application, you can click Ctrl+Shift+M to open a new Side Note on top of the existing OneNote window.

You can also access Side Notes in a larger form through the main OneNote window. Figure 8.4 shows a typical OneNote window with several sections listed at the top of the screen.

note

If you've used Side Notes at all before, you have a Side Notes section visible in your main OneNote window. If you have only recently installed OneNote or have never created a Side Note, you will not have a Side Notes section. To create one, use one of the methods previously described to create a new Side Note and a Side Notes section is created for you.

FIGURE 8.4

Your OneNote window contains a Side Notes section if you've ever created a Side Note.

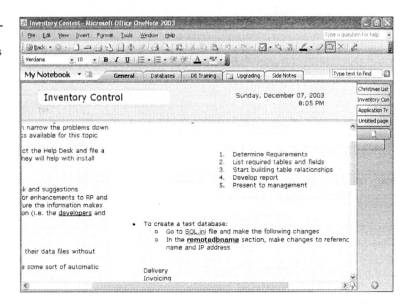

To view a full-size version of your Side Notes, click the Side Notes section tab to display Figure 8.5.

FIGURE 8.5

Side Notes can be viewed in the same window as other notes.

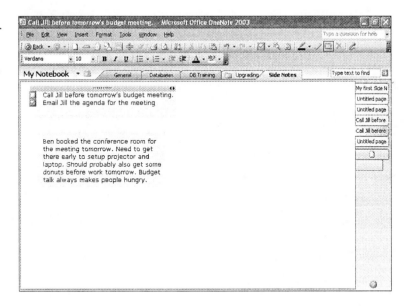

As you can see from the figure, each Side Note you've created has its own page within the Side Notes section.

Working with Your Side Note

Once you've launched the Side Note window using any of the methods mentioned in the section "What Is a Side Note?", you can perform a variety of tasks within that window.

Extending Your Side Note

As you're typing along taking notes, you might eventually run out of room. Generally, Side Notes are used for short, quick notes, but your phone call might run long, or you just might need more space to continue your note. To add additional space to your Side Note, click the Extend Side Note icon next to the horizontal scroll bar, as previously shown in Figure 8.2. This icon will give you an additional amount of space. The exact amount varies, but it's often around the same size as your existing Side Note.

Creating New Side Notes

If you want to create a new Side Note page from the Side Note window, just click the New Page icon (the first icon on the Side Note toolbar). You'll get a new, untitled page in your Side Note window. Once you add a new page, there are only three ways you can return to the previous Side Note page you were viewing. You can delete the new page by clicking the Delete icon on the Side Note toolbar, you can use the previous page button on the bottom right of the OneNote window, or you can maximize the Side Note window and choose your previous page from the page tabs, as explained later in this chapter.

Inserting Note Flags in a Side Note

Just like full-sized notes you create in OneNote, you can add Note Flags to a Side Note as well. To add a Note Flag to a line in a Side Note, Click the note container that has the line you want to flag. You can also highlight the individual line within the note container.

If you want to apply a Note Flag to the highlighted text, click the fifth icon on the Side Note toolbar. The icon will change based on the last Note Flag you used within OneNote. If the last Note Flag you used was Remember for Later, the icon will be a pushpin.

If you want to apply a different Note Flag to the highlighted text, click the drop-down arrow next to the Note Flag icon to display Figure 8.6.

FIGURE 8.6
FIGURE 8.6

You can choose any of your existing Note Flags.

Choose the Note Flag you need from the drop-down list. If you accidentally apply the wrong Note Flag, you can remove it in two ways. You can select the Note Flag again to toggle it off, or you can select Remove Note Flags from Selection.

Adding Audio to a Side Note

Much like other notes in OneNote, a Side Note can be used to store an audio recording along with typed or handwritten text. A typical use for recording audio and text in a Side Note is a telephone conversation or a quick meeting between two coworkers. To start recording audio in a Side Note, click the red record icon on the Side Note's toolbar. A notation is placed in your Side Note that an audio recording is present, as shown in Figure 8.7.

caution

If you choose Remove Note Flags from Selection, you can actually remove the Note Flags from the entire Side Note. Just select all text in the Side Note and choose this option.

FIGURE 8.7

OneNote places a notation about the audio recording on your Side Note.

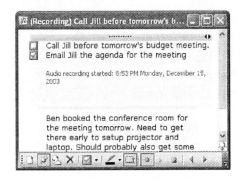

To stop recording audio, click the blue stop button on the Side Note's toolbar. If you're typing or writing while OneNote is recording audio, OneNote records what you're typing during each portion of the audio recording. You can open the main OneNote window, navigate to the Side Notes section, and play back your audio while OneNote highlights the portions of the note you were typing or writing during the audio recording.

Navigating Within Side Notes

You can turn the Side Note window into a full OneNote window at any time by clicking the maximize button on the Side Note window. You can also position your mouse at one of the corners of the Side Note window and drag to make the note larger. As soon as the Side Note gets large enough, it turns into a full OneNote window with the normal toolbars, page headings, and page tabs. You don't have to cause the Side Note window to fill the screen, just make it slightly bigger, as shown in Figure 8.8.

Turning a Side Note into a Standard Note

Within the Side Note window, you can move an existing Side Note into another note section. For example, you might be using OneNote to take notes during business meetings. Another meeting participant calls you on the phone and wants to discuss the agenda for the next meeting. You quickly launch a Side Note and record the phone conversation. But later, you want to move that note from the Side Notes section to the Meeting section. While you have the Side Note open, use the following steps.

1. Click the third Side Note toolbar button, **Move Page To**.

note

Unlike full-sized notes, a Side Note does not have the capability to highlight the portions of a note you were typing or writing during an audio recording, when viewed in the small Side Note window. You need to view a Side Note in the main OneNote window for this functionality.

tip

You can create a new Side Note and begin recording audio directly from the system tray icon. Just right-click the icon and choose Start Recording Audio. OneNote opens a new Side Note window and starts recording your audio note. To stop the recording, close the Side Note or click the stop button on the Side Note toolbar.

2. Choose **Another Section** to display the Move or Copy Pages dialog box shown in Figure 8.9.

3. Choose the section you want to hold your Side Note. You can create a new section or a new folder to house the note by clicking the appropriate button in the dialog box.

4. Once you choose the destination section, the Move and Copy buttons will activate.

5. Click either **Move** or **Copy**. Clicking Move removes the page from the Side Notes section and moves it to the destination section. Clicking Copy places a copy in the destination section while leaving the original in the Side Notes section.

FIGURE 8.8

A Side Note can easily turn into a full-sized note.

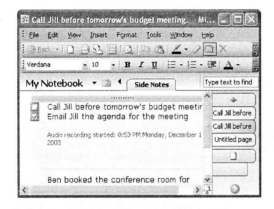

FIGURE 8.9

You can move your Side Note to any other section or create a new section.

If you move an existing Side Note page to another section, you're returned to the last Side Note page created. If you choose Copy, you return to the Side Note window.

Moving or copying pages preserves the page exactly as you created it in the Side Notes window. All audio recordings are preserved and moved with the rest of the page.

Combining Side Notes

As previously mentioned, every time you create a new Side Note, you're actually creating a new page within the Side Note section. If you want to combine some of these pages, you can do so within the main OneNote window. Unfortunately there is no easy way to combine two pages into one, but you can drag and drop or cut and paste note containers from one page to another using the following steps.

caution

If you attempt to move a note container that contains an audio recording by copying and pasting it, the text within the note container will move, but the audio recording will not. You should not use this method to move audio recordings.

1. Open the main OneNote window.
2. Click on the **Side Notes** section.
3. Click on the page tab for the Side Note page you want to delete.
4. To select all note containers on this page, press **Ctrl+A** or choose Select All from the Edit menu.
5. Press **Ctrl+X** (or click the Cut button) to place the selected note containers on the clipboard.
6. Click the Side Note page you want to keep from the page tabs on the right of the screen.
7. Press **Ctrl+V** (or click the Paste button) to paste your note containers on the existing page.
8. Right-click the page tab for the page you want to delete.
9. Choose Delete from the context menu.

You can use this method to combine information on any two OneNote pages, whether they are Side Notes or other pages within OneNote. Remember, if you have audio in a note container you're copying, only the text is copied. The linked audio file isn't copied.

THE ABSOLUTE MINIMUM

In this chapter, you learned how to create Side Notes, a smaller version of a full note. You learned about

- Launching a new Side Note
- Adding text and audio to Side Notes
- Accessing Side Notes from the main OneNote window
- Moving information between Side Notes and other OneNote sections

In the next chapter, we'll cover the various ways you can organize your OneNote information. Once you use OneNote for a few notes, you'll probably end up with a lot of information that's not organized very well. We'll cover the various ways you can organize your information and how you can best use elements of OneNote's structure to organize that information.

IN THIS CHAPTER

- Create folders to store OneNote information
- Create sections within folders
- Create page groups within sections
- Move text within folders, sections, and pages

9

ORGANIZING YOUR NOTE PAGES

You can use a wide variety of programs to take notes. Microsoft Word has a number of features that allow you to take highly formatted notes. Even a program as basic as Notepad can help you keep electronic notes. Since those programs aren't designed primarily as note-taking programs, however, they lack some of the key organizational features that make OneNote so well suited for note taking.

OneNote has a variety of features that allow you to organize any number of pages of notes. Chapter 3, "Using OneNote's Structure to Organize Your Notes," covered creating page groups for multiple related pages, using sections to group all notes on a particular subject or topic, and creating folders to further segregate notes. This chapter covers all of the ways you can work with note pages, sections, and folders.

Creating Page Groups, Sections, and Folders

Before we start exploring the different elements of OneNote discussed in this chapter, we should get our bearings straight. In Figure 9.1, you'll see each element we're discussing in this chapter.

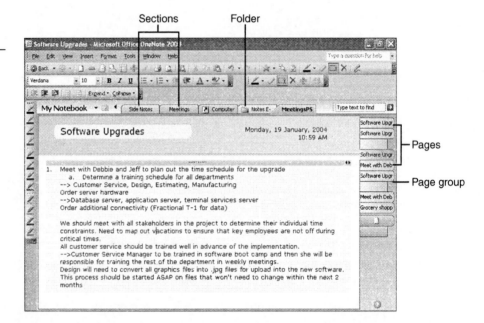

FIGURE 9.1

Your OneNote window might look similar.

Every OneNote installation has one default folder. That folder is called My Notebook. If you examine the My Documents folder on your hard drive, you'll find a folder called My Notebook. Within that folder, you'll find every other OneNote file.

If you examine the My Notebook folder shown in Figure 9.2, and compare it to Figure 9.1, you can begin to relate the structures within OneNote to the individual files and folders in Windows.

As you can see, there's a .one file for each section shown in Figure 9.1 (as well as the sections that aren't shown due to screen size). Each OneNote section has its own file. You might notice that there aren't individual files for each of the pages within OneNote. The information stored in OneNote's pages is actually stored within the section file.

note

You can store OneNote files in other places besides the My Notebook file. However, unless you explicitly place a file in another location, such as a network share or SharePoint server, all files you create in OneNote are stored in the My Notebook folder.

FIGURE 9.2

The My Notebook folder contains a file for each section.

In addition to .one files for each of the sections, there are also folders in OneNote. A folder is a container for section files. You can have multiple pages within a section and multiple sections within a folder.

The other components you'll find in the My Notebook folder are any linked files. For example, you can link a Word document to a OneNote page and OneNote places a copy of that file in the My Notebook folder (or whatever folder you're using to store the files from that particular section). For more information on linking files within OneNote, see Chapter 20, "Office 2003 Integration." Any audio notes you record while in OneNote are stored as separate files in the related folder and linked to the page you were working on when you recorded them. You can find more information about recording and storing audio notes in Chapter 17, "It's Too Quiet in Here—Let's Add Some Sound."

The next sections will explore each of the structural components within OneNote in detail.

tip

It's often helpful to create a folder for wide categories of information. For example, if most of your notes are going to be business related, but some will be personal, consider creating a Personal folder. This way you can store all of your personal information separate from your business information.

Creating Page Groups for Related Notes

A page group is exactly what it sounds like. It's a group of pages. You can think of page groups as several legal pad pages stapled together.

To create a new page group, all you have to do is create a new subpage. To create a new subpage, click the New Subpage tab. This tab is located directly under the new page tab, as shown in Figure 9.3.

FIGURE 9.3

Click the new subpage tab to create a sub-page of the current page.

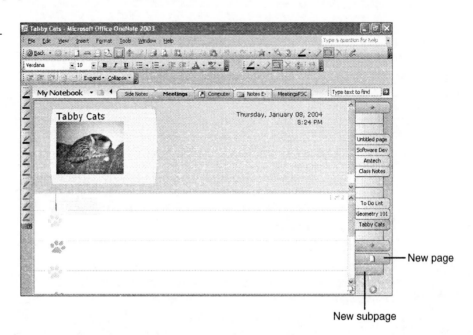

New page

New subpage

The new subpage is placed directly under the page that was currently selected. For example, in Figure 9.3, the subpage will be created under the Tabby Cats page.

The subpage is created with the same title as its master page. The page title won't appear on the subpage's tab, although it will appear in the page header. It also has the same date and time stamp. Even though you can create a new subpage at any time, it will always have the time stamp of your original page.

tip

If you want to change the date and time stamp on a subpage, you can delete the existing entry and type your own date and time stamp.

As you can see from Figure 9.4, the subpage has an additional caption on the right side of the page under the page header that tells you the total number of pages in the page group and the current page you're viewing. You can create any number of subpages under a master page.

FIGURE 9.4

Your subpage lists the current page number and the total number of pages in the page group.

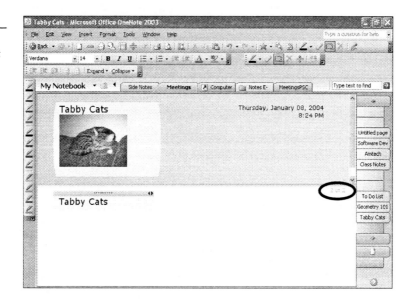

You might wonder why you would want to create a subpage rather than just adding more space to your existing page. Well, there are no firm rules for doing this. However, here are a few common reasons:

- If you create a subpage, you can later turn that page into its own master page by ungrouping the pages.
- You can take an existing master page and easily turn it into a subpage.
- You can control printing of subpages individually.

Using Sections for Categories of Notes

Sections, displayed as individual file folder tabs in a typical OneNote window, can be used to group related information. When you install OneNote, you have default sections for Meetings and General. You can create as many sections as you want. Each section is represented by its own .one file. If you use OneNote for business notes, you can create a new section for each project you're working on.

Creating a New Section

To create a new section, right click an existing section tab and choose New Section, click the New Section button on the toolbar, or select <u>N</u>ew from the <u>F</u>ile menu to display the New task pane, as shown in Figure 9.5.

FIGURE 9.5

You can create new sections, folders, pages, and Side Notes from the New task pane.

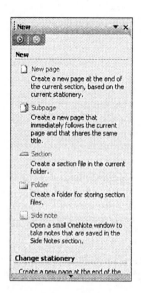

Choose Section in the Task pane to create a new section. When you create a new section, it's inserted directly after the current section you're viewing.

Renaming Sections

When you create a new section, its name (New Section) is highlighted. Just type the name of the section and press Enter or click somewhere else in the section. If you need to rename the section later, right-click the section tab and choose <u>R</u>ename. Type the new name and press Enter or click somewhere in a note page to save your changes.

Using Folders to Organize Multiple Sections

A folder is a container for sections. You can create folders for large categories of notes. For example, create a folder for business notes and a folder for personal notes. If you're using OneNote for school, you can create a folder for each class or a folder for each semester and sections for each class. You have complete control over how your OneNote files are organized.

To create a new folder, display the New task pane by selecting <u>N</u>ew from the <u>F</u>ile menu. Click Folder to create a new folder. When you create a folder, it looks very similar to a section and is displayed in the same place as the section tabs at the top of the OneNote window. However, folders have a folder icon next to their name. Type a name for your folder and press Enter.

tip

You can also choose New <u>F</u>older from the <u>I</u>nsert menu to create a new folder.

Once you create your folder, select the folder's tab. You'll see the message displayed in Figure 9.6.

Once you have a new folder, select New Se<u>c</u>tion from the <u>I</u>nsert menu or just click somewhere in the blank folder to create a new section.

FIGURE 9.6

Your new folder doesn't have any sections yet.

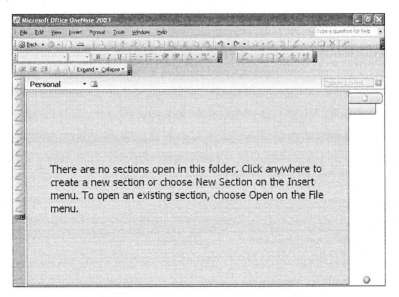

Changing Section Colors

You might notice that when you create a new section, it's not the same color as the previous section. OneNote allows you to create sections with eight different colors (or no color at all). To change your section color, right-click on the section title and choose Section <u>C</u>olor to display the context menu shown in Figure 9.7.

FIGURE 9.7

You can choose
eight different
section colors.

Just click any of the available colors to change the color of the section.

Moving Page Groups, Sections, and Folders

Unless you're incredibly organized with every section, page, and folder you create,
you'll probably need to move some or all of these components to different places.
You can move any of these components using similar steps.

Moving Pages

To move a page or a group of pages, use the following steps.

1. Right-click the page tab to display the page's context menu.

2. Move your mouse or Tablet PC pen over the Move Page To selection to display the context menu shown in Figure 9.8.

FIGURE 9.8

You can move
the page to a
different section
or folder.

3. If the section you need is displayed in the context menu, just click it. If you
don't see the section you need, choose Another Section to display Figure 9.9.

FIGURE 9.9

You can select any available folder or section.

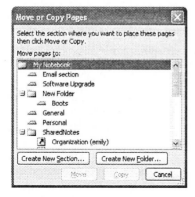

4. Click the destination folder or section and choose either <u>M</u>ove or <u>C</u>opy. If you don't see an appropriate section or folder, you can click the Create New <u>S</u>ection or Create New <u>F</u>older buttons to create the destination folder or section.

Choosing Move will actually move the page to the selected destination section. Copy creates a copy of the selected page and moves it to the destination section.

Moving Sections

In addition to moving pages, you can move entire sections. To move a section, right-click the section tab and click Mo<u>v</u>e. The dialog displayed is very similar to Figure 9.9. You can choose from any available section. When you choose a section, the section you're moving is placed immediately after that section. You can also move the section to a different folder or create a new folder.

Moving Pages Within a Section

You might want to rearrange pages within an existing section. To move a page, click the page once to select it. Click it again and hold down the mouse button. The page tab will turn orange and you can drag the page up or down. As you drag the page, a small black triangle appears letting you know where the page will be released.

note

To move a page group (or just multiple pages), select the pages before you begin the previous steps. To select adjacent pages, click the first page, then hold the Shift key while clicking the last page. To select non-adjacent pages, click the first page, then hold the Ctrl key while clicking the other desired pages.

You can move multiple pages as well. Simply select the first page with your mouse. Hold down the Shift or Ctrl keys to select multiple pages. Once you've selected the pages you need, drag them up or down to the destination location.

Closing Sections

After you've been using OneNote for a while, you'll probably have a lot of open sections. As you can see from Figure 9.10, a large number of sections can make it difficult to read the entire section title. If you have more sections than can fit across the screen, you'll notice black arrows on the sides of the section tabs. Click the black arrows to scroll through the sections.

> **tip**
>
> You can actually perform this operation with a single click. Click and hold the mouse while dragging it slightly to the left to simulate pulling the page out of the stack. Continue to hold the mouse button down and move the mouse up or down to relocate your page.

FIGURE 9.10

Too many open sections can make it difficult to navigate.

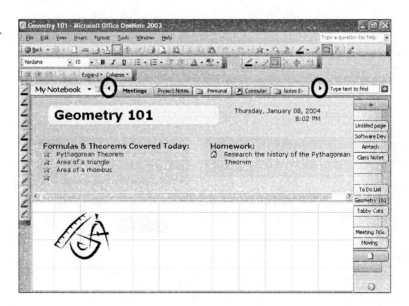

You can close an open section that you no longer need. To close a section, right-click the section's tab and choose Close. The section's .one file remains intact in the My Notebook folder, but the section doesn't display in OneNote any more. You can reopen the section at any time by choosing Open from the File menu and choosing the section's .one file.

The Absolute Minimum

In this chapter you learned about a variety of the structures available within OneNote. You learned

- How you can use page groups to store related notes
- How you can create new sections, rename them, and change their color
- How you can use folders to group multiple sections
- How to manage these components within OneNote
- How to move information between pages, sections, and folders

The next chapter focuses on using fonts and Note Flags to add some structure and organization to your notes.

PART iV

Organizing Information Within Pages

IN THIS CHAPTER

- Format your text with fonts and styles
- Use OneNote to create To Do lists
- Create, customize, and use Note Flags

10

NOTE TAKING 201: AN ADVANCED COURSE

When you take notes on paper, you probably don't write each line or word in exactly the same way. For example, you might underline important topics, circle definitions, highlight to-dos, or even use a different color for certain types of notes. You can do the same thing in OneNote. Through the use of fonts, styles, and different pens on a Tablet PC, you can create highly formatted notes that provide an easy visual representation of the relative importance of different topics.

In addition to using different fonts and styles, OneNote contains a built-in note flagging system. You can create a variety of different Note Flags for different purposes. These Note Flags can be customized to meet your individual needs. In this chapter, we'll cover the use of fonts, styles, and Note Flags to provide a high level of detail for your notes.

Using Fonts and Formatting to Add Style to Your Notes

After a busy session of note taking, you might end up with a very long, boring page of notes, much like Figure 10.1.

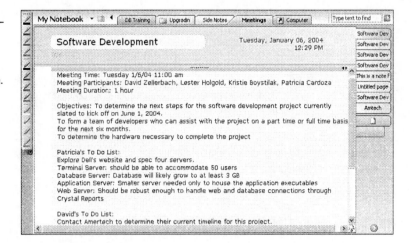

FIGURE 10.1

A long page of notes in the same font can be rather boring.

Looking at Figure 10.1, it's hard to tell where the important tasks, to-dos, or follow-up items are located. You could read through the entire page of notes, but that can be quite time consuming. If you have multiple pages and subpages for a single meeting or project, this can be even more time consuming.

Now examine Figure 10.2. In this figure, you can see the same basic notes as in Figure 10.1. However, in this figure, the notes are highly formatted. Headings are in larger fonts, bolded, and underlined. To-Dos are highlighted. Follow-up items are in italics. Each of these formatting changes provides you with an easier method of finding note items at a later date.

Using varied fonts, highlighting, and styles can be particularly important if you're sharing your notes with others. After all, you might remember that your list of to-dos was created about halfway through the meeting (and therefore is approximately halfway down the note page), but someone else reading your notes won't necessarily know this.

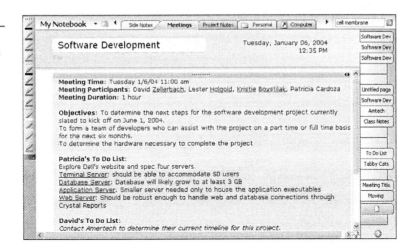

FIGURE 10.2
Formatting, fonts, and styles can greatly increase readability.

Changing Fonts in OneNote

It's easy to change fonts in OneNote. In fact, if you've ever changed fonts in Word, you'll notice it's a very similar operation. You can control a variety of font options through the use of the Formatting toolbar, shown in Figure 10.3.

FIGURE 10.3
You can use the Formatting toolbar to change a variety of font options.

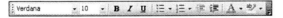

As you're typing, just use the Font and Font Size drop-down boxes shown on the Formatting toolbar to change the font or font size. It's possible to change both of these options anywhere on the note page and even within a word if you want to have individual letters formatted differently.

Figure 10.4 shows a typical page of meeting notes with several different fonts and sizes.

tip

If the Formatting toolbar isn't displayed on your screen, select Toolbars from the View menu and click Formatting from the fly-out menu.

FIGURE 10.4

Varying your
font and font
size can make
reading notes
easier.

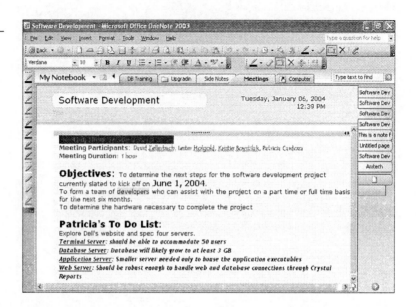

Adding Emphasis to Text

In addition to changing fonts, you can also add
emphasis to text using the bold, italicize, and
underline tools. To do so, simply select the text
with your mouse and click the appropriate toolbar button (either bold, italic, or underline).

You can change the font color in OneNote as
well. An entire page of black text can get a little
boring. To change the font color, click the small
drop-down next to the icon of a capital A to display the color palette. You can choose from any
of the 40 available colors. You cannot create custom
colors within OneNote like you can in other Office programs.

tip

Don't get too carried away
changing fonts and font
sizes. A little change can go
a long way. It can be distracting to read notes where
every other word is in a different style.

Formatting Fonts Using the Task Pane

If you don't want to use the toolbars to format your text, you can access all of the
options we've discussed using the Font task pane. Simply select Font from the Format
menu to display the Font task pane shown in Figure 10.5.

The advantage of using the Font task pane to format your text instead of the toolbar is that you can leave it visible on your screen if you need to make multiple changes within a document. It can also be quicker to use the Task pane to make changes to font and font size while you're typing. If you need to change the font as you're typing along, just choose the font name from the list.

You can also apply three text effects that aren't available from the default Formatting toolbar: strikethrough, superscript, and subscript.

Adding Highlighting to Text

If you want to add some extra emphasis to some of your text, you can use the highlighter. If you're using a Tablet PC, you can switch the pen to a highlighter by choosing one of the four highlighter colors (yellow, blue, green, or pink) from the Pens toolbar. However, you can also highlight using the keyboard and the Formatting toolbar. This option gives you more choices for the highlighter colors.

To highlight a block of text with a particular color, first select the text using the mouse or pen. To highlight in the default color (yellow), just click the highlighting toolbar button. If you want to highlight in a different color, click the small drop-down arrow next to the highlighting toolbar button to display a drop down menu of 15 different highlighter choices as shown in Figure 10.6. Click the desired choice.

tip

As you're typing along, it might be rather distracting to use the mouse to click the buttons on the toobars for bold, italic, and underline. You can use the keyboard shortcuts for these operations as well. Ctrl+B toggles the bold option on or off, Ctrl+U toggles underlining on or off, and Ctrl+I toggles italics on or off.

note

There are several other options you can use on the Formatting toolbar. Directly to the right of the Underline icon, you'll find four buttons that can be used for creating outlines. We'll cover creating outlines in Chapters 14 and 15.

FIGURE 10.5

You can use the
Font task pane
to format your
text.

FIGURE 10.6

OneNote gives
you 15 different
highlighter
colors.

Using OneNote to Create a To-Do List

A popular use of OneNote is to create detailed to-do lists. You might create a to-do list while in a meeting and refer back to it at a later date. If you're working with a shared section, perhaps stored on a SharePoint Team Services Web site, you can keep multiple to-do lists for a project within that section. Each individual user can update their own to-do list, and the project manager can always access anyone's to-do lists.

You can create a to-do list using the text formatting techniques discussed in the previous sections. For example, in Figure 10.2, David's To-Do List contains four items. As David completes these items, he can use the Font task pane to mark each of these items in strikethrough font. When David is done with his to-do list, it might look something like Figure 10.7.

note

Once you change the highlighting color, the new color becomes the default for the note. If you want to highlight another block of text with the same color, just click the button again. You do not need to use the drop-down to choose the color.

FIGURE 10.7

You can use fonts and formatting to format your to-do list.

David has marked off each of his tasks and provided updates where appropriate. This is an easy way to create a to-do list that multiple users can understand. However, OneNote has another helpful feature that can create to-do lists as well as flag notes with a variety of other labels. That feature is Note Flags.

Using Note Flags

A Note Flag is a tool for following up on a particular note or portion of a note. You can flag a phrase, a line, or an entire note container. You can use the Task pane to view a summary of all of your Note Flags across all OneNote sections and even update the Note Flags from within the Task pane.

There are nine Note Flags in OneNote. Unfortunately, you cannot add any more Note Flags, but you can customize the existing Note Flags to meet your needs.

The first five Note Flags are predefined. They are To Do, Important, Question, Remember for later, and Definition. The remaining four Note Flags are undefined. In order to use one of the undefined Note Flags, you'll need to define it. We'll cover customizing the Note Flags later in this chapter.

tip

You can use keyboard shortcuts to apply your Note Flags. The keyboard shortcuts consist of the Ctrl key plus the number of the Note Flag. For example, by default, the To Do Note Flag is listed first. The keyboard shortcut to apply this Note Flag is Ctrl+1. Unfortunately the shortcuts aren't intuitive, but if you use Note Flags on a regular basis, you'll remember which flag corresponds to which shortcut.

Flagging a Line of Text in OneNote

To apply a Note Flag, simply click anywhere in the line of text you want to flag. Select Note Flags from the Format menu to display the pop-out menu shown in Figure 10.8.

FIGURE 10.8

You can choose from a variety of Note Flags.

What happens when you apply a Note Flag depends on the Note Flag. For the five predefined Note Flags, the behavior is summarized in the following list.

- To Do—A blue box is placed to the left of the flagged line. When you've completed the To Do, you can click this box to place a check mark in it.

- Important—A yellow star is placed to the left of the flagged line.

- Question—A purple question mark appears to the left of the flagged line.

- Remember for later—The flagged line is highlighted in yellow.

- Definition—The flagged line is highlighted in green.

note

Your menu might look slightly different. By default, OneNote displays the first five Note Flags and any customized Note Flags. If you haven't customized your Note Flags, you'll only see the first five. If you have customized the remaining four flags, you'll see those custom flags listed as well.

After you've applied Note Flags to your meeting notes, previously shown in Figure 10.2, the notes might look something like Figure 10.9.

FIGURE 10.9

Note Flags can help organize and call attention to your notes.

Removing Note Flags

Even though Note Flags can be quite helpful in organizing your notes, there will always be times you want to remove a Note Flag. You might have accidentally selected the wrong line to flag, or a note you considered important a month ago might not be so important today. To remove a Note Flag, highlight the flagged line and either click the Note Flag toolbar button or select the Note Flag from the menu again. This toggles the Note Flag off. If you want to remove all Note Flags from your page, right-click any flagged line and choose Remove Note Flags from Selection. Your text is retained, but any formatting or icons associated with the Note Flag are removed.

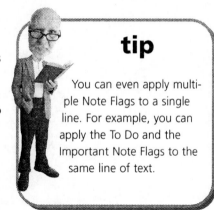

tip

You can even apply multiple Note Flags to a single line. For example, you can apply the To Do and the Important Note Flags to the same line of text.

Marking Note Flags

The To Do Note Flag is a special type of Note Flag. It's the only default Note Flag that has an action associated with it. You can use your mouse and put a check mark in the box, as shown in Figure 10.10.

FIGURE 10.10
You can mark the To Do Note Flags as complete.

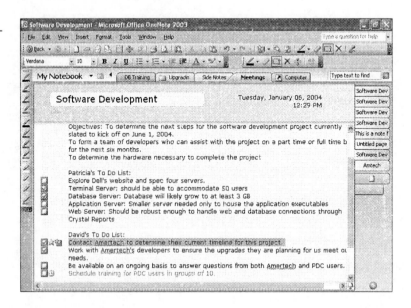

In addition to using the mouse to check the box, you can also right-click the flagged text and choose Mark Note Flags in Selection.

Customizing Note Flags

You can customize any of the nine Note Flags in OneNote. Select Format, Note Flags, Customize My Note Flags to display the Customize My Note Flags task pane as shown in Figure 10.11.

FIGURE 10.11

You can customize any of the nine Note Flags.

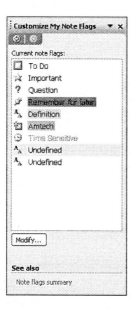

By default, the last four Note Flags are listed as Undefined. You can customize these Note Flags to meet your particular needs. In Figure 10.11, I have customized two Note Flags, naming them Amtech and Time Sensitive. For example, if you need to keep track of notes for three different projects, you can configure a Note Flag for each project. If you're a manager, you could configure a Note Flag for each of your employees. You could then use the Note Flags to mark tasks for each of your employees using their customized Note Flag.

To customize a Note Flag, click the Note Flag and then click Modify to display Figure 10.12.

You can customize several different aspects of a Note Flag. First, you need to enter a Display name. This name will appear in the Note Flag Summary task pane, as well as on the Note Flag menu previously seen in Figure 10.8.

Next, you can choose a symbol to appear to the left of any flagged line. You can choose from 23 symbols in the Symbol drop-down menu. Use the Font Color drop-down menu to customize the font for your flagged text. Any text you flag will automatically change to the color specified.

FIGURE 10.12

Use this dialog
to customize
your Note Flags.

You can also choose a <u>H</u>ighlight Color. All flagged
text will be highlighted in this color. As you change
settings for your Note Flag, you can see a preview in
the Modify Note Flag dialog box. So if you're not
happy with your selections, simply start over.

When you've finished customizing your Note Flag,
click OK to save your changes. Your Task pane
might now look similar to Figure 10.13.

View a Summary of Existing Note Flags

Note Flags make it easy to look at a page of notes
and pick out various types of notes. However, they
can also help you find information across multiple
pages, sections, and folders. Through the use of the
Note Flag Summary task pane, you can view a list
of all existing note flags. You can even print this
summary. To view the summary list, do the
following:

1. If you currently have a Task pane visible in
   your OneNote window, click the title of the
   Task pane to display the drop down.

2. Choose **Note Flags Summary** to display
   Figure 10.14.

3. If you don't have a Task pane visible,
   choose **<u>V</u>iew**, **Tas<u>k</u> Pane**, then choose
   the **Note Flags Summary** task pane
   from the Task pane drop-down.

note

You can customize any
of the existing Note Flags.
However, if you make changes to
a Note Flag you've already used in
your notes, the customizations
won't apply to previously flagged
items.

caution

Once you've customized
a Note Flag, there's no
way to return it to an
undefined state. You can
always change the name
and properties of the Note Flag, but
you cannot reset it to be undefined.

FIGURE 10.13

Once you've customized your Note Flags, you'll see a preview of how they'll appear in the Task pane.

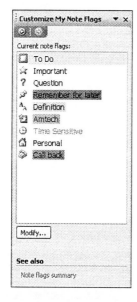

FIGURE 10.14

You can use the Note Flags Summary task pane to display all of your flagged text.

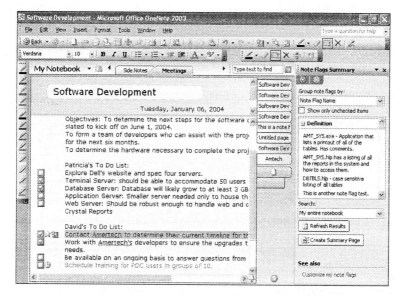

The Note Flags Summary task pane displays all Note Flags in the current section by default. Each Note Flag is displayed in its entirety.

There are a variety of options you can choose within the Note Flags Summary task pane to give you the information you need. By default, all flagged text is displayed grouped by Note Flag Name. You can change this grouping to Section, Title, Date, or

Note Text. Regardless of the grouping you choose, the groups behave similarly. You can click the minus sign next to the group heading to collapse the entire group. To expand a collapsed group, click the plus sign next to the group name.

If you hover your mouse over a flagged note, you'll see a date appear in the ScreenTip. This is the date the note was flagged, not the date the note was written.

To jump directly to a particular Note Flag, click the Note Flag. OneNote will navigate directly to the section, page, and note container that contains the flagged note.

Changing the Note Flags Summary Search Scope

By default, the Note Flags Summary task pane searches the current section for Note Flags. You can change that search scope to a wide variety of options. To find all flagged notes in all open sections, choose My Notebook from the Search drop-down. You can choose to search only selected pages, or only the current page group. You can even change your search and limit it to notes created today, yesterday, this week, or last week.

As you change the search scope, the results should refresh themselves automatically. If for any reason they don't, you can click the Refresh Results button.

Using The Note Flags Summary Task Pane to Create a Summary Page

The Note Flags Summary task pane can display your flagged items in a list; however, if you want to view your flagged items on a larger view, click the Create Summary Page button. This creates a new OneNote page within the current section, as shown in Figure 10.15. This page won't have a title and will display all of your Note Flags grouped by flag type.

The advantage to the summary page is that you can see all of your Note Flags on a full-sized page, rather than in the narrow Task pane. There are a couple of disadvantages to keep in mind. First, as you can see in Figure 10.15, several of the flagged items appear twice. That's because I created two summary pages, one for all flagged notes in the current section, and one for all flagged notes in My Notebook. When you create a summary page, it searches all pages in your search criteria, even if those pages are themselves summary pages.

FIGURE 10.15

You can create a summary page of all your flagged text.

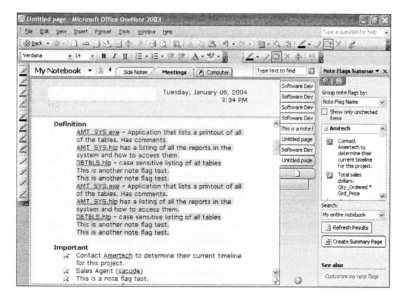

The other disadvantage to creating a summary page is that you cannot tell where your flagged notes originated. Unlike the Note Flags Summary task pane that contains a hyperlink to the flagged text, the summary page contains a copy of the flagged text. There is no way to tell where in your original notes the flagged text is located.

You can print this summary page for your records, or email this page to others. When you're done with the Note Flag Summary page, you can delete it by right-clicking on the page tab and choosing <u>D</u>elete.

tip

The summary page is an actual page in your Notebook. To prevent duplication of Note Flags, it's best to delete this page after you're done using it.

Otherwise, the next time you search for Note Flags, you'll find both the original flagged line and the flagged line that was created in the summary page.

THE ABSOLUTE MINIMUM

In this chapter, you learned how to customize your notes with fonts and Note Flags. You learned

- How to format your notes using fonts and colors to add emphasis and clarity
- How to use formatting to create to-do lists in OneNote
- How to flag notes for different purposes
- How to customize your Note Flags to meet your needs
- How to view a summary of all your Note Flags
- How to create a summary page displaying all flagged notes

All of these topics can help you organize your notes. If you use OneNote for all of your notes, you can quickly succumb to information overload. Using text formatting and Note Flags can help you organize that information and make it manageable. In the next chapter, we'll examine the word processing and editing functionality available in OneNote.

In This Chapter

- Learn how to use OneNote's editing features
- Using and configuring AutoCorrect
- Spell-checking for typed notes
- Spell-checking for handwritten notes
- Using rule lines in your writing

11

Using OneNote's Editing Features

OneNote combines features from several existing programs. It contains some of the word processing features of Microsoft Word, the handwriting capabilities of the Windows XP for Tablet PC Journal, and a variety of features of other third-party programs such as Note Flags, searching, and linked audio.

Since many of OneNote's editing features are loosely based on Microsoft Word, we'll compare Word and OneNote in this chapter.

Word Processing Functionality in OneNote

Microsoft Word is a robust word processing program. With it, you can check spelling and grammar, as well as add bullets and numbering, WordArt, tables, borders, and shading. Figure 11.1 shows several paragraphs formatted with some of these word processing features.

FIGURE 11.1

Microsoft Word has a robust set of editing features.

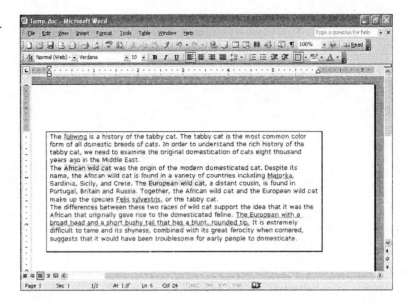

In addition to the shading shown in Figure 11.1, there are several words and phrases underlined in wavy lines. Microsoft Word underlines potential misspelled words in red. In the figure, the word *follwing* is misspelled. In addition, Word doesn't recognize the spelling of Majorka, Felis, or sylvestris.

Microsoft Word does more than simply check for spelling; it also checks for grammar. The underlined sentence that starts with *The European with a broad head* is actually a sentence fragment. Word underlines the entire sentence in green to show you there's something wrong with the sentence syntax.

OneNote has some of the same editing features as Microsoft Word, but is definitely not as robust as Word. Figure 11.2 shows the same text from Figure 11.1 as seen in Microsoft OneNote.

As you can see from the figure, OneNote doesn't have as many editing features as Word. For example, you can highlight text in OneNote, but you can't apply shading like you can in Word. You can't create borders around text or even insert a formatted table.

FIGURE 11.2

OneNote doesn't have as many editing features as Microsoft Word.

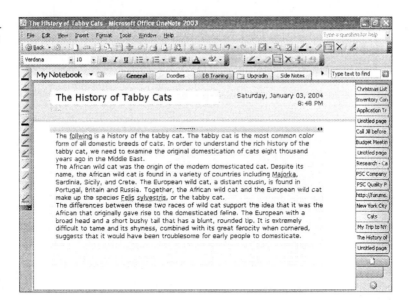

OneNote does include a spell-checker. OneNote will highlight possible misspellings in the same way as Microsoft Word, by underlining the potential misspelling in red. In addition, OneNote doesn't check for grammar, so the fragmented sentence isn't caught in OneNote.

Spell-checking Notes

As you can see from examining Figure 11.2, OneNote does include a spell-checker. You can spell-check both typed and handwritten notes. Much like in other Microsoft Office programs, you can launch the spell-checker by selecting Spelling from the Tools menu or pressing F7 on the keyboard.

Unlike other Office programs, OneNote's spell-checker is displayed in the Task pane on the right side of the OneNote screen, as shown in Figure 11.3.

Much like in other Office programs, you can select from one or many suggested corrections for each misspelled word. If the correct spelling of the word is present, choose it and click Change. If not, you can either click Ignore and add the word later, or change the spelling of the word directly in OneNote. If you change the spelling in your note to a recognized word, OneNote automatically moves to the next misspelled word on the note page. If the word isn't misspelled, as in the case of the word Felis, you can choose Add to Dictionary to permanently add the word to your Custom Dictionary.

FIGURE 11.3

OneNote's spell-checker is displayed in the Task pane.

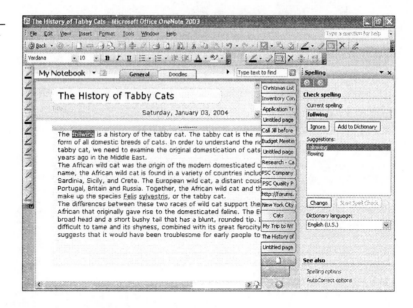

Changing Spelling Options

There are a few spelling options you can configure within OneNote. To configure OneNote's Spelling options, do the following.

1. Choose **Options** from the **Tools** menu.

2. Click **Spelling** on the left side of the Options window to display Figure 11.4.

FIGURE 11.4

You can configure several spelling options in OneNote.

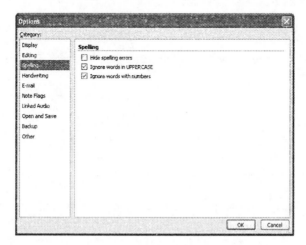

3. You can choose from the following spelling options:

   ▇ Hide spelling errors—If you don't want to know when you misspell a word, check this box. Running a spell check will still find misspelled words, but they won't be underlined in red as you type.

   ▇ Ignore words in UPPERCASE—Words typed entirely in uppercase are often proper names or acronyms. For example, UNLV (a common abbreviation for the University of Nevada at Las Vegas) would be flagged as a misspelled word unless this check box is checked.

   ▇ Ignore words with numbers—Much like words in uppercase, words that contain numbers, such as POP3 (a popular email protocol) or Lotus123 (an old computer program) would be flagged as misspelled unless this box is checked.

4. When you're done adjusting OneNote's spelling options, click **OK** to save your changes and exit the Options window.

Using OneNote's AutoCorrect Feature

Chances are there are spelling mistakes you make all the time. For example, if you're a fast typist, you might often type *teh* instead of *the*. If you type *teh* in Microsoft Word, you'll notice as soon as you hit the space bar, Word changes it to *the*. This feature is known as *AutoCorrect*. Word, Excel, Outlook, PowerPoint, and OneNote all have the AutoCorrect feature. This is the same feature that replaces a lowercase *i* with a capital *I* when the letter is typed by itself.

You can change AutoCorrect's options and add words and phrases to AutoCorrect. Any words or phrases you add to AutoCorrect in OneNote will also appear in Word's AutoCorrect options.

To view OneNote's AutoCorrect options, choose AutoCorrect Options from the Tools menu to display Figure 11.5.

You can change any of the following AutoCorrect options.

   ▇ Show AutoCorrect Options buttons—Unchecking this box prevents OneNote from displaying a list of AutoCorrect options for words you type in OneNote.

   ▇ Correct TWo INitial CApitals—As you're typing along, it's very easy to hold down the Shift key for too long and accidentally capitalize the first two letters of a word. By default, this box is checked. Anytime you type a word with two initial capital letters, OneNote changes the second letter to a lowercase letter.

   ▇ Capitalize first letter of sentences—After you type a period and a space, OneNote will automatically capitalize the next letter typed.

▓ Capitalize names of days—OneNote will always capitalize the days of the week.

▓ Correct accidental use of cAPS LOCK key—If you forget to turn off the CAPS LOCK key after use, OneNote will turn it off for you. OneNote determines that you've forgotten to turn off the CAPS LOCK key if CAPS LOCK is currently on, and you type a word with an initial lowercase letter and the rest of the letters in uppercase.

▓ Replace text as you type—OneNote contains a long list of misspellings and abbreviations. Checking this box allows OneNote to replace potential misspellings and common abbreviations as you type. For example, if you type the three characters *(r)*, OneNote automatically changes it to ® as you type.

FIGURE 11.5

You can add, remove, or examine OneNote's AutoCorrect options through this dialog.

You can add, edit, and remove common AutoCorrect options through this dialog. To add an AutoCorrect entry, do the following:

1. Type the common misspelling in the **Replace** box.

2. In the **With** box, type the proper spelling of the same word.

3. Click the **Add** button to add the pair of words to AutoCorrect.

If you want to remove an AutoCorrect entry, use the scroll bar to find the entry you're interested in. Click to select it, then press the Delete key to remove the entry.

Using AutoCorrect to Speed Typing

You can use AutoCorrect for more than just fixing misspelled words and inserting symbols. If you repeatedly type a long phrase, such as the name of your company, you can create an abbreviation in AutoCorrect to insert the full phrase automatically. For example, if you work for Pacific Life, Car, and Auto Insurance Incorporated, you probably don't want to type that whole company name every time it's needed. You can add an AutoCorrect entry that replaces the letters *plcai* with the full name of the company. Anytime you type *plcai* in OneNote (or any other Office program), AutoCorrect will replace it with *Pacific Life, Car, and Auto Insurance Incorporated.*

Using Rules Lines and Grid Lines to Keep Your Information Neat

If you're using OneNote on a Tablet PC, you might find it difficult to create legible notes without some writing guides. OneNote allows you to add rule and grid lines to your note pages to help you write more legibly. For example, Figure 11.6 shows a typical page of meeting notes without gridlines. As you can see, writing on a slant can poorly affect readability.

FIGURE 11.6

Without writing guides, it's easy to let your writing slant.

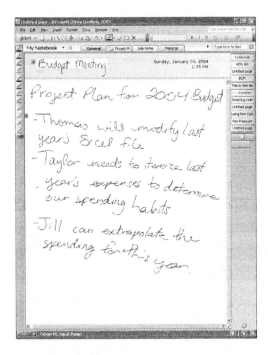

You can add rule lines to OneNote by selecting Rule Lines from the View menu. You can choose from a variety of different types of rule lines. For typical meeting notes, you can choose College Ruled lines. If you want wider lines, choose Standard Ruled or Wide Ruled. Figure 11.7 shows the same meeting notes as previously shown in Figure 11.6 with rule lines.

FIGURE 11.7

Rule lines can help you write legibly.

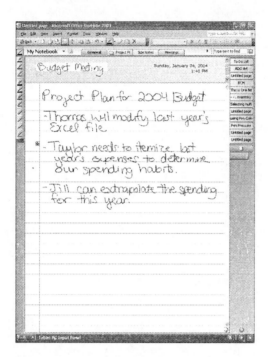

In addition to rule lines, you can also display grid lines in OneNote to give your page a graph paper look. You can choose a small, medium, or large grid.

You can change the type of rule lines at any time by choosing Rule Lines from the View menu and picking a different type of rule or grid line.

THE ABSOLUTE MINIMUM

In this chapter, you learned how OneNote's word processing features can help you take notes. This chapter covered

- The differences between the editing features of Word and OneNote
- Using AutoCorrect to replace mistakes as you type
- Using AutoCorrect to speed typing
- Adding rule lines to OneNote

In the next chapter, you'll learn about drawing pictures and diagrams in OneNote.

12

A Picture Is Worth a Thousand Words

If you're using a notebook or legal pad to take notes, chances are you aren't only writing words. Drawings and diagrams are essential for illustrating complex relationships between business objects or for drawing pictures of structures in science class. Any job that requires diagramming such as architect, interior designer, or engineer can benefit from drawing diagrams and pictures in OneNote. In addition to these more noble tasks, sometimes you just want to doodle.

This chapter introduces you to OneNote's drawing tools and is full of examples of how drawings and diagrams can enhance your note-taking experience.

Drawing Pictures in OneNote

One of the advantages to OneNote is that it's largely free-form. You can enter text and images, paste content from a variety of programs, and even draw pictures. If you're using OneNote for business, you might be thinking the only pictures you'll ever draw in OneNote would be doodles during a particularly boring meeting. However, pictures play a role in all sorts of notes from business to academic to personal. Once you explore the drawing capabilities in OneNote, you might find you'll use these tools more than you ever expected.

The majority of this chapter focuses on using OneNote on the Tablet PC. While the majority of the information contained here can be adapted to a desktop or laptop, it's often significantly harder to draw pictures with a mouse than with the Tablet PC's pen.

Displaying the Drawing Tools

To display OneNote's Drawing and Writing toolbar, shown in Figure 12.1, choose Toolbars from the View menu and choose Drawing and Writing Tools.

There are several buttons you'll use on the Drawing and Writing toolbar, regardless of whether you're using OneNote on a desktop, Tablet PC, or laptop.

- Pen—Use this button to toggle between pen mode and selection mode. For laptops and desktops, selection mode is the default mode.

- Eraser—Use this button to turn the mouse pointer into an eraser. To erase mistakes, just click and move the mouse over the ink. You can only use the eraser to erase ink drawn with the Tablet PC pen or ink drawn with the mouse.

- Selection Tool—Use this button to turn your mouse or Tablet PC pen or mouse pointer into a selection tool. In selection mode, you can click objects (such as note containers) or drag to select multiple objects. This is the default mode for a desktop or laptop.

- Delete—Use this button to delete selected objects.

- Insert Extra Writing Space—As you're writing in OneNote, you might start to run out of room on the page. OneNote doesn't scroll automatically; you'll need to click this button (or the icon on the bottom right of the OneNote page) to add more space to your note.

- Convert Handwriting to Text—This button converts the last handwritten line to text.

FIGURE 12.1

The Drawing and Writing toolbar isn't displayed by default.

If you're using a Tablet PC, drawing with the pen is fairly easy and straightforward. Simply start drawing on the screen. OneNote can automatically recognize whether you're drawing or writing. If you'd prefer, you can also explicitly tell OneNote you're drawing and not writing. You might want to do that if you're drawing a picture similar to Figure 12.2. In this figure, a chemical equation, telling OneNote you're drawing prevents any confusion about the names of the elements being considered text.

When you're using OneNote on a laptop, you're always in selection mode. Even if you use click the pen icon on the toolbar and try to "write" with your mouse, OneNote still treats that writing as a drawing. On a Tablet PC, it's exactly the opposite. When you're using the Tablet PC with its pen, OneNote knows this and automatically switches to pen mode. In pen mode, you can create both handwriting and drawings. OneNote's handwriting recognition engine is smart enough to know most of the time whether you're writing or drawing. However, there might be some times when you want to ensure you're drawing. To tell OneNote you're drawing instead of writing, choose Pen <u>M</u>ode from the Tools menu. From the Pen Mode menu, choose Create Drawings Only. By default, the Pen Mode is set to Create Both Handwriting and Drawings. The Pen Mode menu selection is only available on a Tablet PC device, not on a desktop or laptop running Windows 2000 or Windows XP. Figure 12.3 illustrates the difference between drawing and writing.

FIGURE 12.2

Sometimes, you might want letters and numbers treated as a drawing.

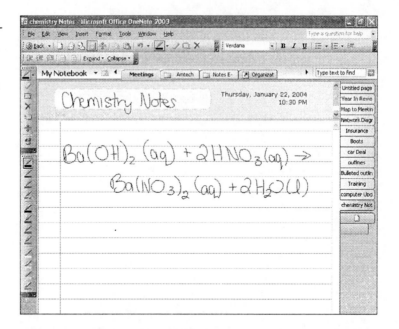

FIGURE 12.3

Selecting drawings and writing produces different results.

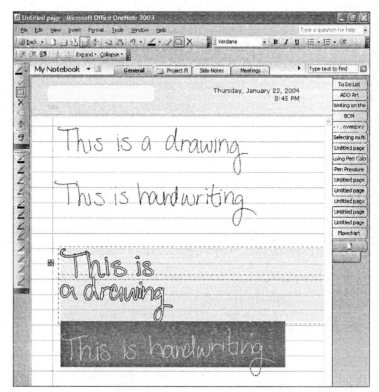

The top two lines, which are not selected, look identical. However, the bottom two lines were written in exactly the same way. When they are selected, you can see the difference. If you examine the drawing selection, you'll notice that the two lines are each their own selection. If you click the Convert Handwriting to Text button on the Drawing and Writing Toolbar, only the bottom selection is converted.

Drawing Pictures in OneNote

Now that you know how to switch between drawing and writing, it's time to draw some pictures. This section covers some examples of the types of pictures you can draw in OneNote.

Diagrams and Flow Charts

Many business processes rely on some sort of flow chart. If you're in a meeting working on a business process, you can document that business process through the use of a flowchart, as shown in Figure 12.4.

FIGURE 12.4

A flowchart can help you capture complicated business information.

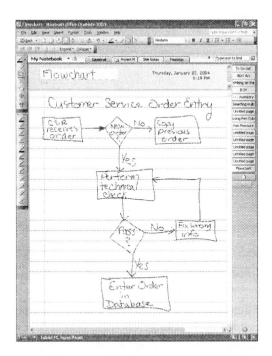

As you can see, you can draw a variety of shapes on your OneNote page. Connect those shapes with arrows and text to complete your flowchart.

Maps and Directions

You can draw anything in OneNote that you can draw on a piece of paper. If you draw a map in OneNote, you can then convert the map to an HTML page and email it to anyone, regardless of whether they use OneNote. Figure 12.5 shows a map drawn in OneNote. Even though it's hard to tell from the image, the author of this map even used a few colors to designate stop lights, stop signs, and the final destination.

FIGURE 12.5

You can enhance your drawings with color.

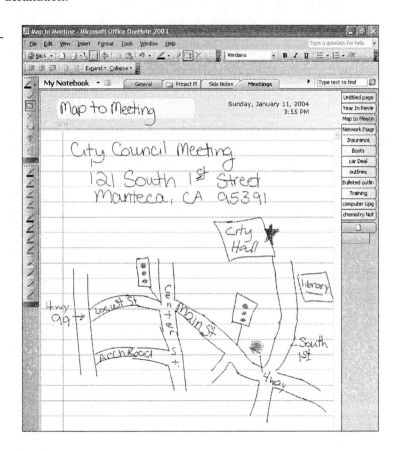

To convert the OneNote page to HTML, choose Save As from the File menu. In the Save as type drop-down, choose Single File Web Page (publish a copy). Choose a location and a name for your Web page and click Save. You can then email the Web page to anyone or publish it on a Web site, as shown in Figure 12.6.

FIGURE 12.6

You can convert
your drawings
into HTML
pages.

FIGURE 12.6

You can convert
your drawings
into HTML
pages.

Add a Bit of Color to Your Drawings

As mentioned in the previous section, you can add color to your drawings. You can
choose from four available pen colors, two pen widths, and four highlighter colors.
On a Tablet PC, you can change colors by simply tapping the appropriate pen selection on the Pens toolbar, as shown in Figure 12.7.

FIGURE 12.7

You can change
pen color and
width to add col-
ors to your
drawings.

Using the highlighter colors, you can fill in shapes and highlight important facts.

Enhancing Your Drawings with Text

You might want to do more than just draw on your OneNote page. For example, in Figure 12.8, a network diagram, you can see how adding text to your drawings can enhance their effectiveness.

As you can see from the figure, some information is better communicated as text. Network addresses need to be exact. Using text to display the addresses can ensure that even if you don't have the neatest handwriting, others can still easily read your notes.

You can also publish your pages as HTML instead of using the Save As command. The difference between the two is the scope of what's converted to HTML. Choosing Save As converts the entire section (all of the section's pages) to HTML. Publishing only converts the selected page (and any associated subpages) to HTML. For more information on the differences between publishing and saving, see "Publishing Notes to HTML," in Chapter 23.

FIGURE 12.8

Adding text to your drawings can help provide clarity.

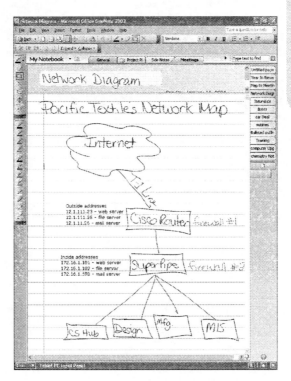

THE ABSOLUTE MINIMUM

In this chapter, you learned that note taking isn't just about text. You learned

- How to add pictures to enhance your notes
- How to add color to your drawings
- How you can enhance your drawings with text

The next chapter covers how to add images and external content to your OneNote notes.

13

USING ONENOTE FOR MORE THAN JUST TEXT

OneNote can accept a variety of input types, from text to handwriting to drawings. However, you can capture more than just words in OneNote. You can also insert a variety of other objects into your OneNote pages.

This chapter will cover inserting all types of objects into your OneNote pages. You can insert Web pages, pictures, and several other object types directly into your OneNote pages. Some of the objects you insert are inserted within the page and others are inserted as links to files stored in your file system.

Inserting Web Pages into OneNote

When using OneNote for school or work, you might find it helpful to insert Web sites with research information or other useful content. For example, Figure 13.1 shows a Google search result inserted into a OneNote page.

FIGURE 13.1

Inserting the results of a Web search can be a helpful time-saver.

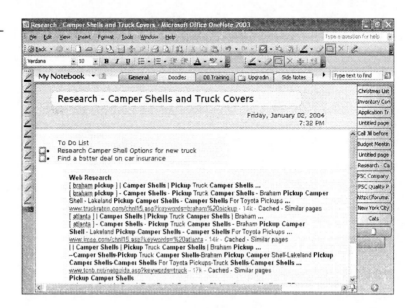

Most Web sites will paste into OneNote without problems, as shown in Figure 13.2.

FIGURE 13.2

Many Web sites can be inserted into OneNote exactly as they appear.

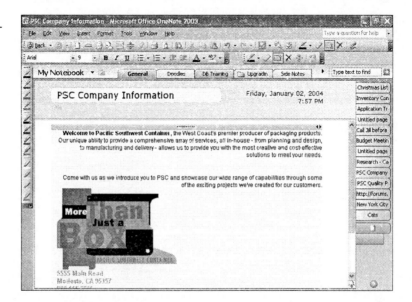

When you insert information from the Web into OneNote, the address of the Web page is inserted directly below the pasted information in the same note container, as shown in Figure 13.3. OneNote saves this information so you can return to the particular Web site at any time from your note page. Just click on the inserted hyperlink to open a new Internet Explorer window of the originating Web site.

Copying and Pasting Web Information into OneNote

To insert information from a Web site into a OneNote page, use the following steps:

1. Navigate to the desired Web site in Internet Explorer.

2. Use the mouse to select (highlight) the information on the Web site you want to insert into OneNote.

3. Choose **Edit**, **Copy**.

4. Switch to OneNote and click anywhere on the note page to create a new note container.

5. Choose **Edit**, **Paste**. The copied information is inserted in the note container.

You can also insert copied information into an existing note container. Just position your cursor within an existing note container before you choose Paste from the Edit menu.

Dragging Information from a Web Page to OneNote

You don't have to go through the hassle of copying and pasting if you want to insert an entire Web page into your OneNote page. You can actually drag and drop the page from Internet Explorer to OneNote.

caution

Not all Web sites insert properly into OneNote. In particular, it's possible you'll lose some formatting such as line breaks and empty space on your notes page. Unfortunately, there isn't a good way to work around this problem. Until you try to paste Web content into OneNote, you won't know whether the page will paste properly.

note

If you copy information from a long Web page, OneNote only remembers the page address, not the spot on the page that contains the copied information. You'll need to scroll down the page to find the copied information.

FIGURE 13.3
The URL of the pasted information is inserted below the pasted information.

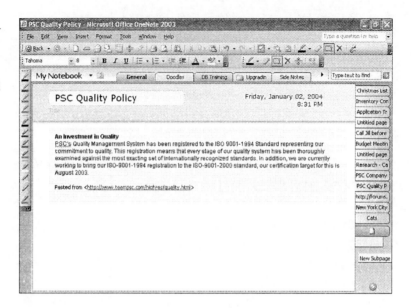

To drag Web content into OneNote, do the following:

1. Select the content. If you want to select the entire Web page, click anywhere on the page and press **Ctrl+A** on the keyboard.

2. Once you have the content selected, click and drag the content onto the OneNote taskbar icon.

3. Once the OneNote window is visible, move your mouse pointer to the appropriate place on your OneNote page and release the mouse button to paste your content.

Controlling How OneNote Inserts Web Content

OneNote includes the Web site address when you copy information from a Web site. At a later time, you can click that URL to return to the Web site that contained the copied information.

tip

You can quickly copy information from the Web to a Side Note. Open a new Side Note by clicking the OneNote icon in the system tray. Then drag and drop selected content from the Web to your Side Note. You can always rearrange the information into another OneNote page at a later time.

If you don't want OneNote to insert the address of the pasted Web content, you can turn this feature off by following these steps:

1. Choose **Tools**, **Options** to display OneNote's Options window.

2. Click **Editing** to display the Editing options shown in Figure 13.4.

3. Uncheck the box marked **Include link to source when pasting from the Internet**.

4. Click **OK** to save your changes.

FIGURE 13.4

You can configure how OneNote inserts pasted Web content.

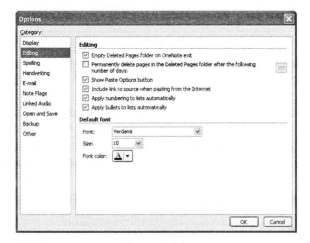

Inserting a Hyperlink into OneNote

If you don't want to insert actual Web content into OneNote, you can insert just the URL for the Web site using one of two methods.

The first method is a standard copy and paste as follows:

1. Click once in the address bar of your Web browser to highlight the Web address.

2. Choose **Edit**, **Copy**.

3. Switch to OneNote.

4. Click where you want the pasted URL to appear, and choose **Edit**, **Paste**.

note

If you have a dial-up connection and aren't connected to the Internet, Internet Explorer will launch your dial-up connection to connect to the Internet.

In addition to copying and pasting a Web address, you can also drag the Web address into OneNote:

1. While in Internet Explorer, position your mouse on the E icon in the address bar.
2. Click and drag the entire address to the OneNote taskbar button.
3. When OneNote becomes the active window, release your mouse button where you want the pasted URL to appear.

If you attempt to insert content from a Web browser other than Internet Explorer, the address of the Web site won't automatically be inserted in OneNote. You'll need to copy and paste the address or drag it into OneNote from the browser.

Inserting Pictures into OneNote

In Chapter 12, "A Picture Is Worth a Thousand Words," you learned how to draw pictures in OneNote. In addition to drawing your own pictures, you can insert pictures or other graphics into OneNote pages. Figure 13.5 shows how a few pictures and graphics can enhance a note.

To insert a picture into a OneNote page, use the following steps:

1. Position your mouse cursor on your OneNote page, either in a new note container or an existing note container.
2. Choose **Insert**, **Picture** to display the Insert Picture dialog shown in Figure 13.6.
3. Click to select the picture you want to insert.
4. Click **Insert**.

tip

This method can be helpful for quickly creating Side Notes. Just leave a Side Note open on the screen. Then drag the Web address from Internet Explorer to the Side Note and release.

You might notice that in Figure 13.7, there are two pictures visible on the note page. The picture on the right is pasted within a note container; the picture on the left is not. You can tell the difference by looking for the note container's handle, only visible in the right figure.

FIGURE 13.5

You can add pictures and images to your note pages.

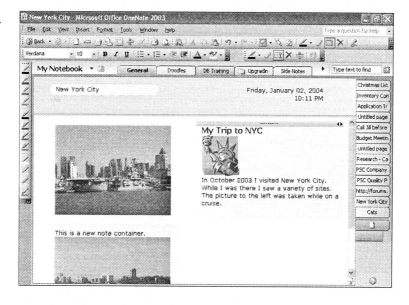

FIGURE 13.6

Choose the picture you want to insert.

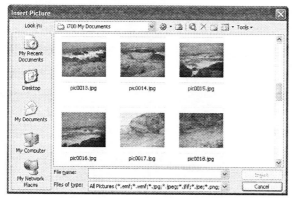

When you attempt to insert a picture, if your cursor is in a note container that contains text or writing, the picture is contained in the same note container. If your cursor isn't currently in a note container when you insert the picture, the picture is inserted directly in the OneNote page.

FIGURE 13.7

You can insert a picture in a note container or by itself.

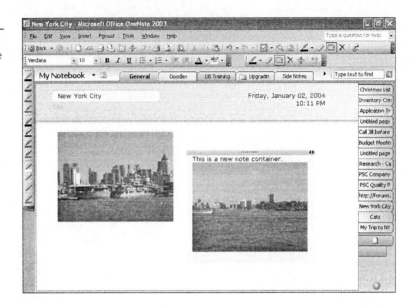

Inserting ClipArt

OneNote doesn't have a ClipArt feature like other Microsoft Office programs, but you can still insert ClipArt into your OneNote page. To insert ClipArt from Microsoft Online, use the following steps:

1. Navigate to the Microsoft ClipArt Web site at `http://office.microsoft.com/ clipart/default.aspx`.

2. Choose a collection or search for a particular image (see Figure 13.8).

FIGURE 13.8

Choose from a variety of ClipArt objects.

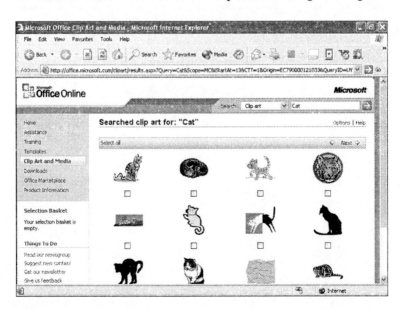

3. Hover over the image you want to insert. A drop-down arrow will appear to the right of the image. Click the arrow and choose **Copy**.

4. Return to OneNote and click to create a new note container (or click within an existing note container).

5. Choose **Edit**, **Paste** to paste the ClipArt into OneNote.

> ## caution
>
> Resizing an image by using the top, bottom, or side handles might distort the image. To prevent distortion use the corner handles.

Resizing Your Images

Once you've inserted a picture or an image into OneNote, you can change the size to fit your needs. Most pictures and ClipArt images, for example, will be much larger than you need them to be. To resize an image, click to select the image. When you do, you'll notice that a dotted border appears around the image and eight small rectangles (called *handles*) appear at the corners and sides of the image, as shown in Figure 13.9. To resize the image, position your mouse pointer over one of the eight handles. Drag the mouse in any direction to resize the image. If you use the corner handles to resize the image, you'll maintain the same relative width and height of the image. If you want to change the width or height independent of each other, use the handles at the top, bottom, or sides of the image.

FIGURE 13.9
You can use the picture handles to resize the picture.

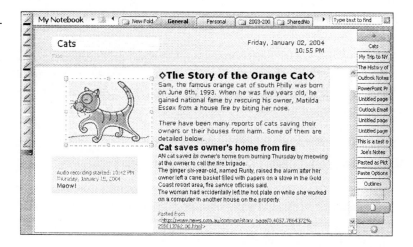

Inserting Other Objects into OneNote

There are a number of other objects you can insert into OneNote pages. For example, you can insert information from Word, Excel, and PowerPoint. For more information on inserting information from other programs, see Chapter 20, "Office 2003 Integration."

Inserting Windows Symbols

OneNote has a wide variety of built-in symbols from Windows you can use within your note pages. To insert a symbol, choose Insert, Symbol to display Figure 13.10.

FIGURE 13.10

You can insert a variety of symbols in your OneNote page.

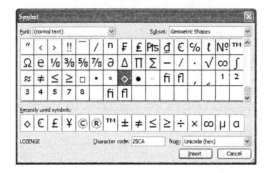

There are a wide variety of symbols available. You can use the scroll bar on the right of the Symbol window to scroll up and down the available symbols. To speed things up a bit, you can use the Subset drop-down box to select a type of symbol, such as Geometric Shapes.

To insert a symbol, click the symbol with the mouse and then click the Insert button. After you insert a symbol, the Symbol window remains open, allowing you to insert more symbols. You can actually click in your OneNote window and move the cursor to another note container or another position within the existing note container and insert another symbol. When you're done inserting symbols, click the Close button.

Inserting Symbols by Using Character Codes

A large number of the symbols available in OneNote can actually be inserted through the use of ASCII codes. An ASCII code is a four-digit numeric code associated with the particular symbol. To see which symbols have ASCII codes associated with them, use the drop-down marked From on the Symbol dialog box. Choose ASCII (decimal). The Symbol dialog only shows symbols that have an ASCII code.

For example, in Figure 13.11, the % symbol has an ASCII code of 37. To use the keyboard to insert that symbol at any time, hold down the ALT key and press 0037 on your number pad. When you release the ALT key, the symbol is inserted.

FIGURE 13.11

You can use a symbol's ASCII code to insert it from the keyboard.

In addition to ASCII codes, you can use a similar method to insert Unicode symbols. As previously shown in Figure 13.10, the Unicode character code for the diamond shape is 25CA. To use your keyboard to enter this symbol, type the Unicode character code in a note container and press Alt+X.

The Absolute Minimum

In this chapter, you learned about a wide variety of items you can insert within your OneNote page. You can insert

- Web content along with the URL for the original Web site
- URLs to return to Web sites you visit at a later time
- Pictures and graphics to enhance your pages
- ClipArt
- Symbols to illustrate mathematical operations

In the next chapter, you'll learn how to create outlines in OneNote. Outlines can help you organize your thoughts and notes. You'll learn how to create a new outline and create an outline from existing text.

14

CREATING OUTLINES IN ONENOTE

Notes can be composed of titles, headings, drawings, diagrams, and references to other information. The chapters in this book cover each of these items. In addition to these items, outlines serve a key purpose in note taking. They can help you organize your thoughts in a hierarchical fashion.

OneNote allows you to easily create outlines in your notes. Automatic numbering, bullets, and different outline styles can help you create a single outline or even nested outlines. We'll explore the differences between creating outlines with a keyboard and creating outlines with the Tablet PC's pen.

The Anatomy of an Outline

Figure 14.1 shows a typical outline using bullets in OneNote. You'll notice the outline has several levels: a title, top-level headings, second-level headings, and third-level headings.

FIGURE 14.1

A typical outline can have many levels.

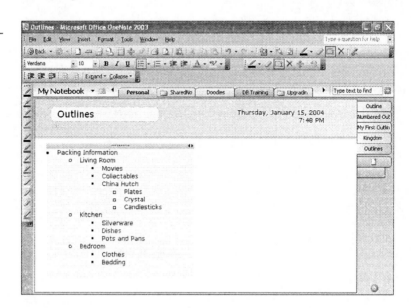

Even though this figure only shows three levels of headings, an outline can have many more levels. You can actually create an outline with any number of levels (I've gone as high as 15). The only drawback to the number of levels you can add is the width of your note container. Once your outline hits the edge of your note container, you can't create any additional levels until you widen your note container. When you create outlines, OneNote associates a different type of bullet for each level of the outline. Even though you can create outlines with more than 10 levels, only the first 10 levels receive a unique bullet type. Levels beyond 10 all receive the same bullet level.

Even if you don't create enough levels to hit the edge of your note container, you might want to limit your outline to around six or seven levels. Creating outlines with too many levels can decrease readability.

You can create outlines manually or let OneNote create them for you. For example, if you type the number 1 followed by a period, OneNote automatically assumes you're creating either a numbered list or a numbered outline. All you have to do to create a numbered outline is press Enter at the end of the first line and press Tab to indent the second line. OneNote automatically turns your typing into a numbered outline.

To turn off automatic numbering, do the following:

1. Choose **Tools**, **Options**.

2. Click **Editing** in the **Category** box to display Figure 14.2.

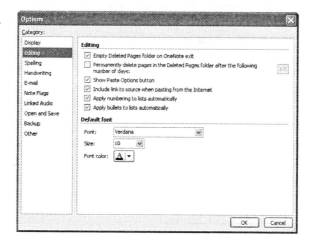

3. Remove the check marks from the boxes labeled **Apply numbering to lists automatically** and **Apply bullets to lists automatically**. You can uncheck one or both check boxes.

4. Click **OK** to save your changes.

The previous steps turn off automatic numbering and outlining. You can still create your outline manually, of course, but allowing OneNote to create the outline automatically is usually much more efficient. If you want to enable the automatic numbering or bullets, just follow steps 1–4 and check the boxes mentioned in step 3.

Bullets Versus Numbering

As mentioned previously, an outline doesn't always need bullets. You can create a numbered outline as well (see Figure 14.3).

The same rules apply to both bulleted and numbered outlines. You can create as many levels as you want, as long as you haven't reached the right edge of your note container.

No matter which type of outline you create (bullets or numbered), OneNote smartly places a different bullet or number format at each level of the outline. For a bulleted outline, there's a different bullet type for the first 10 levels. For a numbered outline, you'll receive a different number or Roman numeral for the first 8 levels of the outline. When your numbered outline reaches the 9th level, the very first number or Roman numeral is used for all subsequent levels.

FIGURE 14.3

You can create a numbered outline or convert a bulleted outline to a numbered outline.

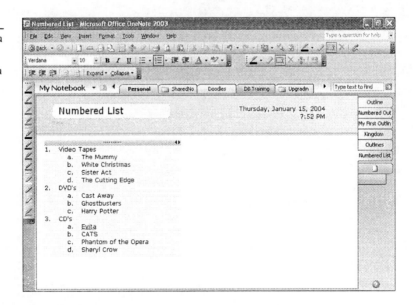

Creating Your First Outline

As previously mentioned, you can let OneNote help you create outlines automatically. To create a simple bulleted outline, use the following steps.

1. Click in your OneNote page to create a new note container.

2. Type the **asterisk** symbol (Shift+8), a **space**, and then some text. As soon as you click the Space bar, OneNote converts the star to a bullet.

3. When you're done typing the line of text, press **Enter**. OneNote puts another bullet on the next line. To indent that bullet and change it's appearance, press **Tab**.

4. Type the second line of text. You've now created an outline, shown in Figure 14.4.

FIGURE 14.4

You can create a basic outline in four easy steps.

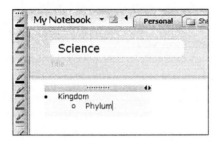

As mentioned previously, to create a numbered out-line, just type the number 1, a period, and a space. OneNote converts the type to a numbered list. Once that happens, you'll notice the AutoFormat icon slightly below and to the right of the 1. Click the drop-down arrow next to the lightning bolt icon to display the choices shown in Figure 14.5.

To continue creating the numbered list, enter your text and press Enter. OneNote will create the second line of the list with the number 2. To turn the list into a numbered outline, just press Tab to turn the number 2 into the letter a, as previously shown in Figure 14.3.

note

Press Tab to indent the outline. If you need to decrease the level of indentation, press Shift + Tab.

FIGURE 14.5
You can tell OneNote to stop creating num-bered lists or undo the cre-ation of the list.

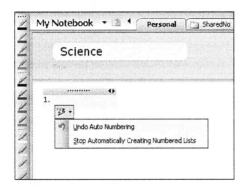

Using the Outlining Toolbar

You might never need more functionality than the previous sections described. You can create multilevel outlines easily with both bullets and numbering without ever customizing your outlines. However, if you want to customize your outlines and explore some advanced functionality, you can display the Outlining Toolbar to help. You can display the toolbar by selecting Toolbars from the View menu and clicking on Outlining. The Outlining toolbar is shown in Figure 14.6.

FIGURE 14.6
The Outlining toolbar can help you control your outlines.

There are several buttons on the Outlining toolbar.

- Decrease Indent—If you're on any level other than the first level of the outline, clicking this button moves the current line one position to the left (so a second level becomes a first level, a third level becomes a second level, and so on). The current line and all lines immediately under the current line are moved.

- Increase Indent—Clicking this button moves the current line one position to the right. This causes a second level to become a third level or a fourth level to become a fifth level. Only the current line is moved.

- Make Body Text—This button allows you to take one or more levels of an outline and make them body text. Body text is the text under a particular section of an outline. For example, in Figure 14.7, the left note container contains a multiple level outline. The right note container contains that same outline after the information directly under the Excel entry was converted to body text.

FIGURE 14.7

Body text isn't indented as much as a regular outline level.

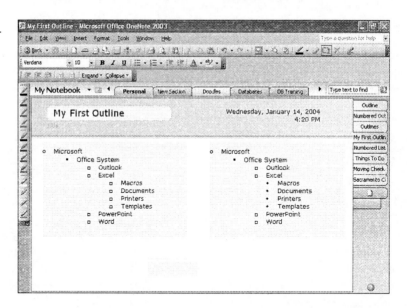

- Show Body Text—When working with your outline, you can show or hide different outline levels. (This functionality is covered later in this chapter.) If you hide one or more levels of the outline, the Show Body Text button shows the hidden body text for the current level.

- Hide Body Text—Clicking this button hides the body text under the currently selected level.

■ Expand and Collapse—You can use these buttons to show or hide different sections of your outline. For example, if you click the Collapse button, a drop-down appears, as shown in Figure 14.8. You can collapse a specific level or collapse the entire outline. If you choose to collapse a specific level, that level is displayed as the top level, and all levels below it will be hidden. If you expand a specific level, all levels above that level are expanded.

FIGURE 14.8

You can expand or collapse any level of the out-line.

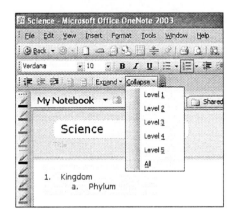

We'll use these functions more later in this chapter and in Chapter 15, "Creating Outlines from Existing Text."

Adding or Removing Outline Sections

After you've completed your outline, you might find you need to add items some-where in the middle of the outline. For example, in Figure 14.9, you might need to add OneNote to the list of software packages included in the Microsoft Office System.

To add OneNote to the list of Office programs, position the cursor after one of the other Office programs (for example, Access) and then press Enter to insert a line. OneNote automatically places the line at the same outline level as the previous line and inserts a bullet. If you need to indent the line further, press Tab. You can then add the text you need to the outline.

You can also remove sections from an outline. For example, in Figure 14.10, there's an extra entry for Order.

FIGURE 14.9

You might need
to add sections
to your outline.

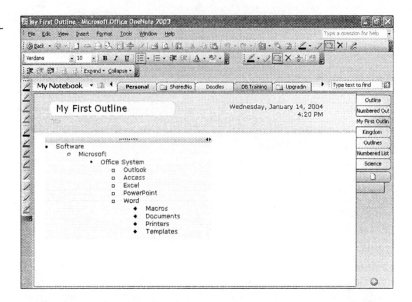

FIGURE 14.9

You might need
to add sections
to your outline.

FIGURE 14.10

You might need
to remove an
entry from your
outline.

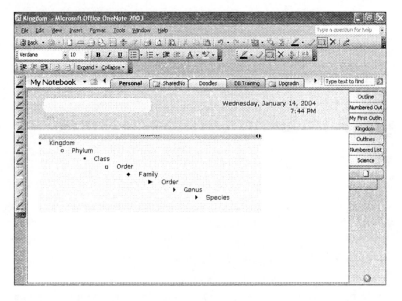

FIGURE 14.10

You might need
to remove an
entry from your
outline.

You can't just select the line and delete it. When you select the line, you'll actually select every line under the selected line. If you select the second Order entry, you'll also select Genus and Species. To remove the second Order entry, you'll actually need to click the line selector twice. The first time you click it, you'll select the line and everything under it. The second time you click it, you'll only select the line in question.

Press Delete on the keyboard to remove the line in question. This process will delete the line, but won't change the indentation of all the subsequent lines. If you need to delete a line and move all of the lower level lines up a level, first click the line you want to delete once to select it and all lower-level lines. Then decrease the indentation level on the selected lines. You can then delete the offending line.

Creating a Numbered List

A numbered list is very similar to an outline. As mentioned previously, whenever you type a number, followed by a period and a space, at the beginning of a new line, OneNote assumes you want to create a numbered list. At the end of the line, when you press Enter, OneNote adds a new line with the next consecutive number in the series. You can cancel the list creation by clicking the AutoFormat Smart Tag and choosing Undo Auto Numbering.

In Microsoft Word, if you want AutoFormat to create a numbered list, you must start that list from the number 1. OneNote doesn't have that restriction. You can start your numbered list with any number, and OneNote's AutoFormat will automatically create the list.

OneNote also allows you to start your numbered lists with a variety of styles. For example, in addition to a number and a period, you can type a number inside parentheses: (1), or a number with a single parenthesis: 1). OneNote also recognizes a wealth of other numbering schemes including i, ii, iii, 1-, 2-, 3-, and a), b), c).

caution

If you click the line twice in rapid succession, you're actually double-clicking the line. Double-clicking collapses the outline. Make sure you pause between the two clicks.

tip

When you're done creating your list, either use the mouse to create a new note container or press Enter twice. The first Enter adds a new line to your list; the second clears that line and list settings.

tip

You can create a bulleted list as well. Just type your first line and click the Bullets button on the toolbar. You can then press Enter to move to the next line and continue your list. You can easily turn your bulleted list into an outline by indenting any of the lines to create multiple levels.

Creating Outlines Using the Pen

So far, all the outlines we've covered have been created using the keyboard. However, you can create outlines with the Tablet PC pen as well. The process isn't as simple with the pen, though. For example, in Figure 14.11, the training outline looks just fine, but if you tried to use the Outlining toolbar to collapse the third level, you'd find that OneNote doesn't recognize the outline levels. That's because when you write directly on the screen, OneNote doesn't always know that each line you create is part of the same line or note container.

FIGURE 14.11

Writing an outline on a Tablet PC presents challenges.

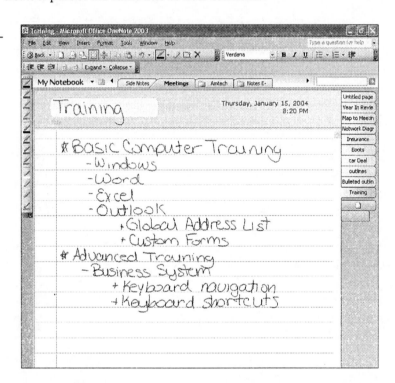

Despite these difficulties, it is possible to create outlines with the Tablet PC pen.

Start your outline by writing the first line of your outline on the screen. Next, click the Bullets toolbar button to place a bullet in front of your line of writing. To add the next line of the outline, place your pen on the next line and indent it slightly. As you start writing, it's likely that OneNote will recognize that the second line is part of the same outline and place a bullet next to the text.

As you continue your outline, you might notice that OneNote doesn't always recognize your indentation. For example, in Figure 14.12, each line of the outline should be one level below the previous level. However, from examining the bullets, you can see that Kingdom and Phylum are on the same level, as are Genus and Species. OneNote doesn't always recognize that you've actually indented a line, even if it appears indented on the screen.

FIGURE 14.12

Writing outlines doesn't always produce perfect results.

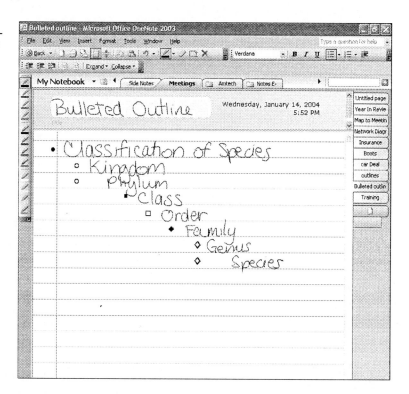

You can edit the outline and correct these mistakes. To indent the Phylum line, place your pen over the line until the line selector appears. Click the line selector with the pen to select the current line and all subsequent lines at lower outline levels. Click Increase Indent level on the Outlining toolbar. This indents all selected lines one level. Repeat this process for the Species line to change your outline into one similar to Figure 14.13.

You'll notice that even after editing your outline with the outlining toolbar, it might still be slightly off center. For example, in Figure 14.13,

tip

If you're just not happy with how OneNote interprets your written outlines, you can always obtain more reliable results by converting your handwriting to text and cleaning up the outline that way.

there's a lot of extra space before Phylum. Unfortunately, when you're writing your outlines, you can't always remedy that problem easily. Typing your outlines will almost always produce more reliable results, however, the convenience of writing your outline might greatly outweigh any idiosyncrasies.

FIGURE 14.13

You can use the Outlining toolbar to edit your outline.

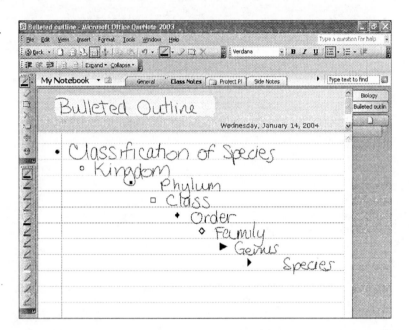

Changing the Style of Your Bullets or Numbering

So far we've created both bulleted and numbered outlines with the default formatting. However, there are a host of styles of both bullets and numbers. You can customize both bullets and numbering. To change an existing bullet style, use the following steps.

1. Select **Format**, **Bullets** to display the Bullets task pane as shown in Figure 14.14.

2. Click anywhere on the line of the outline you want to change.

3. Click the new bullet style from the Task pane to apply the change.

If you want to apply the same bullet style to several levels of the outline, you can use your mouse or Tablet PC pen to select multiple levels of the outline before you choose a new bullet style.

note

You can change the style of any existing bullet, however there's no way to create an entirely new bullet scheme.

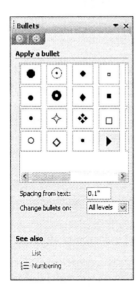

FIGURE 14.14

You can use the Bullets task pane to customize your bullets.

You can change your numbering scheme in a similar fashion. Choose <u>N</u>umbering from the F<u>o</u>rmat menu to display the Numbering task pane, as shown in Figure 14.15.

FIGURE 14.15

Use the Numbering task pane to choose a new numbering style.

To apply a numbering scheme, first select the portion of the outline you want to change. You might want to change the scheme for the entire outline or only for a portion. Once you have the appropriate lines selected, just click the numbering scheme once in the Task pane. The outline's numbering scheme will change immediately.

Customize Your Numbering Scheme

Click Customize Numbering in the Numbering task pane to further customize your numbering, as shown in Figure 14.16.

note

If you select the entire outline but only want to apply the numbering scheme on a single level, use the Change numbers on drop-down to choose the level you need to change.

FIGURE 14.16
You can customize both your sequence and format.

The top box, Apply a sequence, allows you to control the type of numbering you need. For example, you can take a list formatted with 1., 2., 3., 4. and change it to a, b, c, d. Just highlight the entire list, and choose a, b, c, d, e from the Apply a sequence box.

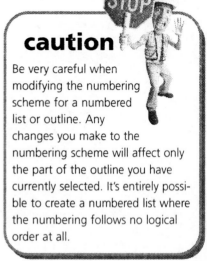

caution

Be very careful when modifying the numbering scheme for a numbered list or outline. Any changes you make to the numbering scheme will affect only the part of the outline you have currently selected. It's entirely possible to create a numbered list where the numbering follows no logical order at all.

After you've chosen a sequence, you can also apply a format. If you don't like a, b, c, d, e, you can change the format to a>, b>, c>, d>, e>.

Be very careful changing sequences and formatting. If you want to affect the entire outline, you'll need to select every line of the outline before you begin. Otherwise, you could end up with two parts of the same outline with different sequences and formats. This can be quite confusing, as shown in Figure 14.17.

Advanced Numbering Settings

There are a couple of advanced settings you can access from the Customize Numbering task pane. You can change the alignment of your bullets or numbers by choosing either Left or Right from the Adjust alignment options. It's difficult to discern the difference between left and right alignment unless you have a numbering scheme that extends into two and three digits. For example, in Figure 14.18, the top numbered list is aligned left and the bottom numbered list is aligned right.

> **caution**
>
> Go slowly when changing the numbering sequence and format on a numbered outline. You can often end up with unexpected results. If you select a sequence or format you don't like, just select Undo from the Edit menu or press Ctrl+Z to undo your changes.

FIGURE 14.17

Changing the sequence for only part of an outline can produce confusing results.

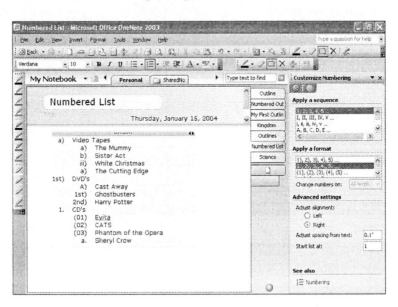

FIGURE 14.18

Aligning your numbering either left or right can give your lists a slightly different look.

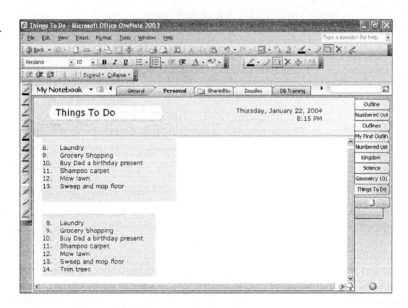

You can adjust the spacing between the number in the list and the text of the numbered item by entering a different value in the Adjust spacing from text box.

If you want to renumber your list automatically, select the entire list and change the value in the Start list at box. OneNote will automatically renumber your list for you.

caution

Renumbering a list doesn't always produce reliable results. Choosing Undo from the Edit menu can quickly undo the last change you made to your outline or list. If you attempt to renumber your list and don't like the results, you can always use this menu option to return to your previous numbering scheme.

note

As with any change you make in the Bullets, Numbering, or Customize Numbering task pane, renumbering your list is an immediate operation. However, it's easy to undo. Either change the number in the Start list at box back to its original value or choose <u>U</u>ndo from the <u>E</u>dit menu.

THE ABSOLUTE MINIMUM

In this chapter you learned how to create an outline from scratch. You learned

- How to create a bulleted outline
- How to create a numbered outline
- How to create a numbered list
- How to customize your bullets and numbering
- How to correctly apply a numbering scheme
- How to renumber your list with a couple of clicks

The next chapter explores some advanced outlining features and shows you how to take existing text and turn it into an outline. While many of the same techniques you learned in this chapter apply to converting existing text into an outline, you'll learn some tips and tricks for taking writing entered on a Tablet PC and turning it into an organized and formatted outline.

IN THIS CHAPTER

- Creating outlines from existing body text
- Changing outlines into body text
- Showing and hiding outline sections
- Changing your outline's format

15

CREATING OUTLINES FROM EXISTING TEXT

Chapter 14, "Creating Outlines in OneNotes," taught you how to create an outline from scratch; now you're ready to learn about how to turn existing text into an outline. You can use OneNote's toolbars, menus, and the mouse or Tablet PC pen to combine note containers, create bullets or numbering, and change indentations.

In addition to turning text into outlines, you can turn outlines into regular text. Finally, we'll cover how to display only certain outline sections and how you can change the format of your outline.

Changing Existing Text into an Outline

As you're typing along in OneNote, you don't always know that what you're typing would make more sense in outline format. You can turn what's called body text (that text that's not part of an outline) into an outline using the Outlining toolbar. Consider the notes in Figure 15.1.

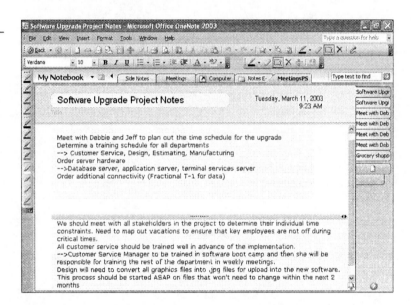

As you can see, there are two distinct note containers on this page. If you need both note containers to be part of the same outline, the first step you'll want to take is combining these two note containers. It's easy to combine note containers. Simply position your mouse over the top of the second note container. You'll see the darker gray container handle appear. Click on this handle and drag the note container upwards until it merges with the first note container. Release the mouse button to combine (or dock) the second note container with the first container.

Now that you have a single note container on the screen, there are several different ways you can turn this large note into an outline. You can use one of the following methods or use a combination of these methods to create your outline.

Converting an Entire Note Container to an Outline

The easiest way to create an outline from existing text is to convert the entire note container to a list (either a bulleted or numeric list) with just a couple of clicks. You can then turn the list into an outline by indenting specific lines. To convert a note container into a bulleted list, click the note container's handle to select all text within the container. Click the Bullets button on the Formatting toolbar to change the text into a bulleted list, as shown in Figure 15.2.

FIGURE 15.2

You can change text into a bulleted list with a single click.

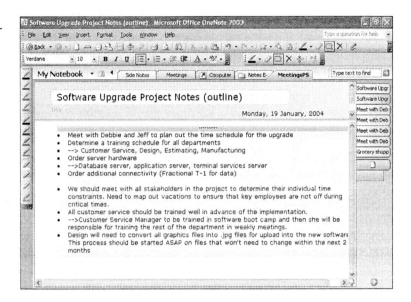

Now that you have a bulleted list, you can turn that list into an outline by choosing sections of text to indent.

Selecting Sections of Text to Indent

Even though the text is now in bulleted form, Figure 15.2 still isn't very readable. From looking at the text, it should be obvious that several of the lines should be indented (or nested) under other lines. To indent these lines, use the following steps.

1. Select the line that you want to indent. You can do this by double-clicking on the line or positioning your mouse pointer to the left of the line and clicking the line handle.

2. Click the **Increase Indent** button on the Outlining toolbar. Each time you click it, you'll indent the line one additional level.

note

If you don't have the Formatting toolbar displayed, choose Toolbars from the View menu and click Formatting. You can also choose Bullets from the Format menu to change text into a bulleted list.

3. Repeat this process for all lines you need to indent. When you're done, your outline might look similar to Figure 15.3.

FIGURE 15.3

Indenting certain portions of your outline increases readability.

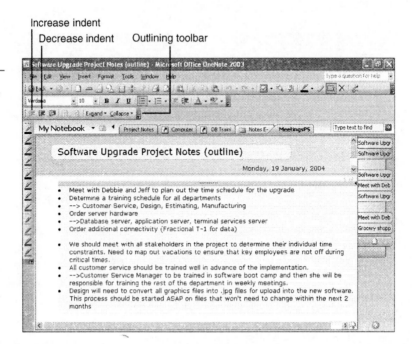

You can use the same sort of process to reverse the indentation of a line. If you accidentally select two lines to indent, or merely want to decrease the indentation of a particular line, select the line and click the Decrease Indent button on the Outlining toolbar. The selected line will decrease one indentation level.

Creating Your Outline Line by Line

If you don't want to convert an entire block of text into an outline at once, you can create your outline step by step. You'll use the same basic techniques as described in the previous section. To begin, highlight the first line of your outline and click the Bullets or Numbering button on the Formatting toolbar. You can then click the next line you want to add to your outline and click the appropriate button again. If you want to create a numbered outline, after you select

tip

You can accomplish the same task by selecting the line and pressing the Tab key on the keyboard. Each time you press the Tab key, you'll indent the line one additional level.

the second line and click the Numbering button, you'll have two lines at the same level (numbered 1 and 2). Select the second line and press Tab (or click the Increase Indent button on the toolbar) to indent the line.

You can continue these steps to create the rest of your outline. Your numbered outline might look similar to Figure 15.4.

FIGURE 15.4

You can create a numbered outline from any text in OneNote.

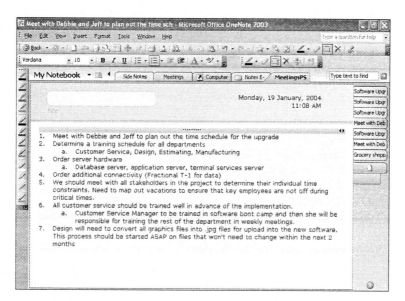

Changing Text from Outline Text to Body Text

Body text is text within your outline that provides more detail to an outline topic. For example, in Figure 15.5, the text beneath the fourth top-level bullet is body text. You can turn any portion of an outline into body text. Simply select the line of text using the line handle and then click the Make Body Text button on the Outlining toolbar. By default, when turning outline text into body text, the text becomes body text under the outline level immediately above it, even if the text was originally at a higher level than the line above it.

In Figure 15.5, if you turned the second bullet and its associated sub-bullets into body text, they would all appear as body text indented under the first bullet.

FIGURE 15.5

You can make body text out of any lines within the outline.

Turning Pen-written Text into an Outline on the Tablet PC

There are some special considerations you'll need to understand when converting written text into outline form. First of all, taking notes on consecutive lines with the Tablet PC pen doesn't always produce notes within the same note container. Secondly, even if two lines are within the same note container, OneNote might recognize them as two completely separate lines, rather than a two-line sentence. For example, in Figure 15.6, the fourth and fifth lines are all part of the same sentence. As such, when put into outline form, they should be considered part of the same bullet. The second topic (MIS) should really be in the same note container as the first, but is actually a new note container.

Before you convert the lines in Figure 15.6 to an outline, you'll first need to manipulate them so that OneNote recognizes which lines are new and which are continuations of previous lines.

First, you can merge the two separate note containers into a single container. To accomplish this, position your Tablet PC's pen over the first

tip

You might need to manipulate the second note container a bit to drop it in the right spot. For example, it's easy to drop the container slightly above where you intended to drop it and insert it between two existing lines.

line of the second note container. You should see the handle for the container (the plus sign with arrows on all sides) appear next to the first line of the note container. Tap the handle once to select the entire container. Tap and hold the Tablet PC's pen over the handle and drag the container upwards until it falls into place below the first note container.

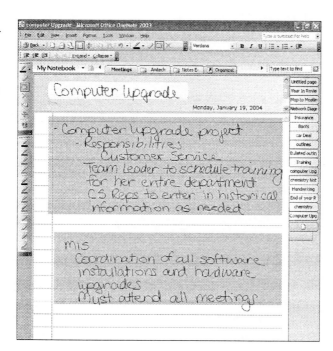

FIGURE 15.6

Writing with a Tablet PC can produce ambiguous note containers.

Now that you have all your lines in one note container, you can tell OneNote which lines are continuations of the previous lines and which represent a new line.

1. To mark a line as a continuation of the previous line, position the Tablet PC pen over the line and hold down the pen to simulate a right mouse click.

2. Choose **Continue Previous Paragraph** from the context menu.

3. Repeat these steps for all lines you need on the page. You're now ready to select the entire block of text and convert it into an outline.

4. Click the handle for the top line of text to select all the text.

5. Click the **Bullets** button on the Formatting toolbar to add bullets to your text, as shown in Figure 15.7.

FIGURE 15.7

Once you've manipulated your note containers, you can turn your text into an outline.

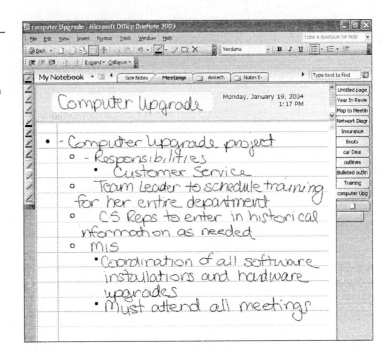

You can use the same process to create a numbered outline or a numbered list. As you work with the Tablet PC, you'll likely find yourself adjusting your writing to avoid some of these typical problems. For example, once you get a feel for how far away two written lines can be and still be in the same note container, you'll probably find that you need to combine note containers less frequently.

Manipulating Your Outline

You can store a vast amount of information in your outline. However, you might not always want to display all that information on your OneNote page. For example, you might want to hide certain sections of an outline in a printout. If you have an outline for tasks for a variety of departments, you can create a printout for each department with only their tasks. You could, of course, copy and paste just the relevant portions of the outline for each department, but it is simpler to merely hide certain portions of the outline.

You can collapse a section of an outline by double-clicking on the top line you want to show. For example, in Figure 15.8, you can hide all levels below Family by double-clicking on the note handle to the left of the word Family. The Genus and Species entries (along with any text in lower levels) are collapsed under the Family level.

FIGURE 15.8

You can collapse
sections of your
outline by
double-clicking
them.

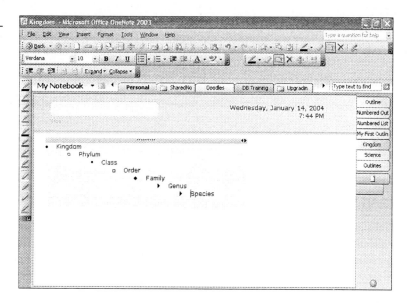

FIGURE 15.8

You can collapse
sections of your
outline by
double-clicking
them.

You can also use OneNote's menus to control which levels of your outline are
shown. You can hide all information under the third level of your outline by selecting the entire outline and choosing <u>V</u>iew, <u>H</u>ide Levels Below Level <u>3</u>. This hides all
the information at level 4, level 5, and so on. No matter how many levels you have
in your outline, the Hide Levels Below menu only shows levels 1 through 5. You can
choose to hide any of these levels through the menu or with the keyboard. To use
the keyboard to hide all levels below level 4, press Alt+Shift+4. This syntax works for
all levels of your outline. If you have eight outline levels and you want to hide all
levels below level six, press Alt+Shift+6.

In addition to double-clicking a line of the outline and using the Hide Levels Below menu, you
can also use the Outlining toolbar to collapse
your outline. Choose the <u>C</u>ollapse button on the
Outlining toolbar and select a level to collapse.
You can also collapse the entire outline by
choosing <u>A</u>ll.

Once you've hidden the levels, you might want
to get them back again. To do this, either select
Ex<u>p</u>and from the Outlining toolbar or double-
click the level you want to expand on the
screen. If you choose Ex<u>p</u>and from the Outlining
toolbar, you can choose to expand just a specific
level or <u>A</u>ll.

tip

If you have an eight-level
outline and you choose to
hide levels below five, you
can show level six again by
pressing Alt+Shift+6. This
shows level 6 again with-
out re-opening level seven
or eight.

Changing Outline Spacing

The last method of manipulating the outline we'll discuss is changing the outline spacing. By default, when using either bullets or numbering, there's a space of 0.1 inches between the bullet and the text. You can change this spacing for both bulleted and numbered outlines, and numbered lists. To alter the spacing for bulleted outlines, first select your outline. Choose Bullets from the Format menu to display the Bullets task pane, shown in Figure 15.9.

FIGURE 15.9

You can control the spacing between the bullet and the text.

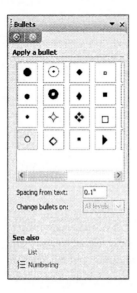

It's possible to adjust the spacing for the entire outline or only one or two lines of the outline. To adjust spacing, select the portion of the outline you're interested in. In the Spacing from text box, enter a number other than 0.1.

Spacing changes can affect more than just the currently selected line. For example, in Figure 15.10, if you select the line that starts with "Office System" through the line that starts with "Word" and change the spacing of the bullets, you won't affect the spacing of the line that starts with "Java," even though it's at the same level as "Office System." However, if you choose the line that starts with "Excel" and its nested bullets of "Macros," "Documents," "Printers," and "Templates," any changes to spacing will affect the "Outlook," "PowerPoint," and "Word" lines as well. You can always choose Undo from the Edit menu if changing spacing produces any unintended consequences.

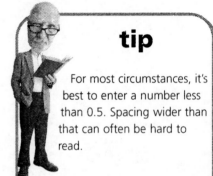

tip

For most circumstances, it's best to enter a number less than 0.5. Spacing wider than that can often be hard to read.

FIGURE 15.10

Changing outline spacing can often have unpredictable results.

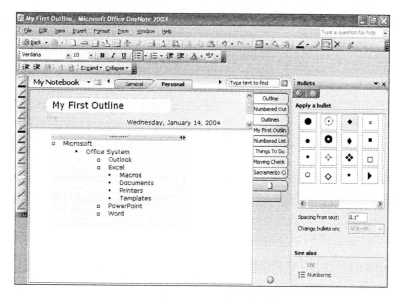

FIGURE 15.10

Changing outline spacing can often have unpredictable results.

Once you've entered a spacing number, press Tab or Enter to apply your changes.

Controlling List Spacing

When working with lists, you have a few other spacing options to control. Choose List from the Format menu to display the List task pane, as shown in Figure 15.11.

FIGURE 15.11

You can control several spacing options for lists.

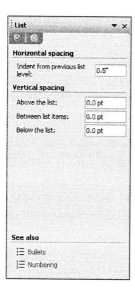

To alter the horizontal spacing, change the number in the box marked Indent from previous list level. This value controls how far the list is indented from the outline level. For example, referring back to Figure 15.5, increasing this value causes the second-level items to indent themselves further under the first-level items.

There are three values you can manipulate for vertical spacing. First, you can control the default space that's present above the list. If you always want there to be a fixed amount of space above your list, regardless of where on the page the list appears, change the value for the Above the list box.

To change the spacing between list items, alter the value in the Between list items box. Finally, to alter the spacing below the list, change the value in the Below the list box. Changing all these values to 8 pt changes Figure 15.5 into Figure 15.12.

FIGURE 15.12
Changing the spacing of your outline can give it a unique look.

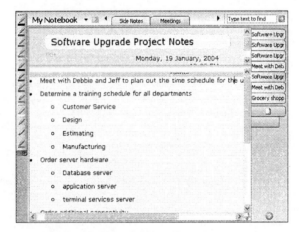

THE ABSOLUTE MINIMUM

In this chapter you learned how to turn existing text into outlines and how to control some advanced features of your outlines. You learned

- How to change standard text into an outline format
- How to indent certain selections of text
- How to customize the look of your outline by collapsing and expanding outline sections
- How to control the spacing of your outlines and lists

The next chapter explains all the various tasks you can perform using note containers within your OneNote pages. You'll learn how to combine note containers, move them between various pages and sections, as well as add lines, tables, and charts to your OneNote pages.

IN THIS CHAPTER

- What's a note container?
- Combine and separate note containers
- Rearrange notes within a container
- Add lines, tables, and charts to your notes

16

WORKING WITH YOUR NOTE PAGE

So far in this book, we've examined a wide variety of the different structural elements of OneNote. You've learned how to create folders to store different types of information, sections to store different categories of information, and pages to store your notes.

This chapter focuses on the most basic element of every page, the note container. A note container is just that—a container that holds text that comprises your note. You can have any number of note containers on a page and there are wide varieties of functions you can use on and in note containers.

Using Note Containers

As you've seen in previous chapters, all notes you take in OneNote, whether on a Tablet PC, desktop, or laptop, are stored in note containers. Figure 16.1 shows a typical OneNote page with three note containers. The note container is the shaded box that contains text, handwriting, graphics or links.

FIGURE 16.1

You can store text, graphics, and links in your note containers.

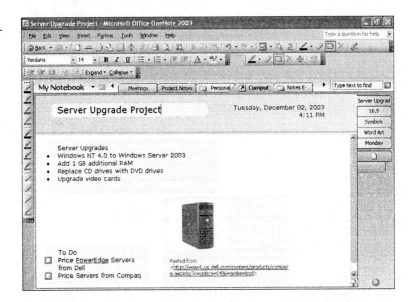

As you can see, note containers can contain a variety of different types of data. They grow in size to accommodate the data stored within them. Anytime you click on a OneNote page, you're either creating a new note container or entering an existing note container. All OneNote notes are contained in note containers.

To create your note container, click somewhere in a blank area of OneNote. You should see a blinking vertical bar where you clicked, representing your cursor.

note

If you have a Tablet PC and are using its pen, you won't necessarily see the note container on the screen when you tap the screen. Rest assured, the note container is still there, however it won't display unless the pen is in selection mode.

In short, you do just about everything in OneNote by using note containers. You can move note containers around on the screen, resize them, combine them, create them, delete them, change their display, copy, paste, and cut them.

Customizing the Display of Note Containers

There are a few customizations you can make to the display of your note containers. Choose Options from the Tools menu to display Figure 16.2.

tip

If you click too close to an existing note container, you won't create a new note container. The cursor will appear within the existing note container. If you really want a new note container, just click a little further away from the existing note container.

The Display category of the Options window allows you to control how dark your note containers are shaded. Use the drop-down to choose the level of note container shading you need. As you can see from Figure 16.3, choosing the darkest shading leaves no doubt as to where the note containers are located on the screen.

FIGURE 16.2

You can control the display of note containers on the screen.

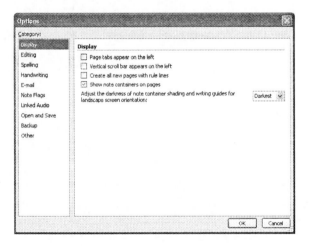

In addition to controlling the shading of the note containers, you can also turn off their display entirely. Uncheck the box marked Show note containers on pages and click OK. The note container is still there, but as you can see from Figure 16.4, it's no longer visible on the page.

FIGURE 16.3

You can vary the note container shading from lightest to darkest.

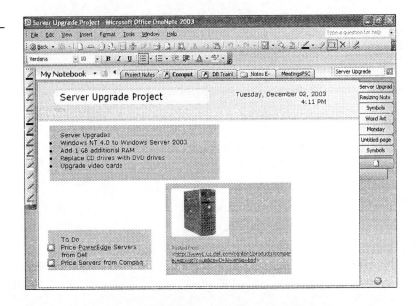

FIGURE 16.4

You can turn off display of the note containers entirely.

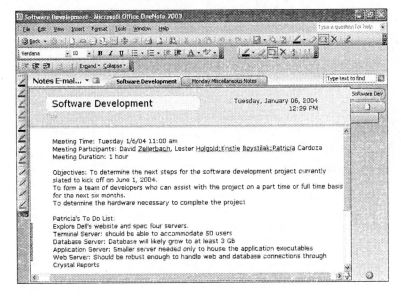

You must click OK to save your changes to the Options settings.

Resizing Note Containers

When you first start typing in a note container, it expands to approximately 75% of the width of the OneNote page. When your typing reaches the end of the line, it automatically wraps to the next line. If you want to resize your note container, just position your mouse or Tablet PC pen over the top of the note container to display the container's handle (the darker gray strip on the top of the note container). Within that strip you'll see two opposite-facing arrows. As you move your mouse pointer over those arrows, the pointer changes into a double arrow. Click and drag left or right to change the size of your note container. Figure 16.5 shows the same text in two note containers of differing sizes.

Note Container handle

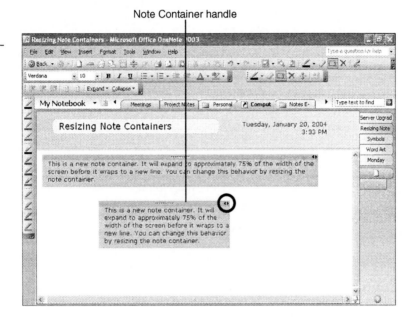

FIGURE 16.5

You can resize your note container by clicking and dragging.

As you resize the note container, the text within the note container wraps properly.

Moving a Note Container Around on the Screen

Using the note container's handle (shown in Figure 16.5), you can move the note container anywhere on your OneNote page. Just position your mouse or Tablet PC's pen over the handle, click and drag the handle to move the note container. You can even move a note container from the note page to the page header. While it's generally not common to store information within note containers in the page header, you might find it useful, as shown in Figure 16.6.

FIGURE 16.6

Sometimes you might want to store information in the page header.

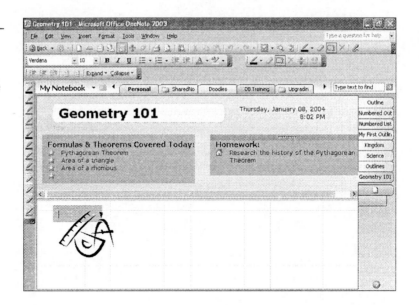

You can also move the note container to another page or section. You can't drag the note container from one page to another. In order to move the note container, you'll need to cut (or copy) it and then paste it at the destination location.

1. Select the note container by clicking the container's handle.

2. Choose **Cut** (or **Copy**) from the **Edit** menu.

3. Navigate to the destination page and choose **Paste** from the **Edit** menu.

You use the same steps to move a note container to another section within OneNote.

Combining Two Note Containers

It's easy to combine two note containers into a single container. Simply use your mouse or Tablet PC's pen to click the note container's handle. Then drag it up or down until it appears to dock (lock on) to another note container. You'll see the two containers combine before you release the mouse.

---

caution

It's easy to drag note containers where you don't want them. In particular, it's easy to drag a note container to the bottom of an existing note container and have it insert itself in the middle of the existing note container. Don't try to rush moving note containers. You'll be able to see where the note container will land before you release the mouse. If it's not the right spot, move it before releasing the mouse.

Rearranging Notes Within a Container

As mentioned in the previous section, when combining note containers, it's easy to drag a note container into the middle of another note container. If you've done this and need to rearrange the lines in a note container, or merely want to rearrange the lines in a list or outline, you can do that rather simply.

Position your mouse or Tablet PC's pen over the line you want to move. As you hover the pointer over the line, you'll see the line handle, as shown in Figure 16.7.

FIGURE 16.7

You can use the line handle to move lines around within a container.

Line handle

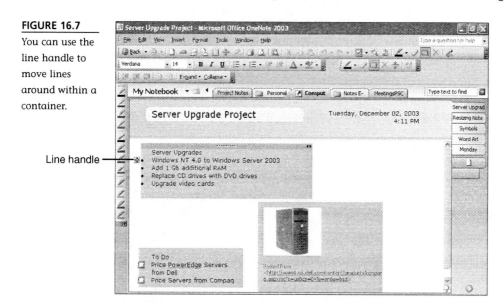

Click once on the line handle to select the line and hold down the mouse button. You can now drag the line anywhere you want on the screen. You can drag it within the current note container or create an entirely new note container.

If you want to select multiple lines at a time, you can use the Shift or Ctrl keys to do this. To select adjacent lines, click the first line's handle with your mouse. Then press and hold the Shift key while clicking the last line's handle. If you want to select lines that are not next to each other, click the first line's handle with your mouse. Press and hold the Ctrl key while clicking to select the second line. You can use these methods with any number of lines. For example, in Figure 16.8, you could select the first, third, and fifth lines from the bottom note container.

FIGURE 16.8

You can select
multiple lines
from the same
note container.

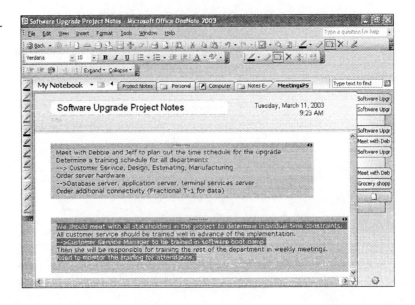

If you drag the selected lines up to the first note container on the page, the lines will be inserted at the bottom of the first note container. If you changed your mind before you released the mouse to drop the lines in their new location and attempted to drag them back to their original location, OneNote would remember that the selected lines had other lines between them and would return the lines to their original position. This positional memory is only preserved until you release the mouse. If you change your mind about the position of the lines after you've released the mouse button, you'll have to move the lines back into position manually.

Making a New Note Container from an Existing Note Container

Much like you can combine two note containers to make a single note container, you can separate one note container into multiple note containers. All you have to do is use the line handle for one or multiple lines and drag the lines away from their existing container. The line or lines will form their

note

You'll see a line handle for every original line. In other words, if you are typing and let OneNote wrap a line of text into two lines, you'll only see one line handle. You cannot move the second wrapped line independently of the first without cutting and pasting it. Whenever you insert a carriage return (by pressing Enter on the keyboard), a new line is created with its own line handle.

own note container. In addition to creating a new note container, you can also move the lines into a different note container.

Adding Lines, Tables, and Charts

Unlike Microsoft Word, OneNote doesn't have a Drawing toolbar. There's no easy way to insert lines, tables, and charts in OneNote. However, like many computer problems, there's almost always a workaround. While these workarounds aren't the most elegant and simple solutions in the world, they will produce successful results.

Drawing a Line in OneNote

If you're using a Tablet PC, it's easy to draw a line. Just use your pen and draw a line across the screen. However, this line won't necessarily be straight (unless you're really good with the pen). If you're on a laptop or desktop, drawing a straight line is even harder.

If you're not on a Tablet PC, you can still switch to pen mode and draw on the screen. Click the pen icon on the toolbar to switch to pen mode. You can now draw on the screen with your mouse. However, even if you're very careful, you'll probably end up with a slightly crooked or curved line, as shown in Figure 16.9.

A circle, rectangle, or other geometric shape can present even more challenges. One of the easiest ways to draw a line is to use a note container and enter the underscore character (_) repeatedly. While this won't produce a very thick line, you can always change the font of the underscores to be large and bold. To display other shapes on your note page, choose <u>S</u>ymbol from the <u>I</u>nsert menu. Use the Subset drop-down and choose Geometric Shapes to display the dialog shown in Figure 16.10.

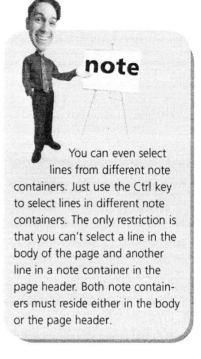

note

You can even select lines from different note containers. Just use the Ctrl key to select lines in different note containers. The only restriction is that you can't select a line in the body of the page and another line in a note container in the page header. Both note containers must reside either in the body or the page header.

note

If you want more information about adding pictures and graphics to your OneNote pages, see Chapter 12, "A Picture Is Worth a Thousand Words."

FIGURE 16.9

FIGURE 16.9

Even the best attempts at drawing a straight line can produce less-than-perfect results.

A line drawn with the pen

FIGURE 16.10

You can insert a variety of geometric shapes in your notes.

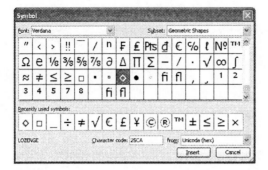

There are a number of geometric shapes you can insert in your notes. Once you've inserted the particular shape you need, you can change the font size to make the symbol larger. Figure 16.11 shows all of the various methods we've discussed in this section for creating lines and shapes.

Using External Tools

If none of the methods available in OneNote meet your needs, you can create your shapes in Microsoft Word and paste them into OneNote. For example, in Word you can create a variety of AutoShapes, including arrows, smiley faces, circles, ovals, and rectangles. You can also fill these images in with color. Once you've created the shapes in Word, you can copy these shapes in Word and paste them into OneNote, as shown in Figure 16.12.

note

You can use the Symbols dialog for much more than geometric shapes. If you need to represent mathematical calculations in graphical form, you can add a variety of symbols into your notes. For more information about using the Symbols dialog, see Chapter 22, "Math in OneNote."

FIGURE 16.11

There are a number of methods you can use to insert shapes in your notes.

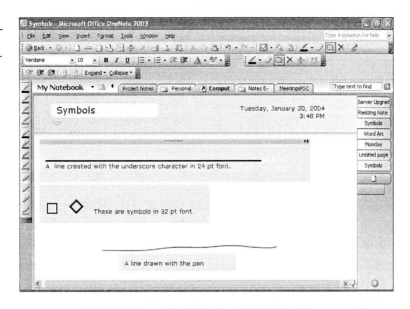

FIGURE 16.12

You can insert Word art into OneNote by copying and pasting.

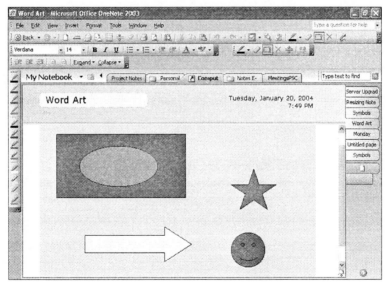

Inserting Tables

If you want to insert a table in OneNote, there are a few ways to do it. If you create the table in Word, you can copy it and paste it into OneNote. There are two ways you can paste the table. You can paste it as text, or you can paste it as a picture. Figure 16.13 shows both options. The first table in Figure 16.13 is pasted as text, the second is pasted as a picture.

Inserting information from Word is covered in depth in Chapter 21, "Importing Information from Other Applications."

You can insert information from Excel in much the same way. Copy the information from Excel, and paste it into OneNote. This works for both tables and charts in Excel.

FIGURE 16.13

You can paste a table as text or as a picture.

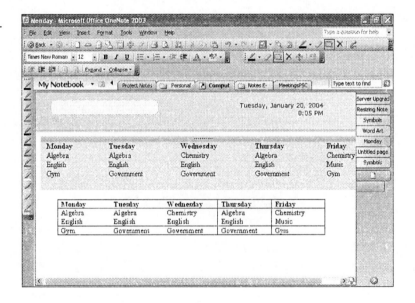

THE ABSOLUTE MINIMUM

In this chapter you learned all about note containers. You learned

- How you can use note containers to store text
- How to move note containers within OneNote
- How to combine two note containers
- How to separate one note container into multiple containers
- How to add lines and other geometric shapes to your OneNote page
- How to add external content to note containers

In the next chapter, you'll learn how to record audio files in OneNote. You'll learn how to save them, share them, and play them within OneNote.

17

It's Too Quiet in Here Let's Add Some Sound

Sometimes, no matter how fast you type or write, you just can't capture everything that happens in the typical meeting. You might have four or five people trying to talk at once, or there might just be too much information to capture at one time. In cases like this, you can use OneNote and your computer's microphone to record audio.

In addition to the basics of how to create audio recordings, this chapter covers a variety of examples of using audio recordings within OneNote.

Recording Audio

As mentioned in the chapter introduction, you can use OneNote's audio capabilities for several purposes. For example, you can record a quick memo from a Side Note with a couple of clicks. You can use audio for added emphasis within a written or typed note. If you have enough hard drive space and battery life on your laptop or tablet, you can even record an entire meeting. Optionally, you can even forego typing or writing notes and only record audio. This enables you to turn your entire concentration over to the meeting. At a later date, you can play back the audio and take more detailed notes.

note

You can use OneNote to take high-quality recordings with the right equipment. If you're going to record audio in a noisy environment, invest in a high-quality microphone.

In order to record audio in OneNote, you'll need both a sound card and microphone attached to your computer. A good number of laptops and just about all Tablet PCs come with both a sound card and a microphone. If your computer doesn't have a microphone, you can usually purchase an easy-to-use external microphone for under $50.

Unlike a simple tape recorder (or even a fancy digital voice recorder or MP3 player), recording audio with OneNote gives you the additional benefit of tracking what you were hearing or saying at the time you wrote or typed the note. Sometimes days or weeks after a meeting, you just can't quite place the context of a particular line of text. If you can replay the audio surrounding that line of text, you can probably remember what that line of text meant.

Using Audio Notes to Interact with Colleagues

If you're sharing notes between coworkers, you can use audio notes to enhance the collaboration. For example, in Figure 17.1, you can see a note page with notes from an ongoing budget project. The note page is divided into two sides, one for each person working on the project. Both sides have attached audio notes to clarify the progress of the budget meeting.

As you can see from the figure, each member of the budget team can record their own audio notes to clarify assigned tasks.

note

In order to share audio recordings, it's best to store the OneNote page on a shared network location. This way the audio files are also stored in the network location and are accessible to all users.

FIGURE 17.1

Using audio can enhance your collaborative efforts.

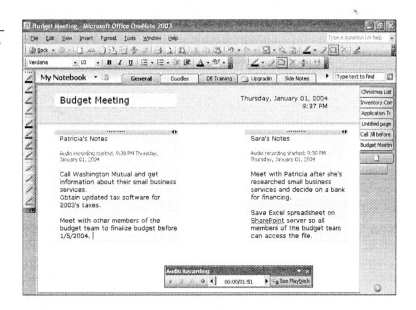

Using the Audio Toolbar

In order to record audio notes, you'll first need to display the audio toolbar. To display the toolbar, select <u>V</u>iew, <u>T</u>oolbars, and click the Audio Recording toolbar to display the toolbar, as shown in Figure 17.2.

FIGURE 17.2

You can use the Audio Recording toolbar to record and play back your audio notes.

The Audio Recording toolbar allows you to start, pause, play, and end a recording. It also contains an audio gauge to show you the total length of the recording as well as the length of the playback so far. The last button on the right side of the toolbar allows you to toggle the highlighting of text you were writing or typing when you recorded the note. We'll cover each of these functions in this chapter.

tip

You can also display the Audio Recording toolbar by right-clicking any existing toolbar and choosing Audio Recording from the pop-up menu.

Recording Your First Audio Note

If you're recording an audio note within the main OneNote program, all you need to do is click the Record button on the audio toolbar. A new note container is created with the date and time of the audio recording. If you want to type or write notes while making an audio recording, you can start typing or writing directly within this note container or you can create a new note container for your typing or writing.

note

It doesn't matter whether you type text in the note container created by the audio recording or a new note container. The audio and the text will still be linked.

You can click the Pause or Stop buttons at any time during your recording. After you click the Pause or Stop buttons, the toolbar will take on a similar appearance to Figure 17.3.

FIGURE 17.3
After you've recorded audio, you'll see a slightly different look to the toolbar.

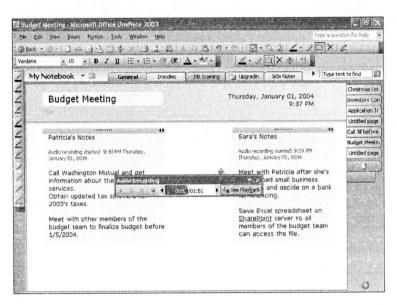

After recording an audio note, the toolbar displays the playback position in the center of the toolbar. For example, in the previous figure, 50 seconds of the audio has played. The recording has a total length of a minute and 51 seconds. We'll cover playback of the audio and audio and note synchronization later in this chapter.

Creating Multiple Audio Notes in the Same Page

You can create any number of audio notes on your note page. Every time you start a new audio recording, OneNote adds a new time and date stamp to the note page even if you're continuing the audio recording in the same note container as a previous recording.

You'll notice that if you create a second audio recording on a note page, the playback counter picks up where it left off. So if your first recording is 30 seconds long, your second recording will start at 31 seconds and continue from there. Although it looks like OneNote is creating one long audio file, the program actually creates a new audio file every time you click the record button or start a new recording from the menus.

Each audio recording is stored in the My Notebook folder. The name of the recording is composed of the name of the current page tab and a numeric component indicating the number of the audio recording. If you need to find the second audio recording on the Doodles page, you'd look for a file called Doodles – 2.WMA.

If you don't have a page title when you start recording an audio note, the note will be named Audio Recording and the appropriate number. You can play back any of the audio recordings outside of OneNote by simply double-clicking on them from the My Notebook folder. The files will open with Windows Media Player or another installed media player.

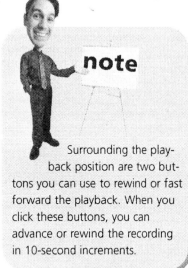

note

Surrounding the playback position are two buttons you can use to rewind or fast forward the playback. When you click these buttons, you can advance or rewind the recording in 10-second increments.

caution

If you like to keep the files on your computer organized, you might be tempted to rename an audio note named Audio Recording to match the name of your page. However, if you change the name of the recording, OneNote won't be able to play it back properly.

Audio Playback and Note Synchronization

One of the most powerful features of OneNote is the ability to synchronize audio and written (or typed) notes. As your audio recording progresses, OneNote remembers the particular line you typed or wrote during each 10-second block of recording time. When you play back the note, OneNote can show you the particular line you were typing or writing by highlighting the line as the audio plays. In Figure 17.4, the particular block of text typed during a portion of the recording is highlighted.

FIGURE 17.4

OneNote can flag the text you were typing during your audio recording.

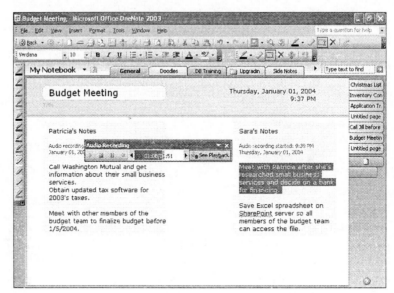

This feature can be especially helpful when you need to remember what exactly you were writing and why you were writing it. You've probably been in a meeting before and written a note and then not remembered exactly what the note meant. Sometimes, particularly if some time has passed since you took the note, you need some help remembering the context of the note. Playing back your audio notes while watching the highlighting of the notes on the screen can sometimes provide enough information for you to respond to the note appropriately.

You can turn off the visual playback of your audio note at any time. Just click the See Playback button on the audio toolbar. The colored shading of the button will disappear. You can toggle the visual playback on or off at any time, even when the audio is currently playing.

Removing Audio Notes from Your Note Page

There are a couple of ways you can remove an existing audio note. OneNote stores audio notes as WMA (Windows Media) files directly in the My Notebook folder. A link to these files is placed in the note page. You can remove an audio note from the page by simply deleting the WMA file from the My Notebook folder. You might expect OneNote to remove the time and date stamp indicating the presence of an audio note when you do this, however that's not the case. OneNote leaves the time and date stamp but removes the speaker icon that indicates the presence of an audio recording.

Figures 17.5 and 17.6 show the difference between a linked audio recording (see Figure 17.5) and the time and date stamp left over when you delete a linked audio recording (see Figure 17.6). You'll only notice the difference between the two when you hover your mouse over the time and date stamp.

FIGURE 17.5

When an audio recording is present, a speaker icon is present.

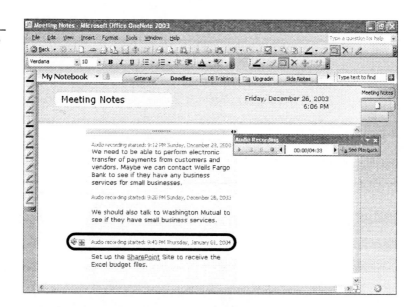

FIGURE 17.6

When you delete an audio record- ing, the speaker icon is removed.

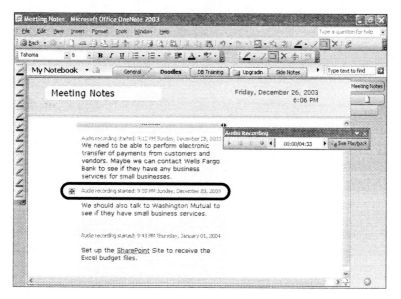

You might think that you can delete an audio recording directly from within the note page. Well, that's not entirely true. If you select the time and date stamp for an audio recording and delete it from the note page, you will only delete the link to the audio recording. The WMA file for the audio recording remains in the My Notebook folder. You can leave the WMA file in the My Notebook folder or delete it manually.

If you want to remove all audio recordings from a particular note page, you can do this through OneNote's menus. Select Audio Recording from the <u>T</u>ools menu (see Figure 17.7).

FIGURE 17.7

You can delete audio recordings from OneNote's menus.

Choosing <u>D</u>elete Recording deletes all linked audio files from the note page. The time and date stamps for the audio files are left in the note page. You can delete them if you want.

Emailing Audio Notes

If you attempt to email OneNote files containing linked audio files, by default, the recipient will receive the note page, but not the linked audio files. If you want to include the linked audio files, use the following steps to change OneNote's options.

1. Choose **Tools**, **Options** from the menu bar.

> **tip**
>
> If you delete a link to an audio file, you can re-establish the link, although you'll lose the ability to see what you were typing when you play back the recording. To re-establish the link, just type the name of the file using this syntax: `file:\\RecordingName.wma`. This references a recording stored in the My Notebook folder.

2. Click **E-mail** on the left side of the Options window to display the E-mail options shown in Figure 17.8.

3. Check the box marked **Attach a copy of linked audio files**.

4. Click **OK** to save your changes.

You can email notes easily by choosing **E-mail** from the **File** menu. We'll cover emailing notes further in Chapter 23, "Sharing and Collaboration."

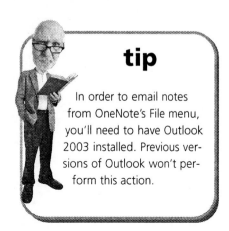

tip

In order to email notes from OneNote's File menu, you'll need to have Outlook 2003 installed. Previous versions of Outlook won't perform this action.

FIGURE 17.8

OneNote doesn't include linked audio files by default when emailing.

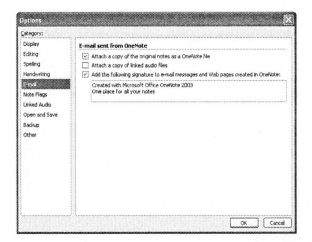

Changing OneNote's Audio Options

There are a few options you can control to enhance your audio experience. Choose Options from the Tools menu and click Linked Audio from the left side of the window to display OneNote's Linked Audio Options dialog, as shown in Figure 17.9.

Many users won't ever need to change OneNote's audio options. If you have a Tablet PC, it probably came with a built-in microphone. To record short snippets of meetings or even entire conversations, you'll probably find the quality of the built-in microphone perfectly adequate. However if the quality of your recordings isn't adequate, you can buy and configure an external microphone.

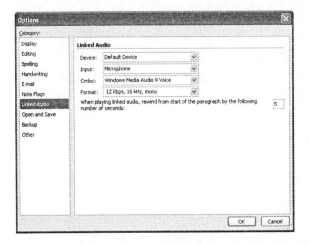

You can configure the following options for linked audio.

- Device—If you only have one sound card or input device, you don't need to change anything in this drop down. If you have multiple input devices, you can choose the one you want OneNote to use by choosing it from the drop-down.

- Input—Most of the time, you'll probably use the microphone to record audio. However, you can also record CD audio or stereo in OneNote as well. For example, you can record a news program on the radio or a short segment of music from a CD within your OneNote note page.

- Codec—Compressor/Decompressor (Codec) is a method for compressing and decompressing (expanding) data. Most users won't ever need to change the Codec method.

- Format—By default, OneNote records audio with a medium-quality format. This means that the recording is a reasonable size and reasonable quality. If you find the files are too large, you can choose a lower-quality format; however, this will reduce the playback quality. If you need a higher-quality format, you can select a new setting. This will increase file size.

- Rewind amount—When you select a paragraph that contains linked audio and choose to play the audio, OneNote rewinds the playback 5 seconds before the start of the paragraph. If you want to change this interval, you can enter any other interval between 1 and 999 seconds.

When you're done changing OneNote's audio options, click OK to save your changes.

THE ABSOLUTE MINIMUM

In this chapter, you learned how to record audio notes in addition to your written or typed notes. You learned

- How to display the OneNote audio toolbar
- How to record multiple audio notes in the same note page
- How to playback your notes and have OneNote highlight the typed or written notes as you listen to the audio
- How to delete one or more audio file links and/or the audio files themselves
- How to configure OneNote to send audio notes via email
- How to change OneNote's audio options

Once you've taken more than a page or two of notes, you'll probably need to search for a word or phrase in your note pages. You might also want to take advantage of a new Office System 2003 feature, researching. In the next chapter, you'll learn about using OneNote's searching and research options.

PART V

GOING FURTHER WITH ONENOTE

- Search for information within your notes
- Jump directly to a search result
- Search handwriting and text
- Use OneNote's research capabilities to find more information

18

NOTE TAKING 301: FINDING AND RESEARCHING INFORMATION

After a few days, weeks, or months, you might amass a large number of folders, sections, and note pages. One of the reasons you might want to use OneNote instead of a spiral-bound notebook is the ability to search your OneNote files for information. You can search text or writing on note pages stored on your computer, on a network drive, or on a SharePoint site.

In this chapter we'll cover the various ways you can find information you've entered in OneNote. We'll also cover a new feature of Office 2003 programs, the ability to research information from a variety of research service sites directly within OneNote.

Using OneNote's Search Feature

All these digital notes won't do you very much good if you can't ever find the information you've entered. If you only have a couple pages of notes in easily organized sections, you can probably just scan the section to find what you need. If you've utilized OneNote's outlining and Note Flag features, it can be even simpler to give your pages a quick scan and find what you need. For example, in Figure 18.1, it's quite simple to find the first To-Do in Patricia's list.

FIGURE 18.1

If your notes are highly organized, performing a manual search can be simple.

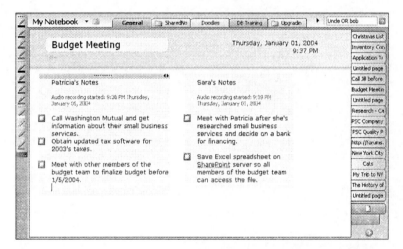

However, if you need to perform a more thorough search of multiple pages in multiple sections, you certainly don't want to examine every page in every section one by one.

Performing a Search

OneNote has a very robust search engine. To perform a search, type the text you're looking for in the text box in the upper right corner of the OneNote window. If you haven't performed a search since starting OneNote, this box contains the words *Type text to find*. If you've performed a search after starting OneNote, the box will contain the last term you searched for. As soon as you click in this box, those words disappear and you can enter your own text.

note

By default, OneNote searches all open sections. To change this behavior, change the scope of your search, as shown later in this section.

Type the search term you're interested in. To start your search, you can use the mouse to click the green arrow next to the search box or press Enter on the keyboard. As shown in Figure 18.2, your search results are highlighted within your current note page. The first result is highlighted in gray, while the other results are highlighted in yellow.

FIGURE 18.2

OneNote highlights your search terms within the current page.

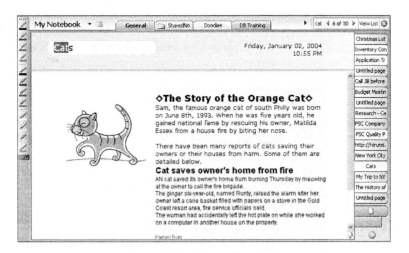

The simple search box changes a bit as well. The search term is displayed on the left of the box along with a counter that displays the total number of occurrences of the search term as well as the number of the currently highlighted result. You can use the left and right arrow icons to cycle through the occurrences of your search term.

In addition to changes to the search box, you'll also notice that some of the page tabs are highlighted in yellow. Those are the pages that contain your search term. You can click on any of the yellow page tabs to switch to the page and view the search results.

If you want to see all of your search results at once, click View List to display your search results in the Task pane, as shown in Figure 18.3.

note

If you search for a word such as *cat*, OneNote will find any occurrences of cat, including those found in words such as concatenation and category. There is no way to change this behavior.

FIGURE 18.3

You can display your search results in the Task pane.

Displaying your search results in the Task pane allows you to see a brief segment of the portion of the page in which your search term is found. To jump right to a page containing your search results, click the summary shown in the Page List Task pane.

You can change how your search results are sorted in the Task pane by choosing either Section, Title, or Date from the Sort list by drop-down box. By default, results are grouped by section and sorted in descending order. To change the sort order, click the ZA (or AZ) button next to the drop-down.

If you have a large number of results, scrolling through the list might be rather time consuming. You can collapse any of the groups to hide the results within that group. Click the minus sign next to the group name to collapse the group. The minus sign will turn into a plus sign. To expand a group, click the plus sign next to the group name.

If you want to change your search scope (which pages or sections you want to search), you can do this through the Page List task pane. Use the Search drop-down and choose Current section, Current folder, Current folder and its subfolders, or My entire notebook. Once you make a change to the search scope, the search is rerun and the new results are displayed in the Page List task pane.

Tips for Conducting a More Effective Search

If you're not getting the results you want from your search, consider the following tips to refine your search.

■ Exact phrases—To search for an exact phrase, such as a proper name or phrase, enclose the phrase in quotation marks. For example, searching for "Christmas Tree" will only find occurrences of the exact phrase. Searching for the phrase Christmas Tree without the quotes will find all instances of Christmas and Tree (in the same paragraph), and any paragraphs that contain words that contain those two words such as Christmastime and trees.

■ Case sensitivity—Searches in OneNote are not case sensitive. The following four search terms will return identical results: window, WINDOW, Window, and wINdow.

■ Find words in the same paragraph—If you want to find occurrences of two words in the same paragraph, you can just type the two words in the search box without quotation marks. However, you can also use the NEAR operator to accomplish the same thing. For example, the search Add NEAR method will display the results shown in Figure 18.4. You can use the NEAR operator with any number of search terms.

FIGURE 18.4

Using the NEAR operator finds two words in the same paragraph.

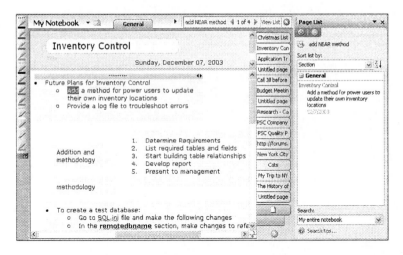

■ Operators—There are three operators you can use to refine your search results. In addition to the NEAR operator, you can use the AND and OR operators in your search. Using the AND operator (as in the search Cat AND Africa) will find all pages with occurrences of both Cat and Africa, as shown in Figure 18.5. Using the OR operator (as in the search cat OR Africa) will find all pages with either of the search terms. Unlike the rest of your search, operators must be capitalized. Otherwise OneNote assumes they are a search term and not an operator.

FIGURE 18.5
You can use the operators AND and OR to further refine your search.

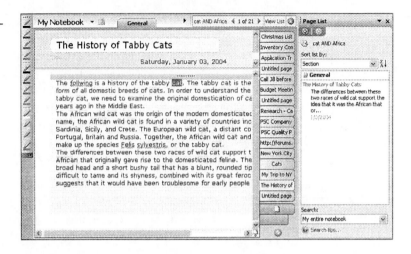

Searching Handwritten Notes

In addition to searching typed notes, you can search handwritten notes as well. The major caveat to remember when searching handwritten notes is that OneNote must be able to recognize your handwriting. For example, in the note shown in Figure 18.6, only three instances of the word *year* were found. However, there are actually five instances of the word on the page. OneNote didn't recognize the handwritten word *year* properly on two occasions.

FIGURE 18.6
OneNote's handwriting search isn't 100% reliable.

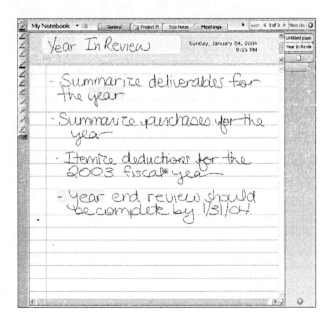

You can increase the chances of OneNote recognizing your handwriting by converting your handwriting to text or writing as neatly and legibly as you can. Without converting the handwriting to text, there's no way you can guarantee OneNote will always recognize your handwriting.

Searching Existing Notes on Your Computer

By default, OneNote searches all currently open sections. If you close one of the sections, your search won't examine the closed .one file. If you don't want to search all open sections, you can change the scope of your search through the Page List task pane. You can search your entire notebook, the current section, the current folder, or the current folder and all subfolders.

Searching Notes on a Shared Workspace Site

If you have OneNote folders or sections stored on a SharePoint Portal Server or SharePoint Team Services site, you can search those as well. Simply ensure that the search scope is set to My entire notebook, and any open sections stored on a Shared Workspace site or network location will be searched. If the section isn't currently open, OneNote won't search it. We'll cover storing OneNote files on a Shared Workspace site in Chapter 23, "Sharing and Collaboration."

Using OneNote's Research Library Pane

Office 2003 introduced a new feature, Research. Users can open the Research pane from all Office applications and search for information on any topic from a variety of free and paid sites. This can be particularly helpful for those using OneNote for college classes, or work research projects.

To launch the Research pane, select Research from the Tools menu. The Research pane is displayed in Figure 18.7.

tip

If you need some extra help keeping your handwriting straight and legible, you can add rule lines to your OneNote pages. Select Rule Lines from the View menu and choose from any of the six line or grid options.

tip

You can also launch the Research pane by right-clicking on a word on your page and choosing Look Up.

FIGURE 18.7

The Research pane allows you to search free and paid sites.

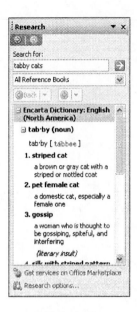

If you opened the Research task pane with a word highlighted on your page, or by right-clicking a word and choosing Look Up, your search term is already in the Search for box. If it isn't, to start your research, enter the topic in the Search for box and click the green arrow. Your results are displayed within the Research pane, as shown in Figure 18.8.

FIGURE 18.8

The Research pane displays search results from a variety of locations.

There are a number of free sites that are searched automatically. They include Encarta dictionary, thesaurus, and translation services.

Searching Free Online Sites

The only sites searched initially are the free online sites. For example, in Figure 18.8, searching for the phrase *tabby cat* displays a number of entries for *tabby*. The first entry is a definition for tabby that includes a pronunciation. Clicking the pronunciation opens the Encarta pronunciation key. To return to your search results, click the Back button.

You can use the plus and minus buttons next to various components of your search results to expand and collapse the results for easy readability.

Translation

If you need to translate a word or phrase into another language, you can do that within the Research pane as well. Just enter the word or phrase in the Research pane, use the drop-down immediately below the Search for dialog, and select Translation. Click the green arrow to display your results. If a match is found in the translation service, it's displayed in the Translation section of the Research pane as seen in Figure 18.9.

FIGURE 18.9

You can translate words or phrases into other languages.

The default translation is from English to French. You can change both the originating and ending languages by using the drop-downs. As you change one or the other, your results change as well.

You can change a few options for the translation service by clicking on the Translation options hyperlink in the Research pane to display Figure 18.10.

FIGURE 18.10

You can choose the available languages for your translation.

You can choose from 16 different translation options. When you've finished making changes to your translation options, click OK to exit the dialog box.

Encarta Encyclopedia

If you don't find what you need in the Encarta dictionary, you can search the Encarta Encyclopedia. You'll need to choose Encarta Encyclopedia from the drop-down box in order to utilize it. When you do, your search results change, as shown in Figure 18.11.

The Research pane only displays a small amount of the information available from the Encarta Encyclopedia. You can display more information by clicking on one of the topics displayed in blue in the Research pane. For example, clicking on II. Origin of Species in the Research pane opens the Web page displayed in Figure 18.12.

FIGURE 18.11

The Encarta
Encyclopedia
can help with
your research.

FIGURE 18.12

You can display
in depth
research in your
Web browser.

You can choose any of the research options available in the drop-down. Each will likely show you slightly different information. Experiment to find the research site that works best for you.

Adding More Research Sites

If the currently available research sites don't meet your needs, you can add other research sites by following these steps:

1. Click **Research Options** to display the dialog shown in Figure 18.13.

FIGURE 18.13

You can add more research services to OneNote.

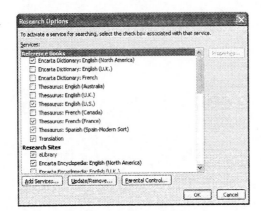

2. Scroll through the list of available research services and check the boxes next to the ones you want to add.

3. If you don't see the service you're interested in, click **Add Services**. You can choose from a list of advertised services or type in the address of a service. There are a number of currently available services, and more are added all the time. It's quite possible that more subscription services will appear in the future. These services may require you to pay a monthly or yearly subscription fee.

4. When you've added your custom service address, click the **Add** button to add the service to the main Research Options dialog box.

5. Click **OK** to save your changes.

The Absolute Minimum

Once you amass a significant amount of information in OneNote, it can be difficult to quickly find information by scanning pages. In this chapter, you learned how to search for information within OneNote. One of OneNote's strengths is its ability to search through a variety of information stored in a variety of locations. You learned

- How to search typed and handwritten notes
- How to search notes on a SharePoint site
- How to use Office 2003's new Research capabilities to find additional information on a topic
- How to add and change Research sites

In the next chapter, you'll learn how to personalize OneNote to meet your needs.

19

Personalizing OneNote

In previous chapters, you've learned how to use OneNote to take hand-written, typed, and audio notes. You've created bulleted and numbered lists and outlines and organized your notes with note flags, highlighting, and different colors of ink. In this chapter, you'll learn how to customize your OneNote installation by creating new toolbars that contain your more frequently used commands.

Customizing OneNote's Look and Feel

Many people never customize any Microsoft Office product. They simply install the product and learn to use the toolbars and menus as they normally appear. There's nothing wrong with that practice, but it's a lot like always stepping over a box in the middle of your hallway instead of moving the box out of your way. If there are menus or toolbar buttons that you use all the time, you can create new toolbars or customize existing toolbars in order to display your most frequently used commands at your fingertips.

Configuring OneNote for a Left-handed User

Particularly when using OneNote on a Tablet PC, a left-handed user might prefer to display the page tabs on the left side of the screen rather than on the right side. To customize the display of the page tabs, choose Options from the Tools menu. On the Display options tab, shown in Figure 19.1, check the box marked Page tabs appear on the left.

FIGURE 19.1

You can customize OneNote for a left-handed user.

If you also want the scroll bar on the left side of the screen, check the box marked Vertical scroll bar appears on the left. When you've made these changes, your OneNote window will look similar to Figure 19.2.

FIGURE 19.2
Switching the page tabs and scrollbars to the left can make it easier for left-handed users.

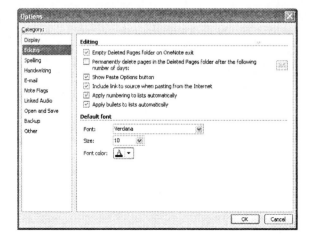

Changing the Default Font

All notes you create in OneNote start out with the same font. By default, that font is 10 point Verdana. You can change the default font by choosing Options from the Tools menu. Click Editing from the Category list to display Figure 19.3.

FIGURE 19.3
You can change the font OneNote uses for all its notes.

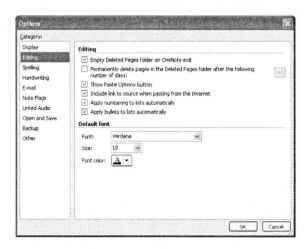

Use the Font, Size, and Font color options to set the default font for your OneNote pages. Click OK to save your changes.

Displaying Full Menus

In Office 2002, Microsoft introduced a new menu system. After studies revealed that the majority of people didn't use all of the commands available on a program's menus, Microsoft customized the menus to show only recently used commands. So, for example, instead of showing the full OneNote File menu, as shown in Figure 19.4, a customized menu was displayed, as shown in Figure 19.5.

FIGURE 19.4

The full File menu from OneNote.

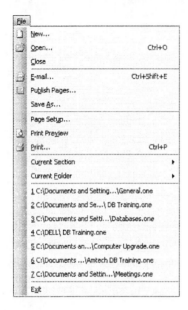

FIGURE 19.5

A customized File menu shows only recently used commands.

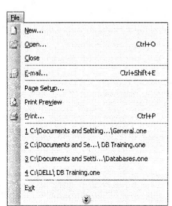

As you can see from comparing the two figures, several commands are left off the customized menu. Some users love the change, preferring not to see the more obscure menu choices on a regular basis. Other users prefer to always see the full menu structure.

When you install OneNote for the first time, your toolbars are by default customized to only show recently used commands. If you like the customized menus, but want to view a command that's not initially available, you can wait a few seconds for the entire menu to display or click the two small arrows at the bottom of the menu to immediately display the full menu.

If you prefer to always show full menus, use the following steps to change your menu preferences.

1. Position your mouse on a blank area of the menu bar (such as just to the right of the Help menu).

2. Right-click to display the context menu shown in Figure 19.6.

FIGURE 19.6

The Menu and Toolbar context menu allows you to customize your menus and toolbars.

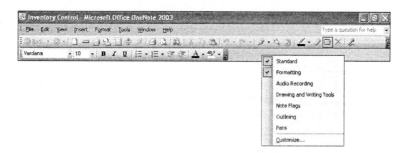

3. Choose **Customize** to display the Customize dialog.

4. If it's not already selected, click the **Options** tab to display Figure 19.7.

FIGURE 19.7

You can change the display of your menus through the Customize dialog.

5. To always show full menus, check the box marked **Always show full menus**.

6. Click **Close** to save your changes.

Displaying the Toolbars in OneNote

Like almost all programs that run in Microsoft Windows, OneNote has several toolbars that contain buttons for many of the commands you use within the program. There are actually seven different toolbars you can display within OneNote, as shown in Figure 19.8.

If you display all of these toolbars on the screen at once, as in Figure 19.8, your screen will probably seem a bit cluttered. You might not need the majority of those toolbars on a regular basis; after all, the commands available on the toolbars are also available within OneNote's menus. You can show or hide any of these toolbars at any time. To show or hide a toolbar, right-click on a blank area of a toolbar or menu to display the toolbar context menu previously shown in Figure 19.6. Any of the toolbars with a check next to them are currently displayed; those without a check next to them are hidden. To display a toolbar that's not currently displayed, just click on its name. A check will appear next to the toolbar's name and the toolbar will appear on the screen. To hide the toolbar, click its name again. The check will disappear and so will the toolbar.

note

Your choice to display full menus persists across all Office programs. For example, if you want to display full menus in OneNote, your menus in Word, Excel, Outlook, Access, and PowerPoint will also display full menus.

note

There's actually an eighth toolbar you can display in OneNote, the Side Note toolbar. It's always visible when viewing Side Notes. To learn more about Side Notes, see Chapter 8, "Creating Side Notes."

Moving Toolbars Around the Work Area

You can move any of OneNote's toolbars around the work area. Toolbars can be either docked or undocked. A *docked* toolbar normally appears either at the top of the screen or along the left side of the screen. If you reduce the size of the OneNote window, the toolbars remain in the same location. An *undocked* toolbar generally appears over the OneNote page or page header, much like the Audio Recording toolbar in Figure 19.8.

You can dock an undocked toolbar or undock a docked toolbar whenever you want. Docking an undocked toolbar is quite easy. Position your mouse pointer on the top of the undocked toolbar (in the darker area next to the toolbar's title). Click and drag the toolbar either up towards the existing menus or to the left side of the screen. When you move the toolbar to a position where it can be docked, it will appear to "snap" into place. Release the mouse and the toolbar will stick in place, docked.

note

The toolbar you display might not appear where you expect. For example, the Pens toolbar appears on the left side of the screen. The Audio Recording toolbar typically "floats" over the existing OneNote window.

FIGURE 19.8

You can display seven standard toolbars within OneNote.

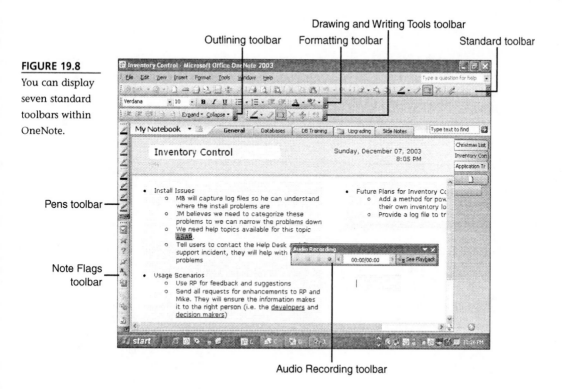

Outlining toolbar   Formatting toolbar   Drawing and Writing Tools toolbar   Standard toolbar

Pens toolbar

Note Flags toolbar

Audio Recording toolbar

Undocking a docked toolbar is only slightly more complicated. Every docked toolbar has a toolbar handle, as shown in Figure 19.9.

Toolbar handle

FIGURE 19.9

Every toolbar has a toolbar handle you can use to move the toolbar on the screen.

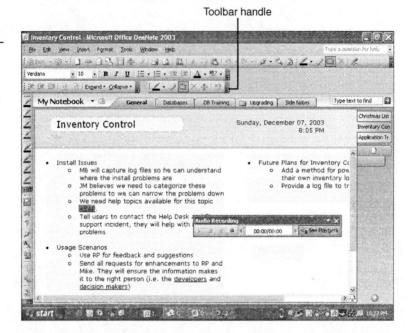

To undock or move the toolbar, position your mouse directly over this toolbar handle. Click and hold the mouse button while moving the toolbar around on the screen. You can dock the toolbar in a different location or undock it and let it float over your OneNote window.

Customizing Toolbars

There are a number of customizations you can make to the toolbars in OneNote. We'll cover a few of them in this section. If you have a very high screen resolution, the toolbar buttons might appear quite small. If you want your toolbar buttons to appear larger, you can change your buttons from small icons to large icons using the following steps.

caution

When you undock a toolbar, you'll see an X on the right side of the toolbar. Clicking this X closes the toolbar. If you accidentally close a toolbar and want to display it again, follow the steps listed in the "Displaying the Toolbars in OneNote" section to display the toolbar.

1. Position your mouse on a blank area of the toolbar or menu.
2. Right-click and choose **Customize** from the context menu.
3. Click the **Options** tab of the Customize dialog box.
4. Check the box next to **Large icons** and click **Close**.

Your toolbars should now look similar to Figure 19.10.

FIGURE 19.10

Large icons can
make it easier to
view your tool-
bars.

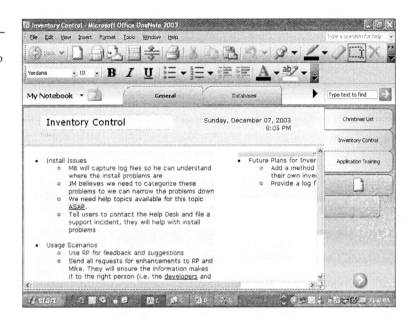

Creating Your Own Toolbars in OneNote

In addition to customizing the size of your toolbar
buttons, you can create your own toolbars or
rearrange the buttons on existing toolbars. After
you've used OneNote for a while, you might find
that you typically use a dozen toolbar buttons on
a regular basis. You can create a custom toolbar
with only those commands and hide all other
toolbars.

To create a custom toolbar with several key commands, use the following steps.

1. Position your mouse over a **blank area**
   of an existing toolbar or menu.

caution

Choosing Large icons
within OneNote also
causes all of the toolbars
in other Office applica-
tions (such as Word and
Excel) to display large icons. You
cannot choose Large icons in one
Office program and Small icons in
another Office program.

2. Right-click and choose **Customize** from the context menu.

3. Click the **Toolbars** tab (see Figure 19.11).

FIGURE 19.11

Use this dialog to create a new toolbar or to choose which toolbars to display.

4. Click the **New** button to create a new toolbar.

5. Type a name for your new toolbar and click **OK**. Your new toolbar is displayed next to the Customize dialog as shown in Figure 19.12.

New toolbar

FIGURE 19.12

Your new toolbar won't have any buttons when you create it.

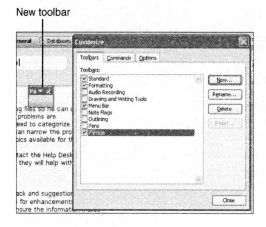

Now that you've created a new toolbar, you can move it around on the screen and add buttons to it.

Adding Toolbar Buttons

The steps for adding toolbar buttons are the same whether you're working with an existing toolbar or a new, empty toolbar. The following steps add some buttons to your newly created toolbar, however you can add buttons to any existing toolbar using the same steps.

1. Position your mouse over a **blank area** of an existing toolbar or menu.

2. Right-click and choose **Customize** from the context menu.

3. Click the **Commands** tab (see Figure 19.13).

FIGURE 19.13

You can add a variety of commands to your custom toolbar.

4. To choose a command to add to your custom toolbar, select the **category** from the left list box. When you select a category, a list of commands appears in the Commands list box.

5. Scroll down the **Commands** list box until you find the command you want to add to your toolbar.

6. Click and drag the command onto your new toolbar (or to an existing toolbar). As the command moves to an available position on the new toolbar, a black vertical bar (I-beam) will appear on the toolbar, as shown in Figure 19.14. This bar lets you know where the toolbar button will appear on the toolbar. Release the mouse button to place the command on the toolbar.

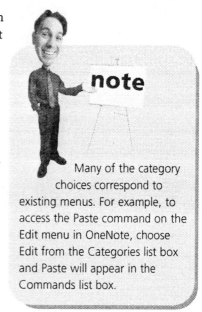

note

Many of the category choices correspond to existing menus. For example, to access the Paste command on the Edit menu in OneNote, choose Edit from the Categories list box and Paste will appear in the Commands list box.

I-beam

FIGURE 19.14

You can choose where to put your new toolbar button.

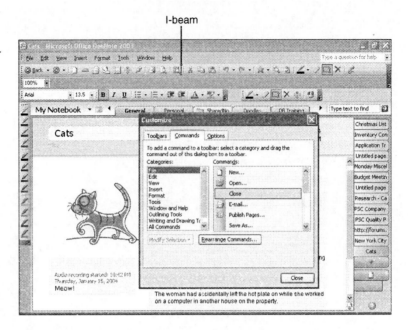

You can use the previous steps to add any number of buttons to your new toolbar. Once you have more than one button on your toolbar, you might want to change the order of buttons on your new toolbar or any existing toolbar as described in the next section.

Moving Toolbar Buttons

To move a toolbar button on a toolbar, display the Customize dialog box by right-clicking on a blank area of the toolbar and choosing Customize from the context menu. Once the Customize dialog is displayed, you can position your mouse button over any existing toolbar button on any toolbar you currently have displayed on your screen. Click and drag the button anywhere on any existing toolbar. A vertical bar appears as you move the toolbar button indicating the current position of the button. Release the mouse button when the vertical bar appears where you want the toolbar button to stay.

Removing Toolbar Buttons

To remove a toolbar button from a toolbar, display the Customize dialog box by right-clicking on a blank area of the toolbar and choosing Customize from the context menu. Position your mouse pointer over the toolbar button you wish to remove. Click and drag the toolbar button away from the toolbar. When you see a black X just below the mouse pointer, you can release the mouse and the toolbar button will be removed from the toolbar.

THE ABSOLUTE MINIMUM

In this chapter you learned how to customize OneNote to make it easier for you to find the commands you need. You now know how to

- Change your toolbars to display full menus instead of the most recently displayed commands
- Hide and display the seven toolbars available in OneNote
- Change your toolbar buttons from small to large
- Create your own custom toolbars
- Add and remove buttons from toolbars

Next you'll learn about the integration between OneNote and the rest of the Microsoft Office family.

In This Chapter

- Using OneNote with other Office 2003 applications
- Creating Outlook tasks from OneNote
- Word and OneNote: better together
- Using OneNote information in presentations

20

Office 2003 Integration

OneNote is one of the newest members of the Microsoft Office 2003 System. As the name implies, the Office System is designed to be a suite of products that work together to enhance productivity. As a new product, OneNote is missing much of the integration present in other Office programs. For instance, there's no built-in way to save OneNote files as Microsoft Word documents, or insert an embedded object into OneNote such as an Excel spreadsheet control.

This chapter will cover the limited built-in Office 2003 integration as well as show you some of the workarounds you can use to add some integration of your own. Even though there's no built-in way to convert OneNote files to Word documents, that doesn't mean it can't be done. It's actually relatively simple. We'll cover integration with Word, PowerPoint, and Outlook.

Can OneNote Work with My Other Office Applications?

The answer to that question is yes, of course it can. However, once you move beyond the initial question into the mechanics of the integration, you might start to wonder what type of integration is possible. After all, you *can't* do any of the following natively with OneNote:

- Link OneNote Notes to an Outlook Contact
- Set reminders in OneNote to appear both in OneNote and your Outlook Calendar
- Convert OneNote Notes to Microsoft Word documents
- Link a OneNote page to a PowerPoint presentation

However, simply because there's no one-button method of performing these tasks, that doesn't mean they can't be done. Before we delve into any of these items, we'll talk about the integration OneNote does have, creating Outlook tasks.

Creating Outlook Tasks from OneNote

If you have both OneNote 2003 and Outlook 2003 installed, you can integrate the two by creating Outlook tasks directly from OneNote. You might want to create an Outlook task for any items you create in a to-do list. You can also assign tasks to others directly from OneNote. For example, in Figure 20.1, the meeting notes have to-dos listed for three individuals: Sally, Joe, and Trish. Trish, the note taker, can create Outlook tasks from OneNote and send those tasks to herself as well as to Sally and Joe.

To create an Outlook task from Trish's first to-do item, use the following steps.

1. Position your cursor on the line item you want to use for the body of the task. This can be a single line in a note container or an entire note container. If you need to select more than one line, you'll need to highlight all necessary lines.

2. Click the **Create Outlook Task** button on the standard toolbar as shown in Figure 20.2. There is no way to create an Outlook task from the menus.

   When the Outlook Task form appears, as shown in Figure 20.3, the high-lighted line or note container appears in the body of the task item. The subject of the task defaults to the selected line or the first line if multiple lines are selected.

FIGURE 20.1

You can create Outlook tasks for yourself and others.

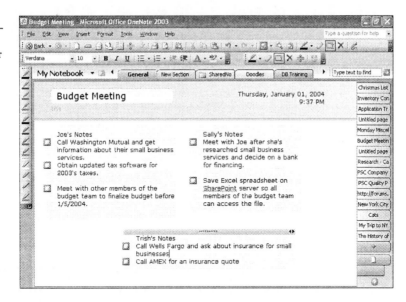

Create Outlook Task button

FIGURE 20.2

Click the Create Outlook Task toolbar button.

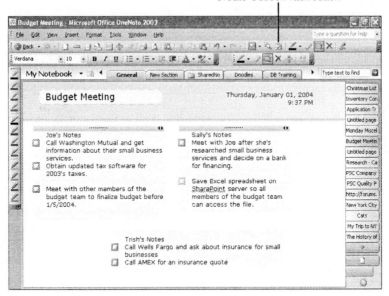

FIGURE 20.3

Your Outlook task contains the selected line(s) in the body.

3. Enter dates in the **Due Date** and/or **Start Date** fields for the task.

4. If you want a reminder for the task, check the **Reminder** box and choose a reminder date and time.

5. Click **Save and Close** to save the task to your Outlook task list.

Advanced Task Options

There are a number of advanced functions you can perform with your Outlook task that you created from OneNote. Two items in particular you might want to do are assign the task to another user and create a recurrence pattern to the task.

Assign the Task to Another User

;assigning" to users>the task to another user, follow the previous steps 1 through 5. Then click the Assign Task button in the task's toolbar to alter the task as shown in Figure 20.4.

Click the To button to display your Outlook Contact list or the Global Address list, as shown in Figure 20.5.

You can choose any valid recipient in your Contact list or Global Address list and click the To button to add the person to the task assignment. Click OK when you're done to return to your task.

note

If you don't change the default reminder and due date for the task, when you click Save and Close you'll likely see an immediate reminder pop up on your screen. The reminder date and time default to today at 8 a.m. If it's any time past that, the reminder is seen as past due and pops up immediately. To avoid this, change the reminder date or time before saving.

FIGURE 20.4

You can assign
the task to
another Outlook
user.

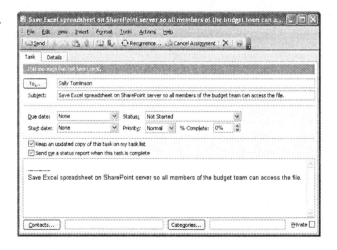

FIGURE 20.5

Choose a valid
recipient from
your Global
Address list or
Contacts folder.

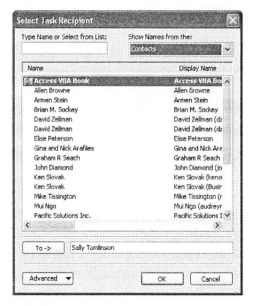

There are two default options you can modify when assigning a task to another person.

- Keep an updated copy of this task on my task list—If you check this option, a copy of the assigned task will remain in your Tasks folder. If you assign the task to someone in the same Exchange organization, you'll get updates whenever they modify the task.

- Send me a status report when this task is complete—This option, checked by default, sends you a message when the assignee completes the task. Uncheck this box if you don't want updates when the task is completed.

Set Up a Recurring Task

Outlook 2003 allows you to set up a recurring task directly from OneNote 2003. To setup a recurring task, follow the previous steps 1 through 5. Click the Recurrence button on the toolbar to display Figure 20.6.

FIGURE 20.6

You can create recurring tasks in Outlook 2003.

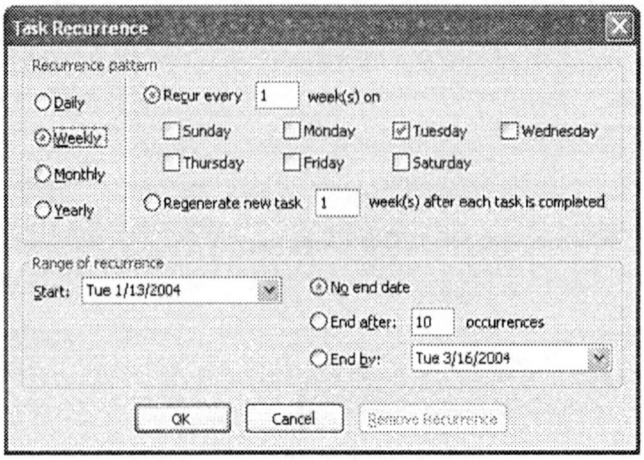

You can choose a daily, weekly, monthly, or yearly recurrence pattern for your task. For example, to create a task that occurs every Monday, Wednesday, and Friday, choose a weekly recurrence pattern and check the boxes for Monday, Wednesday, and Friday. To create a task that occurs the last Friday of every month, choose a monthly recurrence pattern. Use the drop-downs and option buttons to select the last Friday of every 1 month.

In addition to setting the pattern, you can also define a recurrence range. If the task should end after a specific date or after a certain number of recurrences, you can specify those options as well.

When you're done setting recurrence options, click OK on the Task Recurrence dialog and then click Save and Close to save your task.

Linking a OneNote Section to an Outlook Contact

One of the benefits to keeping your contacts in Outlook is that you can record a number of different types of activities you have with the contacts.

note

It is possible to create a recurring task that you assign to another person. To do this, follow the instructions in "Assign the Task to Another User" and "Set Up a Recurring Task."

Outlook can do much of this automatically through its Journal feature. Outlook can keep track of the Word documents, Excel files, Access databases, and PowerPoint presentations. It can also automatically track your emails to contacts.

In addition to the automatic tracking, you can also enter a variety of activities manually. For example, you can create a journal entry for each phone call you make to a client. It can be helpful to create a journal entry for each document you prepare for a client and link that document to the client's contact record. You can then use the contact's Activities page to list all activities you've had with that contact, as shown in Figure 20.7.

FIGURE 20.7

You can view all activities associated with a contact.

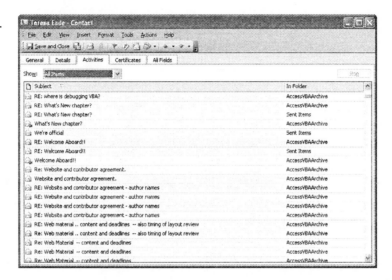

OneNote isn't one of the Office programs you can automatically track with the Journal. However, you can use a bit of fancy footwork to link a OneNote section to an Outlook Contact. To create this link, use the following steps.

1. In Outlook, create a new Journal entry by choosing **File**, **New** and then selecting **Journal Entry** as shown in Figure 20.8.

2. Enter a **Subject** for your Journal entry (the title of your OneNote section is a good choice).

3. Choose **Document** from the **Entry type** drop-down.

4. Click the **paper clip** icon on the toolbar to browse for an attachment.

5. Navigate to the **C:\Documents and Settings\UserName\My Documents\My Notebook** folder, as shown in Figure 20.9.

FIGURE 20.8
You can enter a variety of information about your Journal entry.

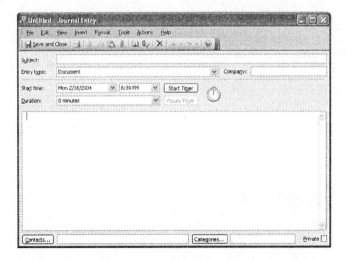

FIGURE 20.9
The My Notebook folder contains your section files.

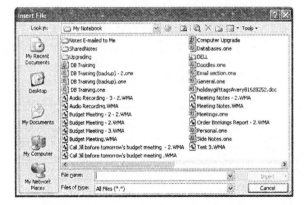

6. Choose the section you want to link and click the down arrow next to the **Insert** button.

7. Choose **Insert as Hyperlink**. This creates a link to the file.

8. Click the **Contacts** button at the bottom of the Journal form to display Figure 20.10.

tip

If you insert the item as an attachment, you're inserting a copy of the item. Inserting a hyperlink ensures that any changes you make to the original section are reflected any time you click the link.

FIGURE 20.10

You can insert a link to a contact record.

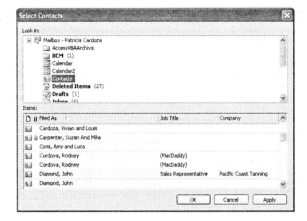

9. Choose a contact and click **OK**. Your Journal entry should now look like Figure 20.11.

FIGURE 20.11

Your Journal entry contains a link to a OneNote section.

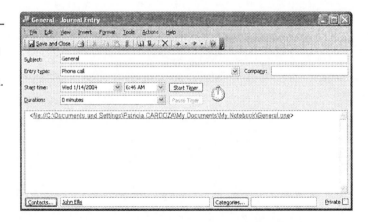

10. Click **Save and Close** to save your Journal entry.

You can now open the contact record you chose in step 9 by opening your Contacts folder and double-clicking the contact. Switch to the Activities tab for the contact. Once you open the Activities tab, Outlook will search for any Journal entries or other Outlook items linked to that Contact. The Journal entry you just created will be available. You can open it from the Activities page, click the hyperlink, and OneNote will display the section.

Converting OneNote Notes to Microsoft Word

There might come a time when you need to convert an existing OneNote file to another format, such as Microsoft Word. For example, if you need to send your OneNote notes to a colleague who doesn't have OneNote, and you think there's a chance he'll want to edit the notes, you should consider converting the notes into another format, such as Microsoft Word.

If you need to convert a OneNote page into Microsoft Word, the easiest method of doing this is to select all the text on the OneNote page and copy it. To do this, press Ctrl+A while in the page to select all of the text. Choose <u>C</u>opy from the <u>E</u>dit menu to place your text on the Office clipboard.

> **note**
>
> When you click the Contacts button, you'll see the contents of the Contacts folder. If you have multiple Contacts folders and want to find a contact in a different folder, choose the folder from the Look in list at the top of the Select Contacts window.

To insert this copied text into Word, open Word and choose <u>P</u>aste from the <u>E</u>dit menu. After pasting your OneNote page into Word, your Word document might look like Figure 20.12.

FIGURE 20.12

You can insert OneNote content into Microsoft Word.

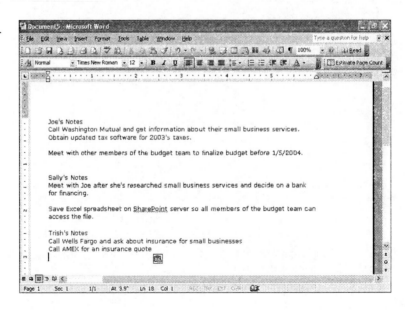

Inserting Word Information into OneNote

In addition to converting OneNote files to Microsoft Word, you can also insert Word files into OneNote. You can copy and paste information from Word into OneNote or insert entire Word documents into OneNote and link them to your note pages. To insert content into OneNote from Word, just highlight the desired content and choose Edit, Copy. Switch to OneNote, click to create a note container (or click in an existing note container), and choose Edit, Paste.

caution

You can also simply drag and drop the content between Word and OneNote. However, be careful with this method as it will actually *move* the content from Word to OneNote, rather than copying the content.

Inserting Word Content As an Image

One of the advantages to pasting content from a Word document into OneNote is you can take advantage of some of Word's formatting features that aren't available in OneNote. For example, you can create tables and borders in Word and paste that information directly as an image. To insert Word content as an image into OneNote, first copy the information to the Office clipboard by selecting Edit, Copy. Then use the following steps to paste your content as an image.

1. Switch to OneNote and navigate to the destination note page.
2. Choose **Edit**, **Paste** to insert the copied content into OneNote.
3. Once you paste the content into OneNote, you should see a small clipboard at the bottom of the pasted content. Position your mouse over that clipboard and click the drop-down arrow next to the icon to display the options shown in Figure 20.13.

FIGURE 20.13

You can choose to paste content as text or as a picture.

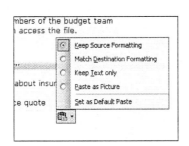

4. Choose **Paste as Picture** to insert the content directly into OneNote retaining all the formatting and special Word features as shown in Figure 20.14.

FIGURE 20.14

Inserting content as a picture retains features not supported in OneNote.

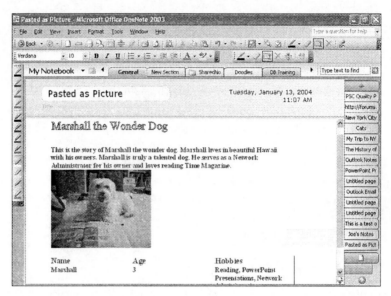

The only drawback to pasting content as a picture is that you won't be able to edit the content later.

Other Paste Smart Tag Options

So far in this chapter you've learned how to paste content directly and as a picture. However, there are three other options available from the Paste Options Smart Tag. To access the Paste Options Smart Tag, paste content into OneNote and hover your mouse over the small icon of a clipboard. Click the drop-down arrow to display the Smart Tag options. The three other options we'll talk about are Keep Source Formatting, Match Destination Formatting, and Keep Text Only. For an example, we'll copy and paste the text from the Word document shown in Figure 20.15.

Keep Source Formatting

Choosing the Keep Source Formatting option retains all of the original formatting. However, when you use this option, you still might not get the same results that pasting as a picture provides. For example, in the previous figure, the title Marshall the Wonder Dog was formatted with shadow formatting. Since OneNote doesn't support shadow formatting, the text size and color are retained, but not the shadow.

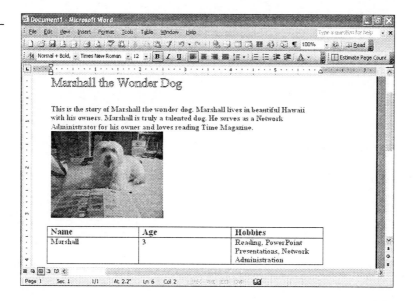

Match Destination Formatting

The Match Destination Formatting option changes the formatting of the pasted text to match the formatting of the current note container.

Keep Text Only

Choosing the Keep Text Only option preserves none of the original formatting. The font color and size are reduced to OneNote's default. If you're copying tables or text with borders and shading, these are not pasted.

Figure 20.16 shows the four different paste options you can choose when pasting text from Word (or another application) into OneNote.

Dragging and Dropping Files into OneNote

Sometimes you might not want to insert actual content from a document into OneNote. However, you might want to include a link to the file in your note page so that you can refer to the file at a later date. The easiest way to insert a link to a file into OneNote is to drag the file from a folder on your computer onto the OneNote taskbar button. Once the OneNote window activates, you can drop the document anywhere on the OneNote page and create a link, as shown in Figure 20.17.

FIGURE 20.16
The four different paste options all show different results.

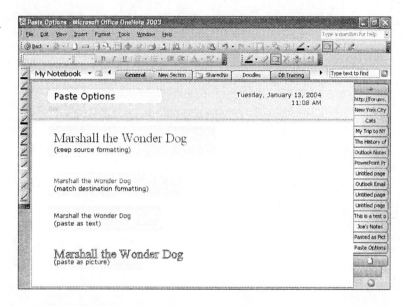

FIGURE 20.17
A link to another file can be inserted anywhere in your OneNote page.

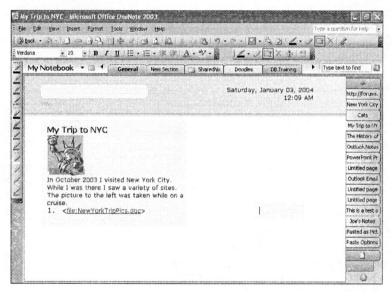

When you need to open the file, you can just click on the link. This technique works for more than just Word documents. You can insert links to Excel files, PowerPoint presentations, Adobe Acrobat files, images, and audio files. If your computer contains the appropriate program to open the linked file, you'll be able to open the file with a click.

As you can see from the figure, the file doesn't have a path associated with it. It's referenced by the syntax <file:filename>. When you drag a file from somewhere on your computer or external disk into OneNote, a copy of the file is actually placed in the My Notebook folder. So when you click the link in OneNote to open the file, you're only opening a copy of the file. If you updated the file after you inserted the link into OneNote, you won't see the updates. If you update the file linked in OneNote, your original file won't reflect those changes either.

note

Usually when creating hyperlinks, you can't use spaces in the link. However, since you're enclosing the link in the brackets, spaces are perfectly acceptable.

In order to work around this problem, you can insert your own manual hyperlinks to files in OneNote. Creating your own hyperlink enables you to click on the link and go directly to the copy of the file you need.

For example, if you keep a copy of your budget spreadsheet in a Budget folder on your hard drive, you can create a link to that file by typing the link in a note container with the following syntax: `<file://pathandfilename>`. For example, to point to a spreadsheet in the My Documents folder, you might use the following syntax: `<file://c:\Documents and Settings\Sara\Budget\2004Budget.xls>`.

Using OneNote in PowerPoint Presentations

In the next chapter, we'll cover how to insert PowerPoint slides into OneNote. However, you can also insert OneNote content into PowerPoint. This section actually applies to any other Office application you can paste data into, but we'll use PowerPoint as the example.

To select all notes on a particular note page, choose Select, All from the Edit menu to highlight all of the page's text. You can then choose Edit, Copy to place the text on the Office clipboard.

If you don't want to choose all the text on your note page, you can choose only certain lines or note containers. To choose an entire note container, hover your mouse over the note container to display the container handle. The handle is the dark gray bar at the top of the note container. Click the handle to select the entire note container.

If you want to select multiple note containers, hold down the Ctrl key while clicking multiple container handles.

To select two non-consecutive lines in a note container, hover your mouse over the first line you want to copy. You'll notice a small icon to the left of the line. This icon looks like a plus sign with arrows on all four ends. Click this icon to select the line. You can then hold down the Ctrl key to select other lines in the same manner.

Once you have highlighted the lines you need to copy, choose Edit, Copy. You can then switch to PowerPoint (or any other Office application) and choose Edit, Paste. Figure 20.18 shows a PowerPoint slide with content pasted from OneNote.

FIGURE 20.18

You can paste content from OneNote into PowerPoint.

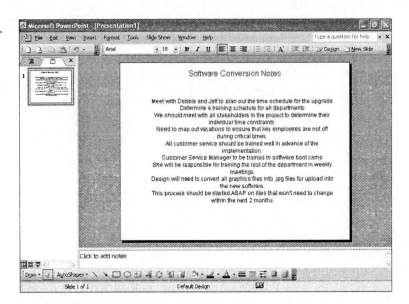

THE ABSOLUTE MINIMUM

In this chapter you learned about OneNote's ability to integrate with other Office applications. You learned

■ How to create Outlook tasks directly from OneNote

■ How to insert OneNote content into Microsoft Word

■ How to insert Word content into OneNote as text

■ How to insert Word content into OneNote as an image

■ How to insert links to other documents into OneNote

■ How to integrate OneNote with your PowerPoint presentations

The next chapter covers importing information from other Office programs. You can import information from a variety of sources to create notes with the most complete information. Importing spreadsheets, Outlook information, or Word tables and graphics allows you to store information about entire projects in OneNote.

IN THIS CHAPTER

- Determine what other information should be inserted within your OneNote page
- Insert linked information into OneNote
- Copy information into OneNote
- Insert online content into OneNote

21

IMPORTING INFORMATION FROM OTHER APPLICATIONS

When you're taking notes on a legal pad or notebook, you are limited to what you can write or affix to the piece of paper. If you need to take a printed document or spreadsheet and insert it in your notes, you'll need to either staple or tape the paper to the notebook page or copy the entire contents of the document by hand into your notes.

OneNote makes inserting information from other applications significantly easier. You can copy a variety of information from other applications, including the Internet. You can insert portions of Word documents, Excel spreadsheets, PowerPoint slides, images, Web sites, and even information from non-Office applications such as Adobe Acrobat.

Importing Information from Other Applications

OneNote doesn't have any built-in importing or exporting functionality. Unlike other Office applications, you'll need to rely on manually copying and pasting most of the information you need from other applications. Even though this might seem a bit archaic, OneNote does have some tricks up its sleeve to make this process highly functional.

Changing Outlook Notes to OneNote Notes

An often-asked question in OneNote support forums is whether OneNote has any relation to the Notes functionality in Outlook 2003. The short answer is no; there's no relationship between Outlook notes and OneNote notes. However, if you need to transfer Outlook information into OneNote, you can do that using the following steps.

1. Select the destination page to receive your inserted notes.

2. Open Outlook 2003 and switch to the Notes folder using the Navigation pane, as shown in Figure 21.1.

FIGURE 21.1

You can move your Outlook notes into OneNote.

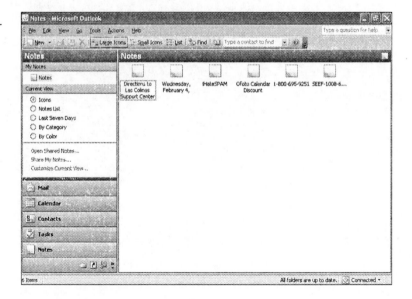

3. Open the Outlook Note in question and use your mouse or pen to highlight the text you need.

4. Drag the highlighted text to the Windows taskbar and hover the mouse or pen over the OneNote entry to activate OneNote.

5. When you find the place on the screen you want to drop your note text, release the mouse button or pen button to paste the note text, as shown in Figure 21.2.

You can also use the Edit menu and the Office clipboard to copy the contents of Outlook notes. Then you can switch to OneNote and paste the note text (Edit, Paste).

tip

If you find yourself using the previous steps often, you might find it faster to open a new Side Note and drag and drop your text onto the Side Note. Since Side Notes remain on top of other applications by default, this can enable you to quickly see the content you dropped onto the note.

FIGURE 21.2

You can paste all your Outlook notes into OneNote.

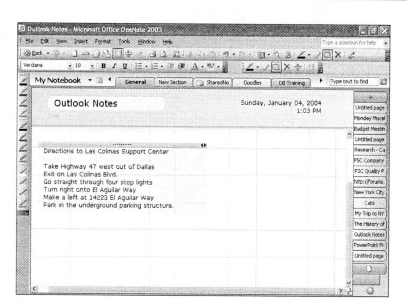

When pasting information from Outlook to OneNote, you'll lose some key information, such as the time and date the note was originally created. You can insert this information manually or use the following steps to insert a table view of all your Outlook notes into OneNote using the following steps.

1. In Outlook 2003, switch your Notes view to a table view such as Notes List or By Category, as shown in Figure 21.3.

FIGURE 21.3

You can switch your view to a table view before copying into OneNote.

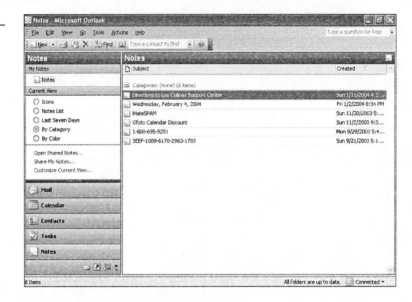

2. Choose **Select All** from the **Edit** menu in Outlook to highlight the entire list of notes.

3. Drag the selected list from Outlook to the OneNote entry in the Windows taskbar.

4. Drop the selected list onto your OneNote page to create a list of your notes as shown in Figure 21.4.

FIGURE 21.4

You can insert a table for your Outlook notes.

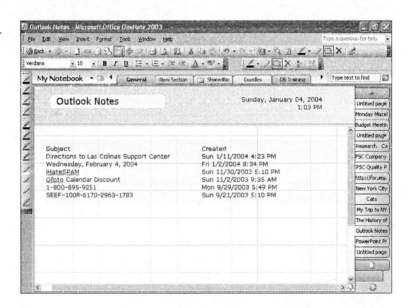

When you insert this table view into OneNote, you can view the subject and creation date of each of your Outlook notes. You can then use the previous instructions to copy the text of your notes into OneNote. If you want to add some formatting to your notes, you can create an easily understood page that contains all of your Outlook notes. When you're done, your OneNote page might look like Figure 21.5.

FIGURE 21.5

You can insert all of your Outlook notes into OneNote.

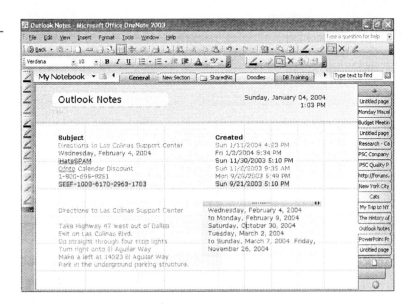

Inserting Outlook 2003 Emails into OneNote

In addition to inserting your Outlook notes into OneNote, you can use similar methods to insert email messages into OneNote. To insert some summary information about your email message into OneNote, just drag the email from the Outlook Inbox to the OneNote Taskbar button and drop it into OneNote. In order to drag the contents of the email into OneNote, you'll need to open the email message first. Use the Edit menu and choose Select All to select the text of the email. Switch to OneNote, and paste the text of the email into a note container (Edit, Paste). You can paste text from any number of emails in to OneNote. When you're done, your OneNote page might look similar to Figure 21.6.

FIGURE 21.6

You can insert emails from Outlook into OneNote.

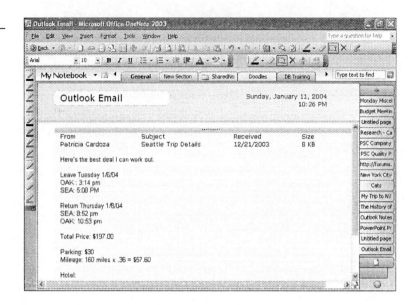

Inserting PowerPoint Content into OneNote

In addition to Outlook information, you can insert PowerPoint slides into OneNote. This way you can use OneNote to take notes on a PowerPoint presentation and have all of your notes in one location.

To import a PowerPoint slide into OneNote, open PowerPoint and view your presentation in Normal or Slide Sorter view. Use your mouse or Tablet PC pen to select the OneNote slide you want to insert into your OneNote page. Drag the slide down to the OneNote button on the Windows taskbar to activate OneNote. You can drag and drop your slide anywhere on your OneNote page as shown in Figure 21.7.

tip

PowerPoint has an annotation feature you can use to take notes along with slides. However, this leaves you with some notes in OneNote and some notes in PowerPoint. Importing your PowerPoint slides into OneNote ensures that all of your notes remain in one location.

FIGURE 21.7

You can insert a
PowerPoint slide
into OneNote.

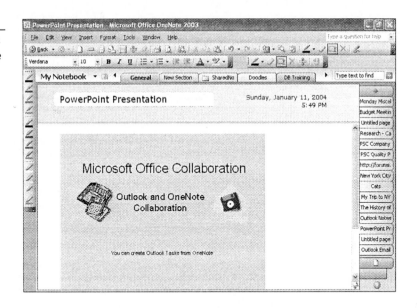

If you want to insert an entire presentation into OneNote, you can hold down the Shift key while selecting the first PowerPoint slide and the last PowerPoint slide. Then you can repeat the drag-and-drop process. Your results might look similar to Figure 21.8.

In addition to inserting PowerPoint slides into OneNote, you can also insert the PowerPoint outline into OneNote. Inserting the outline instead of the actual slides gives you more room in PowerPoint to take your notes. Unfortunately, you can't drag and drop the outline into OneNote like you can drag the slides. In order to insert the outline, you'll have to use the following steps.

1. Switch to **Outline** view in PowerPoint.

2. Click the first slide in Outline view.

3. Hold down the **Shift** key on the keyboard and click the last slide.

4. Select **Edit, Copy** to copy the entire outline.

note

The following section requires that you have a copy of some version of PowerPoint installed on your computer as well as a copy of the presentation you want to import. You cannot accomplish these steps with the free PowerPoint viewer. PowerPoint 2003 is not required; a previous version will work.

5. Switch to OneNote. Click in a note page and choose **Edit**, **Paste** to display Figure 21.9.

Working with Imported PowerPoint Slides

It can be slightly cumbersome to take notes on an entire PowerPoint presentation while inserting full-sized PowerPoint slides into your note pages. After all, the slides take up more than half the visible OneNote page. If you want more room for your notes, you can resize the PowerPoint slide in OneNote. Just click or tap once on the inserted PowerPoint slide. This puts a dotted blue line around the PowerPoint slide. Resize handles (small squares) are present at all four corners and in the middle of each side. Just click any of the resize handles and drag to change the slide's size.

note

If you try to drop your PowerPoint slide onto your OneNote page and all you get is a circle with a line through it, your insertion point is probably somewhere between the page title and note page. Move the mouse to another location on the OneNote page before you release.

FIGURE 21.8

If you want to take notes on an entire presentation, you can insert all the slides into OneNote.

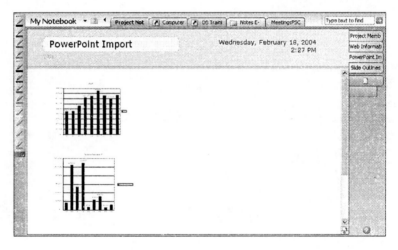

FIGURE 21.9

Pasting the slide show outline in OneNote allows you to take detailed notes.

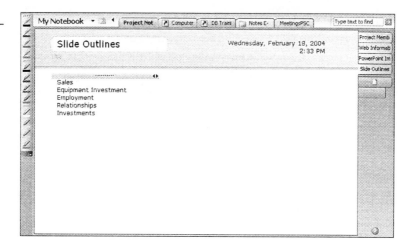

Copying Information from a Web Page to OneNote

In addition to inserting information from Outlook and PowerPoint, you can also insert information from the Internet into your OneNote note pages. It's very easy to insert information from Internet Explorer. You can copy and paste the information or simply select the information and drag and drop the selection directly onto your OneNote page. To copy and paste the information, simply open Internet Explorer to the Web page you need. Select the text you need, and choose Edit, Copy. Switch to OneNote and navigate to the page you want to receive your pasted information. Choose Edit, Paste to insert the copied text, as shown in Figure 21.10.

caution

The previous steps move a slide from PowerPoint to OneNote. If you want to leave your PowerPoint presentation intact, select the slide from the Slide Sorter or Outline view and choose Copy from the Edit menu. Switch to OneNote and choose Paste from the Edit menu.

FIGURE 21.10

Inserting
Internet infor-
mation also
inserts a link to
the source infor-
mation.

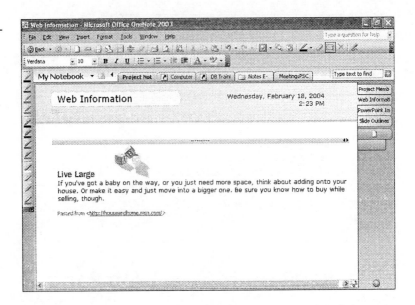

When you paste text from Internet Explorer, you'll
notice that at the bottom of the pasted information,
you'll find the link to the originating Web site. If
you don't want the link inserted in OneNote when
you paste Internet information, do the following:

1. Choose **Tools**, **Options**.
2. Click **Editing** in the Category box to display Figure 21.11.
3. If you don't want the link included when
   you paste Internet information, uncheck the
   box marked **Include link to source
   when pasting from the Internet**.
4. Click **OK** to save your changes.

note

When pasting informa-
tion from Internet Explorer
into OneNote, you might notice
formatting variations between the
originating Web page and the
destination OneNote document.

FIGURE 21.11

You can control a variety of OneNote's editing features.

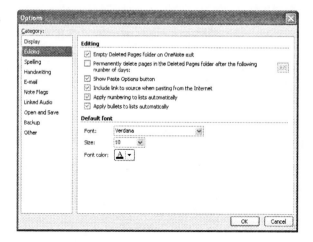

THE ABSOLUTE MINIMUM

In this chapter you learned how to import information from a variety of sources into OneNote. You learned

- How to insert Outlook items into OneNote
- How to insert PowerPoint slides into OneNote
- How to insert Internet information into OneNote

This chapter covered Outlook, PowerPoint, and the Internet. The next chapter covers math in OneNote, including how to use Word and Excel to enhance OneNote's functionality.

22

Math in OneNote

A comprehensive note-taking program should include the capability to insert any type of information within the note. In previous chapters we've covered how you can import information from Outlook, PowerPoint, and Internet Explorer into OneNote. When inserting information from each of these programs, you inserted either graphics or text into OneNote.

This chapter covers inserting a different type of information into OneNote—calculations and other mathematical information. As in previous chapters, even if there isn't a built-in way to capture the information in OneNote, there are workarounds that will help you capture all of your necessary information in an easy-to-understand format.

Are There Mathematical Tools in OneNote?

In a word—No. There are no built-in tools in OneNote for performing mathematical calculations. You can't enter 2 + 2 = and have OneNote answer with 4. However, that doesn't mean you can't work around this limitation. Even without explicitly developed mathematical features, you can still use OneNote for calculations, mathematic class notes, and facts and figures.

Of course you can always take mathematical notes in OneNote by hand. Figure 22.1 shows some handwritten notes on the Tablet PC with mathematical calculations written in the note page.

FIGURE 22.1

You can write detailed calculations in OneNote, but it won't calculate them for you.

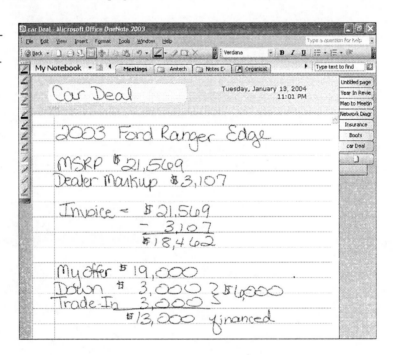

You can also enter calculations on a laptop or desktop computer. Use the Tab key to line up your columns, as shown in Figure 22.2.

This functionality is exactly the same as the functionality you'd get on a legal pad or spiral notebook. So while OneNote can't perform the calculations for you, it's very possible to type or write out detailed calculations in your notes.

FIGURE 22.2

FIGURE 22.2

You can type
your equations
and use the Tab
key to line up
columns.

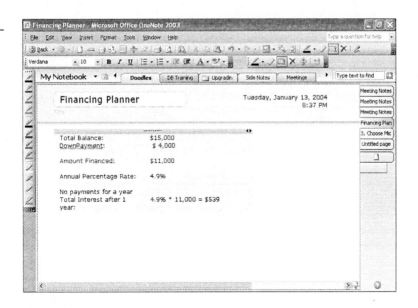

Using Symbols to Enter Equations

If you need to display complex equations in OneNote, you can insert symbols
between your numbers. Consider the following equation: The square root of 25 is
not equal to 10 divided by 2.1. To enter this complex equation, use the following
steps.

1. Enter the basic equation without symbols. For our example, enter 25 10 2.1.

2. Position your cursor before the number 25 using your mouse or Tablet PC's
   pen.

3. Choose **Insert**, **Symbol** to display Figure 22.3.

FIGURE 22.3

You can choose
from a variety of
mathematical
symbols.

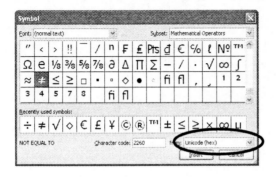

4. Choose **Unicode (hex)** in the **from** drop-down box. This displays the **Subset** drop-down in the upper right corner of the Symbols box.

5. Select **Mathematical Operators** from the Subset drop-down box.

6. Choose the **Square Root** symbol and click **Insert**.

7. Move the Symbol dialog over as needed so that you can see the numbers you typed in step 1.

8. Use your mouse or Tablet PC pen and click between the 25 and the 10. (You can leave the Symbol dialog open and still click and type within your note.)

9. Choose the **Not Equal To** symbol and click **Insert**.

10. Move your cursor between the 10 and the 2.1.

11. Choose the **Division Sign** symbol and click **Insert**.

12. Click the **X** to Close the Symbol dialog box.

Your equation should now look like Figure 22. 4.

FIGURE 22.4

You can enter a variety of symbols in your notes.

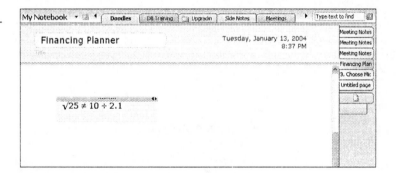

Your equation: $\sqrt{25} \neq 10 \div 2.1$

Using Microsoft Word's Equation Editor to Perform Math in OneNote

If you need actual mathematical functionality with a wider range of symbols, you can utilize Microsoft Word's Equation Editor to perform calculations. Then you can insert the results from the Equation Editor into OneNote. The resulting equation won't appear much different than the same equation created using the Symbols dialog, however you do have a wider range of symbols you can insert using Microsoft Word. To launch the Equation Editor and perform a calculation, use the following steps.

1. Open Microsoft Word and create a new, blank document.

2. Select **Insert**, **Object**.

3. Choose **Microsoft Equation 3.0** from the **Object** type list and click **OK** to display Figure 22.5.

Now that you have the Equation Editor open, just type your equation in the blank field that appears on the Word document. Click the appropriate button on the toolbar whenever you need to insert a symbol. To create the equation from the previous example, you would first click the second button on the bottom row of the toolbar and choose the square root button, then type **25**. Next click the first button on the top row, choose the not equal to button, and type **10**. Last, click the fourth button on the top row and choose the division sign. Now type **2.1**. Click anywhere outside of the Editor box to commit the entry.

If you want to edit your entry before you insert it into OneNote, just double-click the equation to reopen Equation Editor.

When you're done, you'll have a nicely formatted equation in Microsoft Word. To insert this equation into OneNote, click once to select the equation object. Choose <u>C</u>opy from the <u>E</u>dit menu. Switch to OneNote and choose <u>P</u>aste from the <u>E</u>dit menu to insert the equation. Click the Paste Options Smart Tag, as shown in Figure 22.6 and choose Paste as Picture to paste the equation into OneNote as shown in Figure 22.7.

note

Equation Editor isn't always installed when you install Office. If it's not available, you can add it to your Office installation. From the Windows Control Panels, choose Add/Remove Programs. Then choose Microsoft Office and choose Change. You can add any Office feature in this manner, as long as you have your Office CD.

note

You can also right-click the equation and choose <u>E</u>dit to reopen Equation Editor.

FIGURE 22.5

You can choose a variety of mathematical symbols to create your equation.

FIGURE 22.6

Use the Paste Options Smart Tag to choose how the equation is added to OneNote.

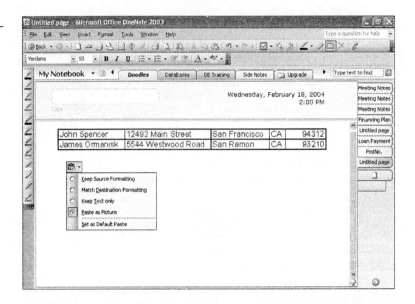

FIGURE 22.7

Insert your equation object as a picture.

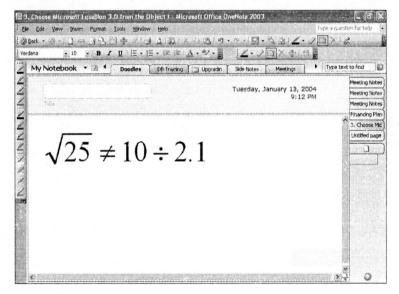

Inserting Excel Spreadsheet Components

No program in Microsoft Office has more flexibility and functionality for mathematical operations than Microsoft Excel. If you need to actually perform and display the results of calculations in your note pages, you should consider entering the equations in Microsoft Excel and then inserting the Excel spreadsheet component into OneNote. For example, you can use an Excel template to calculate a car loan and its payments, as shown in Figure 22.8.

To insert this table into OneNote, use the mouse or Tablet PC pen to select the cells to insert. Choose Copy from the Edit menu to copy the cells to the Office clipboard.

Switch to OneNote and click in a note page to create a new note container (or click within an existing note container). Choose Paste from the Edit menu to insert the data. You can use the Paste Options Smart Tag to control how the information is pasted into OneNote. The default option is to keep source formatting, as shown in Figure 22.9. While this produces text you can edit, it eliminates the cell gridlines that help keep the information readable.

When you paste content as a picture in OneNote, the picture won't be pasted in a note container unless your cursor was already positioned in a note container before you chose Paste from the Edit menu.

You don't have to insert your equation as a picture; however, often this produces a cleaner-looking object.

FIGURE 22.8

You can use an
Excel template
to calculate auto
loan payments.

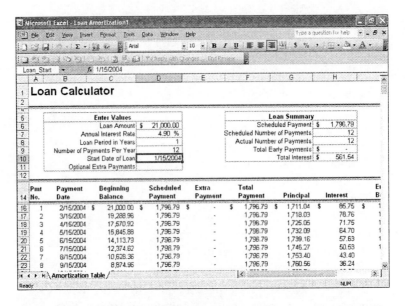

FIGURE 22.9

Pasting informa-
tion from Excel
can produce dif-
fering results.

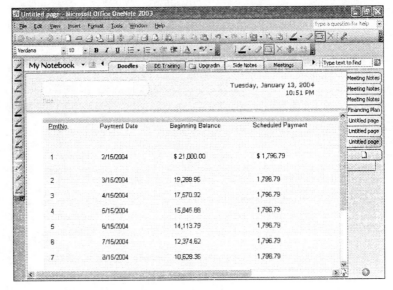

If you choose Paste as Picture from the Paste Options Smart Tag, as shown in Figure 22.10, you'll retain all of the gridlines and formatting from Excel, but you won't be able to edit the information later.

note

For more information about importing information from other programs into OneNote, see "Importing Information from Other Applications," Chapter 21.

FIGURE 22.10

Pasting Excel information as a picture retains all formatting.

Pmt No.	Payment Date	Beginning Balance	Scheduled Payment	Extra Payment	Total Payment	Principal
1	2/1/2004	$ 15,000.00	$ 448.89	$ -	$ 448.89	$ 387.64
2	3/1/2004	14,612.36	448.89	-	448.89	389.22
3	4/1/2004	14,223.14	448.89	-	448.89	390.81
4	5/1/2004	13,832.32	448.89	-	448.89	392.41
5	6/1/2004	13,439.92	448.89	-	448.89	394.01
6	7/1/2004	13,045.91	448.89	-	448.89	395.62
7	8/1/2004	12,650.29	448.89	-	448.89	397.23
8	9/1/2004	12,253.05	448.89	-	448.89	398.86
9	10/1/2004	11,854.19	448.89	-	448.89	400.49
10	11/1/2004	11,453.71	448.89	-	448.89	402.12
11	12/1/2004	11,051.59	448.89	-	448.89	403.76
12	1/1/2005	10,647.82	448.89	-	448.89	405.41
13	2/1/2005	10,242.41	448.89	-	448.89	407.07

Loan Payments

Tuesday, January 13, 2004
10:03 PM

THE ABSOLUTE MINIMUM

In this chapter you learned how to enter mathematical equations in OneNote. Although you can't perform calculations directly in OneNote, you can use several different tools to approximate these functions. You learned

- How to use symbols in OneNote to insert mathematical symbols into your notes

- How to use Microsoft Word's Equation Editor to create mathematical operations in Word that you can copy and paste into OneNote

- How to insert Microsoft Excel spreadsheet components into your OneNote pages

In the next chapter you'll learn how to share your notes with others through the use of a network share or Windows SharePoint services.

In This Chapter

- Email your notes to other users
- Publish notes to HTML
- Share notes in (almost) real time
- Use notes as a shared whiteboard

SHARING AND COLLABORATION

One of the good things about a legal pad or spiral notebook is that it's easy to share with those around you. If you're in a meeting, you can easily slide your notebook across the table to share with a colleague. However, using a notebook or legal pad makes it very difficult to share notes with those not in your immediate vicinity.

This chapter will show you how you can use OneNote to share notes between colleagues, publish the notes to the Internet, or share notes in almost real time with other users using a SharePoint site or network location.

Emailing Notes

One of the simplest ways to share information between users is through email. There are several ways you can share notes via email in OneNote 2003. If you have Outlook 2003 installed, you can share notes within an email message. If you don't have Outlook 2003, you can still email OneNote files much like you can email Word documents or Excel spreadsheets.

Sending a Note by Using Outlook 2003

You can send a note page by using Outlook 2003 in several simple steps.

1. Choose the note page by selecting its page tab.

2. Select **File**, **E-mail** to display a screen like the one shown in Figure 23.1.

FIGURE 23.1

You can send a OneNote page embedded within an email.

3. Click the **To** button to display the email address book, as shown in Figure 23.2.

4. Double-click to choose a recipient for your email message. Alternatively, select the recipient and click either the **To**, **CC**, or **BCC** buttons to add the recipient to the specified address field.

FIGURE 23.2

Choose a recipient from your Contacts folder or Global Address List.

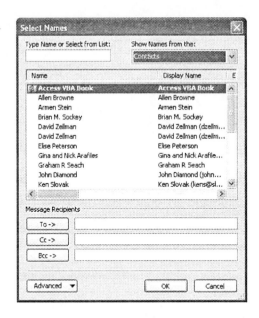

5. Click **OK** when you're done adding recipients to your email message.

6. When you return to the email message, the cursor is placed in the Introduction field. You can type a short introduction to your email for your recipients.

7. When you're done composing your introduction, click **Send a Copy**.

When your recipient receives your emailed page, it will look similar to Figure 23.3.

note

You don't have to select an address from your address book. You can simply type the email address in the To, Cc or Bcc fields.

FIGURE 23.3
Your recipient
will receive the
OneNote file
attached and
embedded in the
email.

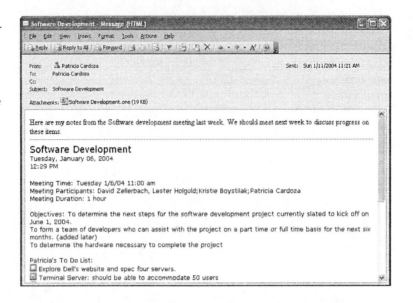

As you can see from the figure, the OneNote file is
included in two ways. First, the text of the note is
included in the body of the email message. Second,
the .one file is attached to the email.

Viewing Emailed Notes in OneNote

If you receive an emailed OneNote file, as in the
previous figure, you can open the attached .one file
by double-clicking it. Outlook asks you if you want
to open or save the file. If you choose to open the
file, it is displayed in a separate folder within
OneNote as shown in Figure 23.4.

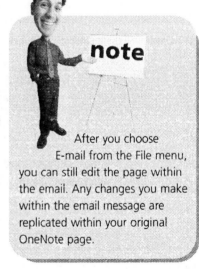

After you choose
E-mail from the File menu,
you can still edit the page within
the email. Any changes you make
within the email message are
replicated within your original
OneNote page.

Any notes you receive via email are stored in a separate folder, Notes E-mailed to Me. You can view and edit those files just like any other files in OneNote. Even if you already have a copy of the same .one file stored somewhere else in OneNote, the emailed .one file is stored in a separate folder.

When you receive and open a .one file contained within an email, the emailed page is displayed in its own section, called Software Development. Each emailed note page is stored in its own section within the Notes E-mailed to Me folder.

If you don't have OneNote installed on your computer, you'll still be able to view the OneNote content displayed within the message, but you won't be able to double-click and open the .one file.

Customizing the OneNote Email Signature

If you scroll to the bottom of an emailed note, as shown in Figure 23.5, there's a signature included by default with all emailed notes.

FIGURE 23.4

Notes you receive through email are displayed in a separate folder within OneNote.

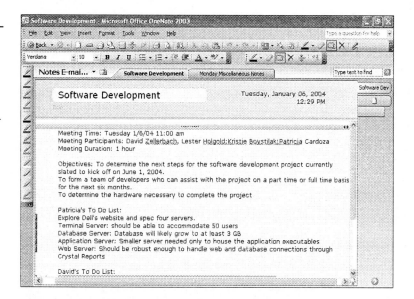

FIGURE 23.5

All emailed notes have an included signature.

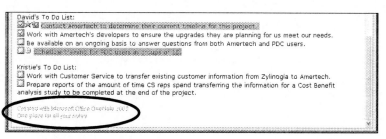

You can change that signature from OneNote's Options dialog. To hide or change the signature, use the following steps.

1. Select **Tools**, **Options** to display the Options window.

2. Choose **E-mail** from the **Category** list to display Figure 23.6.

FIGURE 23.6

You can change the signature included with OneNote emails.

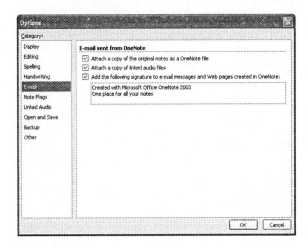

3. If you want to change the signature, you can edit the signature in the box provided.

4. To remove the signature entirely, uncheck the box marked **Add the following signature to e-mail messages and Web pages created in OneNote**.

5. When you're done editing or removing the signature, click **OK** to save your changes.

Changing the Way OneNote Handles Emailed Notes

There are two other options you can control through OneNote's E-mail Options dialog. You can prevent a copy of the .one file from being included in your email. From within the E-mail Options dialog, uncheck the box marked Attach a copy of the original notes as a OneNote file. If you do this, recipients will not receive the .one file with the email.

If you remove the .one file from the email message, you're preventing the recipient from actually opening the page within OneNote. The page won't appear in your recipient's Notes E-mailed to Me folder, and they won't be able to edit the note page. For example, in Figure 23.7, the note page has several check boxes included as part of a To Do list.

FIGURE 23.7

Your recipient
can still view the
OneNote content
if the .one file
isn't included.

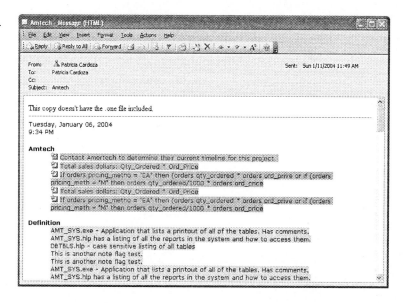

Even if the recipient chooses <u>E</u>dit Message from the message's <u>E</u>dit menu, they can't mark the check boxes as complete. They can edit the text of the message, but short of copying and pasting the entire content, there's no intuitive way to bring the note text back into OneNote.

The last option you can control when emailing notes is the inclusion of linked audio files. As discussed in Chapter 17, "It's Too Quiet in Here—Let's Add Some Sound," you can record audio notes in OneNote if your computer has a microphone. By default, when you email a OneNote page that contains a linked audio file, that file isn't included with the page. You'll still see a reference to the audio recording in the page, as shown in Figure 23.8, however hovering the mouse over the reference won't display the clickable speaker icon you can use to play the audio recording.

tip

You should only remove the .one file from an email if your recipient doesn't have OneNote.

FIGURE 23.8
By default,
linked audio
files aren't
included in your
emailed notes.

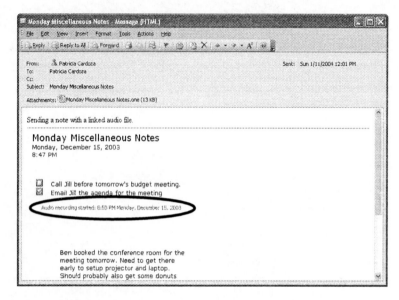

If you want OneNote to include linked audio files when you email notes, check the box marked Attach a copy of linked audio files in the E-mail Options dialog box. Now when you email a note to another user, two attachments are included with the note, as shown in Figure 23.9.

FIGURE 23.9
When you
include linked
audio files, both
the .one file and
the audio file
are attached to
the email.

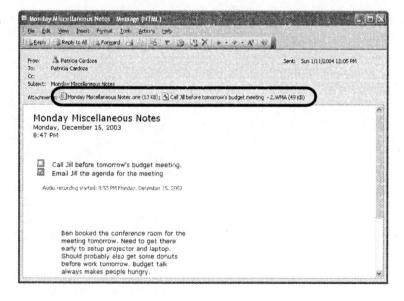

Sending Notes via Email Without Outlook 2003

If you don't have Outlook 2003, you can still share OneNote notes with others. However, you won't be able to use the E-mail command from OneNote's File menu. You'll need to attach the .one file to your email message much like any other type of file.

If you email the .one file, you're actually emailing an entire section to another user. Individual pages aren't stored as files within Windows. If you need to email just one page to another user, there are several ways you can accomplish this.

The recipient will have to double-click the attached .WMA file to play the audio recording. Unlike within OneNote, they can't just click on the link to the audio recording.

- Publish the note page to HTML
- Copy all of the text on the page and paste it into Word or another word processing program
- Move the page to its own new section, and then email the one-page section to another user

If you want to move the note page (or a copy of the page) to a new section, use the following steps.

We covered exporting OneNote note containers into Word in Chapter 20, "Office 2003 Integration." We'll cover publishing the note page to a single Web page later in this chapter.

1. Right-click the note page's tab on the right side of the OneNote screen.
2. Choose **Move Page To** from the context menu.
3. Select **Another Section** to display the Move or Copy Pages dialog box (see Figure 23.10).
4. Choose **Create New Section**, enter a section name, and then click **OK**.
5. You can choose either the Move or Copy button to move your page.

Once you have a new section, you can attach the new section's .one file to an email message.

FIGURE 23.10

You can move a
copy of a page
to a new section.

Emailing OneNote Files to Non-OneNote Users

If the recipient of your email message has OneNote 2003, they'll be able to open the attached .one file directly in OneNote. If they don't have OneNote 2003, however, they won't be able to open the .one file.

When your recipient views the email, if you haven't attached the .one file, they'll see something similar to Figure 23.11.

FIGURE 23.11

Even a non-
OneNote user
can view notes.

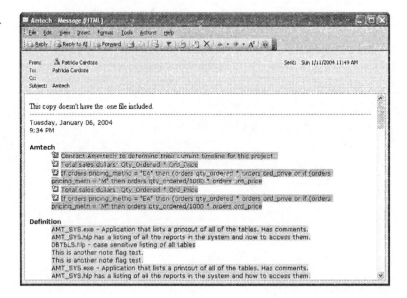

Saving Notes As Web Pages

OneNote 2003 includes the ability to save notes to a Web page format. You can then include them on a Web server or email them to others.

The format OneNote uses for its Web page files isn't true HTML. It's actually an .mht file (a file type Microsoft developed to include both text and graphics in the same file). This file views quite well in Internet Explorer, but doesn't always display properly in other browsers such as Netscape or Mozilla.

To save the file as a Web page, do the following:

1. Choose **File**, **Save As** to display the dialog shown in Figure 23.12.

note

If you include the .one file in your email to a non-OneNote user, they won't be able to open it. However, they can still view the note page details within the email message.

FIGURE 23.12

You can choose a file location and file type.

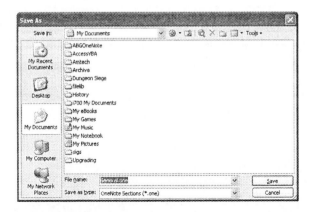

2. Use the **Save as type** drop-down to choose **Single File Web Page (Publish a Copy)(*.mht)**.

3. Type a name for your file in the **File name** box and click **Save**.

When you view your page in Internet Explorer, it will look something like Figure 23.13.

As you can see from the figure, there are some elements from OneNote that don't translate perfectly. In particular, highlighting can often appear off center in an .mht file, and audio files aren't included in the Web page. At the bottom of the Web page, you'll find the same text that appears when you email a OneNote page. By default that text is "Created with Microsoft Office OneNote 2003. One place for all your notes."

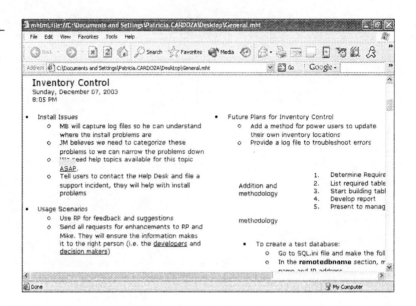

As previously mentioned, OneNote .mht files don't always display well in alternate browsers. In particular, images aren't included reliably, and fonts can sometimes appear wrong.

Publishing Notes to the Web

In addition to saving notes to Web pages, you can also publish notes to Web pages as well. There's one key difference between publishing notes to Web pages and saving notes to a Web page. When you save a note to a single Web page file, you're saving all pages within the active section to the file. When you publish your notes to a Web page, you're only publishing the currently active page.

You can publish to a file on your desktop or to a Web server. To publish a file, use the following steps.

1. Choose **File**, **Publish Pages**.

2. Type a name for your file (the name defaults to the name of the current page).

3. Click **Publish**.

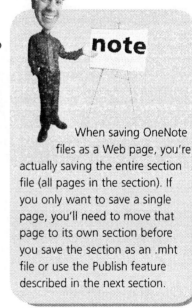

note

When saving OneNote files as a Web page, you're actually saving the entire section file (all pages in the section). If you only want to save a single page, you'll need to move that page to its own section before you save the section as an .mht file or use the Publish feature described in the next section.

A published page looks almost identical to a section saved as an .mht file. The only difference is that when you save as an .mht file, you see the entire section (all pages). Publishing only chooses the currently selected page.

Collaborating with Others

There are several ways you can use OneNote to collaborate with others. You can put a section (a .one file) in a network location where multiple users can access it. You can save a .one file to a SharePoint site and make it accessible for multiple users. You can also use OneNote as a type of shared whiteboard.

Locking Notes for Editing

A frequently requested feature for OneNote (and other programs) is to be able to have multiple users work on the same document in real-time. OneNote doesn't quite support that functionality, but it comes close. Two users can have a .one file open at the same time. Unfortunately, only one user can make changes to a OneNote file at a time. When the first user opens the .one file for editing, a lock is placed on the file. This lock allows another user to open the file for viewing, but not for editing. In order for the second user to edit the file, the lock must be released.

By default, OneNote locks a file for five minutes. This means that if Joe opens a OneNote file and makes changes to it, Sally can't open the file for editing until five minutes after Joe's last change. Sally can view the file, and she'll see all of Joe's changes within five minutes of when he makes them.

If Joe doesn't make changes for five minutes, the file lock is released. Sally can then make her own changes. If Joe attempts to make changes at that time, he can't, because Sally has locked the file. Five minutes after Sally's last change, the file lock is released again, Joe will see Sally's changes, and he can make changes again.

You can change the number of minutes OneNote locks a file for editing.

1. Choose **Tools**, **Options** to display the Options dialog box.

2. Choose **Open and Save** from the **Category** list to display Figure 23.14.

note

In order for the file lock to be released, Sally and Joe must not make changes to any OneNote page in the current section. The OneNote section must remain inactive for the file lock to be released.

FIGURE 23.14

You can config-
ure the number
of minutes
OneNote holds a
file lock.

3. In the **Accessing files from multiple
   locations** section, enter a number
   between 1 and 99999 for the number of
   minutes OneNote waits before releasing a
   file lock.

4. Click **OK** to save your changes.

Merging Edits Between Multiple Users

When two users open the same .one file, the
words (Read Only) appear in the title bar for the
OneNote application. If two users (for instance,
Sally and Joe) are using OneNote to make
changes to the same page or section, there has to
be a way for changes to be merged between users.

In order for Sally to view Joe's changes, all she has to do is wait.
After the specified number of minutes, Joe's
changes will appear and the (Read Only) caption
in the title bar disappears.

Figuring out which user has access to the .one file
can be rather complicated. If both Sally and Joe
have OneNote open as the active application,

tip

You can't set the file locking interval to 0. If you need
to have two users accessing
the same .one file, it's best to
leave the file locking interval
somewhere around two or
three minutes. One minute
can often be too short as the
other user might just be thinking
of something to type.

caution

When you change the
file locking interval, the
change won't apply
until you close and then
reopen the OneNote
application.

control of the .one file will reside with the user who opened the file first. The trick to collaborating with OneNote is that the shared section must be inactive for the number of minutes specified in the Options dialog box before the file locks release themselves. If Sally opens the file first, makes changes, and then leaves OneNote as the active window on her computer with the shared section displayed, Joe won't ever be able to edit the file. If, however, Sally switches sections or minimizes the OneNote window (or her screen-saver kicks in), Joe will be able to access the file.

> **tip**
>
> If you think enough time has passed and the changes don't show up on your copy of the shared page, try clicking another section and clicking back. Sometimes this is enough to refresh OneNote's view.

When a file lock is released and updates are made visible to both users, there's no fanfare or indication that the file has changed. If you're sharing a OneNote file with another user, it might be best to have some indication of what's changed. You can have each user type or write in a different color, or put their initials next to any new notes. This way, each user is aware of the information the other user added to the note page.

Using OneNote As a Shared Whiteboard

As the previous section alluded to, it's possible to use OneNote as a shared whiteboard. If you need to use OneNote in this manner, consider reducing the file locking interval to a very small interval, maybe two or three minutes. This short amount of time should be long enough to prevent control from being released too soon (such as if a user is merely thinking about what they want to type) while short enough to not make collaboration a painfully slow process.

In Figures 23.15 and 23.16, you can see two versions of the same OneNote page. The first version is Sally's OneNote page with some diagrams and text. The second figure is Joe's version of the same OneNote page after he's made some changes to it. In these examples, each user has made changes in their own color and left notes for each other on what has been done to the page. This can be an effective method of collaboration for colleagues in separate locations.

FIGURE 23.15
Sally can start
the collabora-
tion.

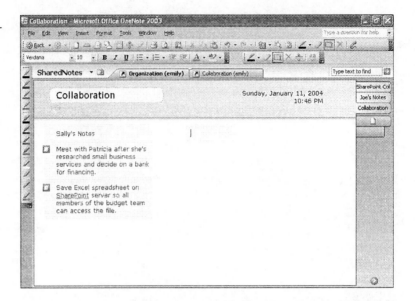

FIGURE 23.16
Joe can add his
own notes and
text.

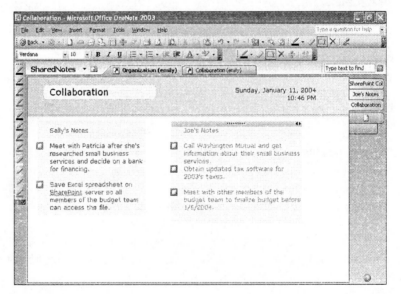

Using OneNote with SharePoint Team Services

SharePoint Team Services and SharePoint Portal Server are two products from
Microsoft designed to facilitate document sharing and collaboration. You can save
your OneNote section files to a SharePoint Portal Server or SharePoint Team Services
Web site using the following steps.

1. Navigate to the section you want to save on your SharePoint site.

2. Choose **File**, **Save As** to launch the Save As dialog in OneNote.

3. Choose **My Network Places** from the left pane.

4. Find and double-click the SharePoint site you have access to. You can usually access a SharePoint site with the address of `http://sitename/foldername`. Check with your systems administrator to find out the name of your SharePoint site.

5. Choose the **Document Library**, as shown in Figure 23.17.

FIGURE 23.17

Choose the Document Library you need from your SharePoint site.

6. Type a name for your OneNote section (or accept the default) and click **Save**.

Your section is now stored on your SharePoint site. When you open a section stored on a SharePoint site, it opens with the SharePoint Workspace Task pane, as shown in Figure 23.18.

You can use the Shared Workspace task pane for a variety of purposes. It shows the following information:

■ Members—All users who subscribe to your SharePoint site are listed, along with their online status. New members can be added, and email can be sent to all members through this pane.

■ Tasks—You can create tasks that all users can access. Members of the Shared Workspace can add new tasks or edit existing tasks.

note

The Shared Workspace task pane won't appear unless you've opened or saved a document from a Shared Workspace.

■ Documents—All OneNote section files as well as any other document types are listed in this view. You can change the sort order, add a new document or even add a new folder for documents.

■ Links—Members of the Shared Workspace can add external links to the site.

FIGURE 23.18

Opening a page on a SharePoint site displays the Shared Workspace task pane.

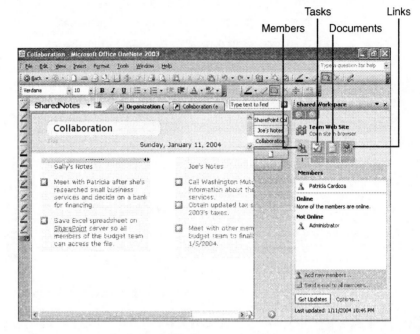

You can click the Get Updates button to refresh the data in the Shared Workspace task pane. If you suspect that another user has added information, documents, or tasks to the SharePoint site, click the Get Updates button. Any updated information will be transferred to your local computer.

There are several options you can configure through the Options hyperlink at the bottom of the Shared Workspace task pane as shown in Figure 23.19.

The Service Options dialog box allows you to configure several options for how OneNote (or any other Office program) deals with information stored on the site. If you don't want to display the Shared Workspace task pane when opening a document stored on a Shared Workspace, uncheck the box marked The document is part of a workspace or SharePoint site.

FIGURE 23.19

You can change some of the options for your SharePoint site.

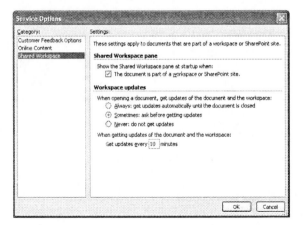

You can also configure how often updates are downloaded from the SharePoint site. By default, OneNote will ask you if you want to get updates to the document; however, you can choose to always get updates or to never get updates. If you either choose Always or Sometimes, OneNote will check for updates every 10 minutes. To change this interval, type a value between 1 and 999 minutes.

To save your changes to the service options, click OK. Using a SharePoint site to store .one files can be an easy way to allow multiple users access to a variety of OneNote sections.

caution

When viewing pages on a Shared Workspace, users are subjected to the same file-locking issues as when opening a OneNote file on a network share.

THE ABSOLUTE MINIMUM

In this chapter you learned about a variety of OneNote's collaborative features. You learned

- How to email your notes to others and how to customize the way OneNote handles the notes you send via email
- How to publish a single page or an entire section as a Web page
- How you can use OneNote as a collaborative tool and share information with users in almost real-time
- How to merge information from two different users in a single OneNote page or section

Using these collaborative features, you can further enhance your note-taking experience. You can take notes and access them from a variety of locations and share them with others inside and outside your organization.

A

KEYBOARD SHORTCUTS

OneNote Shortcuts

This appendix lists a variety of keyboard shortcuts for working within OneNote. There are shortcuts for editing content, moving around in pages, and opening and closing OneNote files.

Shortcuts for Entering and Changing Content

Table A.1 lists the various shortcuts you can use to enter and edit the content within your OneNote pages. Many of these shortcuts operate the same within any Microsoft Office 2003 System program.

> **note**
>
> Some of these short-cuts include symbols that are available on the numeric keypad. However, the shortcuts won't work if you're using the symbols on the numeric keypad. Use the symbols elsewhere on the keyboard. In other words, to use the + symbol in a shortcut, use the one on the same key as the = symbol, not the one on the numeric keypad.

TABLE A.1   Shortcuts for Editing Content

Shortcut	Description
Ctrl+A	Select all text and ink on a page
Ctrl+X	Cut the active selection to the clipboard
Ctrl+C or Ctrl+INS	Copy the selection to the clipboard
Ctrl+V or Shift+INS	Paste the contents of the clipboard at the insertion point
Ctrl+Z or Alt+Backspace	Undo the last action
Ctrl+Y or Alt+Shift+Backspace	Redo the last action
ESC	Cancel selection of the current page or selection
Insert	Turn overstrike mode on or off
Alt+Shift+Up Arrow	Move selection up
Alt+Shift+Down Arrow	Move selection down
Alt+Shift+Left Arrow	Move selection to the left
Alt+Shift+Right Arrow	Move selection to the right
Ctrl+Shift+-	Select the current paragraph and subordinate paragraphs
Alt+I,N	Add or remove space on the page
Shift+Delete	Permanently delete the selection (when one or more pages are selected)

Text Formatting Shortcuts

Within any Office application, there are a handful of shortcuts that allow you to format your selected text quickly. Those shortcuts are listed in Table A.2.

TABLE A.2   Shortcuts for Formatting Text

Shortcut	Description
Ctrl+B	Bold
Ctrl+I	Italic
Ctrl+U	Underline
Ctrl+-	Strikethrough
Ctrl+=	Subscript
Ctrl+Shift++ (plus sign)	Superscript
Ctrl+L	Left justify
Ctrl+E	Center
Ctrl+R	Right justify

Working with OneNote Pages

The shortcuts listed in Table A.3 are unique to OneNote. They allow you to work with the various pages in OneNote, adding, moving, and manipulating your pages.

TABLE A.3   Shortcuts for Working with Pages

Shortcut	Description
Ctrl+N	Add a new page at the end of the section
Ctrl+Shift+N	Add a new subpage to the current page group
Ctrl+Shift+A	Select the current page
Alt+Shift+Up Arrow	Move the selected page tab up
Atl+Shift+Down Arrow	Move the selected page tab down
Ctrl+T	Move the insertion point to or away from the page header
Ctrl+Shift+. (period)	Increase the size of the page header
Ctrl+Shift+, (comma)	Reduce the size of the page header
Alt+Ctrl+X	Increase or reduce the size of the page header
Ctrl+PageUp	Go to the previous page in the section
Ctrl+PageDown	Go to the next page in the section
Alt+Home	Go to the first page in the section

TABLE A.3 (continued)

Shortcut	Description
Alt+End	Go to the last page in the section
Alt+PageUp	Go to the first page of the currently displayed set of pages
Alt+PageDown	Go to the last page of the currently displayed set of pages
PageUp	Scroll up the current page
PageDown	Scroll down the current page
Ctrl+Home	Scroll to the top of the current page
Ctrl+End	Scroll to the end of the current page
Ctrl+Down Arrow	Go to the next paragraph in a note container
Ctrl+Up Arrow	Go to the previous paragraph in a note container
Ctrl+Alt+Up Arrow	Move the insertion point up in the current page or expand the page up
Ctrl+Alt+Down Arrow	Move the insertion point down in the current page or expand the page down
Ctrl+Alt+Left Arrow	Move the insertion point left in the current page or expand the page left
Ctrl+Alt+Right Arrow	Move the insertion point right in the current page or expand the page right
Alt+Down Arrow	Move to the next note container
Home	Go to the beginning of the line
End	Go to the end of the line
Alt+Left Arrow	Return to the last page visited
Alt+Right Arrow	Go forward to the next page
Alt+Ctrl+Shift++	Zoom in
Alt+Ctrl+Shift+-	Zoom out

Working Within Notebooks

The shortcuts listed in Table A.4 allow you to navigate and manipulate data within notebooks.

TABLE A.4   Shortcuts for Working Within Notebooks

Shortcut	Description
Ctrl+O	Open a section
Ctrl+Shift+G	Open a menu of folders and sections in the parent folder
Ctrl+P	Print
Ctrl+Tab	Go to the next section
Ctrl+Shift+Tab	Go to the previous section

Shortcuts for Flagging Notes

The keyboard shortcuts listed in Table A.5 flag notes within pages.

TABLE A.5   Shortcuts for Flagging Notes

Shortcut	Description
Ctrl+1	Apply the To Do flag
Ctrl+2	Apply the Important flag
Ctrl+3	Apply the Question flag
Ctrl+4	Apply the Remember for Later flag
Ctrl+5	Apply the Definition flag
Ctrl+6, Ctrl+7, Ctrl+8, Ctrl+9	Apply a particular custom flag you create
Ctrl+0	Remove all Note Flags from the current selection
Ctrl+Shift+K	Create a Microsoft Office Outlook 2003 task

Shortcuts for Using Lists and Outlines

The keyboard shortcuts listed in Table A.6 allow you to create lists and outlines within OneNote.

TABLE A.6   Shortcuts for Using Lists and Outlines

Shortcut	Description
Ctrl+/ or Ctrl+Shift+O	Create a numbered list
Ctrl+. or Ctrl+Shift+L	Create a bulleted list
Alt+Shift+1	Displays the current group in the outline through Level 1
Alt+Shift+2	Displays through Level 2
Alt+Shift+3 through Alt+Shift+9	Displays Levels 3 through 9

TABLE A.6   (continued)

Shortcut	Description
Alt+Shift+0	Expand all levels
Shift+Tab or Alt+Shift+Left Arrow	Decrease indenting by one level
Tab or Alt+Shift+Right Arrow	Increase indenting by one level
Ctrl+Shift+0	Remove from outline and make body text

Other Miscellaneous Shortcuts

The shortcuts listed in Table A.7 allow you to perform a variety of additional tasks within OneNote.

TABLE A.7   Miscellaneous Shortcuts

Shortcut	Description
Ctrl+Shift+E	Create a new email message in Microsoft Office Outlook 2003
Ctrl+F	Move the cursor to the Find box
Enter	While the Page List task pane is displaying search results, this moves to the next search result
Ctrl+M	Open a new OneNote window if OneNote is already open
Windows Key+N	Opens a new Side Note if OneNote is closed but the tray icon is visible
Windows Key+Shift+N	Opens OneNote if it's closed (but the tray icon is still visible)
Ctrl+Shift+M	Opens a small OneNote window for Side Notes when OneNote is already open

OneNote Resources and Help

OneNote is a relatively new program, but that doesn't mean there aren't a variety of resources you can use if you need help. You can obtain help from the Microsoft newsgroups, the Internet, and Microsoft Product Support Services.

Accessing the Microsoft Newsgroups

A newsgroup is a collection of messages on a particular topic. These messages are submitted to the news server by users. The questions asked by some users are answered by others. You can view newsgroups in a news reader (a piece of software such as Outlook Express or Opera) or on the Internet.

Using Web-based Newsgroups

To access the official Microsoft newsgroups on the Internet, use the following steps.

1. Open your Internet browser and navigate to
   `http://support.microsoft.com/newsgroups/default.aspx`.

2. Once you've chosen a language, you'll see an entry for each category of Microsoft software. Click the plus sign next to the category to expand the category. To find Microsoft OneNote, click the plus sign next to Office. Scroll down to the OneNote entry and click the plus sign.

3. Click OneNote General Questions to display Figure B.1.

FIGURE B.1

You can view the existing questions in the newsgroup or ask a new question through the Web interface.

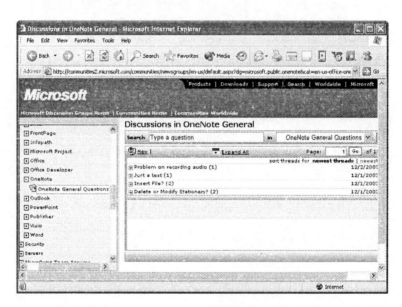

To ask a new question, click the New button to display Figure B.2. Type your question and click Send.

Accessing the Newsgroups from a Newsreader

If you have a newsreader such as Outlook Express on your computer, you can download existing messages and send new messages through Outlook Express. To add the Microsoft newsgroups to your Outlook Express installation, use the following steps.

1. Select **Accounts** from the **Tools** menu.

2. Click **Add**, **News**.

3. Enter a display name for your news account. This name can be as simple as "Anonymous." You should never use your email address as your display name. Click **Next**.

4. Enter an email address for use in the newsgroups and click **Next**.

5. Enter the NNTP (network news transfer protocol) server for the Microsoft newsgroups. The server you should enter is `msnews.microsoft.com`. Leave the **My news server requires me to log on** check box unchecked. Click **Next**.

6. Click **Finish** to complete your newsgroup setup and click **Close** from the Accounts dialog.

tip

When asking a question in the newsgroups, it's helpful to always include your operating system version as well as the specific build number of OneNote you're using. You can find the build number by selecting Help, About Microsoft Office OneNote while in OneNote. The build number is usually in the format of (11.5510.5606) .

When you click Close, you'll be prompted to download newsgroups from the news server. Choose Yes to download newsgroups. You'll see all 1,500+ newsgroups in the Newsgroup Subscriptions dialog. To narrow down your search, type the name of the program you need assistance with in the Display newsgroups which contain text box. The list is case sensitive and no capitals are used in newsgroup names, so for OneNote newsgroups, enter onenote. Double-click the newsgroup name to subscribe.

When you've subscribed to newsgroups, your Outlook Express installation should look similar to Figure B.3.

To ask a question in Outlook Express, click New Post in the upper left corner of the toolbar. Click Send to send your message to the newsgroup.

tip

You should always use a fake email address for this step. If you use your real email address, it's quite possible that you'll start to receive spam (unsolicited commercial email). You can use just about anything as a fake email address. For example, if your email is john@sample.com, try changing it to john@DONTEMAILMEsample.com.

FIGURE B.3

You can subscribe to a variety of newsgroups in Outlook Express.

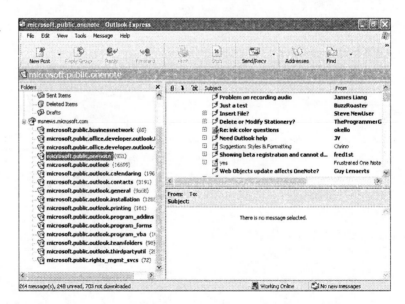

Using Microsoft Product Support Services

If you can't find your answers on the Microsoft newsgroups, you can open a personal support incident with Microsoft Product Support Services (PSS). Every Microsoft

Office product, including OneNote, comes with two free support incidents you can use to obtain help with problems. If you need additional support incidents after the first two, you can open them, but you will have to pay for each additional incident.

To open a support incident with Microsoft PSS, visit `http://support.microsoft.com` and choose Contact Microsoft. You can choose to open an incident via telephone or online.

Other Support Options

In addition to newsgroups and Microsoft Product Support Services, you can search a variety of other Web sites for information about OneNote. Some Web sites I recommend are

- Google—Visit `www.google.com` to search the Web for OneNote information.
- OneNote FAQ—OneNote MVP Ben Schorr has an extensive OneNote Frequently Asked Question page at
  `http://home.hawaii.rr.com/schorr/Computers/OneNoteFAQ.htm`.
- Microsoft's OneNote Info Center—Microsoft has compiled a variety of helpful resources for OneNote located at
  `http://support.microsoft.com/default.aspx?scid=fh;EN-US;1note2003`.

C

OneNote System Requirements and Installation

Generally, Microsoft programs are incredibly easy to install. All you have to do is put the CD in the CD drive, wait for the CD to autoplay, and click the Install button. OneNote isn't that much different. However, before you install OneNote, make sure your computer meets at least the minimum system requirements. For optimum performance, your computer should meet the recommended system requirements as well.

If you've already installed OneNote, or it came preinstalled on your laptop or Tablet PC, you can skip this appendix. We'll cover the minimum system requirements for OneNote, as well as installation instructions.

OneNote Minimum System Requirements

Before you install OneNote on your computer, be sure your computer meets the minimum system requirements that are outlined in Table C.1. These requirements apply whether you're on a Tablet PC, desktop, or laptop.

TABLE C.1   OneNote Minimum System Requirements

Component	Requirement
Processor	Intel Pentium 133 megahertz or higher
Memory	64MB RAM plus 8MB for every open application
Hard Drive	245MB available free space for typical installation (includes 130MB of temporary space needed for installation)
Media Drives	CD-ROM or DVD drive
Audio Devices (for recording and playback of audio notes)	Microphone, speakers, Windows Media Player 8.0 or later, and Microsoft DirectX 8.1 or later
Display	Super VGA (800 × 600) or higher resolution
Operating System	Windows 2000 SP3 or higher OR Windows XP

OneNote Recommended System Requirements

Keep in mind that Table C.1 lists the minimum system requirements. A computer with those specifications will definitely run OneNote, but might not run it well (particularly if you're trying to run more than just one application at a time). If you want to ensure that OneNote runs well on your computer, consider installing OneNote on a computer with at least the requirements outlined in Table C.2.

note

You'll notice some of the requirements are the same in both tables. Typically, the two components that have the greatest effect on system performance are processor speed and RAM.

TABLE C.2   OneNote Recommended System Requirements

Component	Requirement
Processor	Pentium III Processor
Memory	128MB RAM plus 8MB RAM for each open application
Hard drive	Up to 280MB available free space for a complete installation
Media drives	CD-ROM or DVD drive
Audio devices (for recording and playback of audio notes)	Microphone, speakers, Windows Media Player 9 or later, and Microsoft DirectX 9.0a or later
Display	Super VGA (800 × 600) or higher resolution
Operating system	Windows 2000 SP3 or higher OR Windows XP

Installing OneNote on Your Computer

Microsoft Office OneNote is available as a standalone product. To install OneNote on your computer, use the following steps.

1. Close all open programs on your computer. Open programs can sometimes lock certain files and prevent them from updating properly.

2. Insert the OneNote CD in your computer's CD or DVD drive. The CD should autoplay and display the Microsoft Office OneNote 2003 Installation Wizard.

3. Enter your 25 character product key for OneNote. You can find the product key on the back of OneNote's CD case or on the Certificate of Authenticity. When you've entered the product key, click **Next** to display Figure C.1.

4. Enter your full name, your initials, and the name of your organization. Your name and organization are displayed on the splash screen each time you launch the application. Click **Next**.

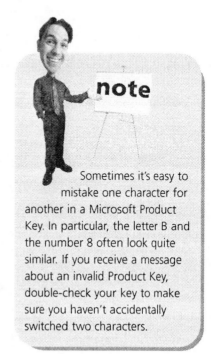

note

Sometimes it's easy to mistake one character for another in a Microsoft Product Key. In particular, the letter B and the number 8 often look quite similar. If you receive a message about an invalid Product Key, double-check your key to make sure you haven't accidentally switched two characters.

FIGURE C.1

Enter your name, initials, and organization carefully; you'll see them each time you launch OneNote.

5. You must accept the End-User License Agreement (EULA) before installation can proceed. Check the box marked **I accept the terms in the License Agreement** and click **Next** to display Figure C.2.

FIGURE C.2

You can choose from three pre-configured installation types or choose a custom installation.

6. You can choose from three installation types or choose a custom installation. Choosing a Custom Install displays Figure C.3. The different installation types are

▓ **Typical Install**—The most commonly used OneNote components are installed. Some advanced components, such as certain stationery, are not installed. These components are either installed when first used (requiring the CD) or can be installed through the Add/Remove Programs function within Control Panel.

▓ **Complete Install**—All components of OneNote are installed. This option requires the most space on the hard drive but minimizes future requirements for the OneNote CD.

▓ **Minimal Install**—Only the minimum required components are installed. Templates, stationery, and other advanced features are not installed. This installation type is only recommended if you have very little free hard drive space.

▓ **Custom Install**—Selecting this option allows the user to choose which components are installed.

FIGURE C.3

You can choose which components to install.

7. A component with a dark gray icon, such as the Office Shared Features icon in Figure C.3, contains some components selected for installation and other components not selected for installation. To view subcomponents, click the plus sign next to the component name. To install a component, click the small down arrow next to the name of the component and select either **Run from My Computer** (installs the selected component only) or **Run all from My Computer** (installs the selected component and all subcomponents). You can prevent a component's installation by selecting Not Available. Click **Next** when you're done customizing your installation.

8. On the next screen all you'll see is merely a confirmation screen. To install OneNote, click **Install**. You'll see an installation screen with a progress bar. This screen might display for several minutes while OneNote 2003 is installed.

9. When the installation completes, a confirmation screen is displayed. You can select the check box to **Check the Web for updates and additional downloads**. While not required, this is often a good idea in case service packs or patches have been released for OneNote. When you're done, click **Finish**.

You're now ready to begin using OneNote 2003!

There's another installation option you can choose—Install on First Use. Choosing this option installs the selected component the first time it's needed. While this can be a good way to save space, it does require you have the installation CD handy if you ever try to use a component that's not already installed.

When installing OneNote, you don't need to install the optional components such as Handwriting Fonts, Tours, or some Help components. You can also leave out some of the Office Shared Features such as Proofing Tools.

THE FUTURE OF ONENOTE

OneNote: Future Plans

This is the first version of Microsoft OneNote that's been released. OneNote is a unique type of program. Before the release of OneNote and the Windows Journal application for the Tablet PC, there really were not any good Microsoft options for note-taking programs. Note takers were limited to Microsoft Word, WordPad, NotePad, or a Pocket PC device with a variety of programs (such as Pocket Word or Notes). There were a handful of other third-party note-taking applications on the market, but none that utilized the Tablet PC's inking capabilities as well as OneNote. OneNote and the Windows Journal application changed the face of note taking. The Windows Journal was the first of these new types of note-taking applications, but OneNote improved upon the capabilities of the Windows Journal by adding rich multimedia capabilities and offering the possibility for some basic integration with other Office applications.

For the first time, users could integrate handwriting, drawing, audio, video, and online content. With OneNote, users can create detailed multilevel outlines, add pictures, and content from Web pages, and more.

OneNote Features—Users Want More

OneNote has many helpful features, but the product is still in its first version. Microsoft performs many usability studies when creating a new product or a new version of an existing product. However, no study can identify all of the ideal features for any application. In addition, the development cycle for any product must always include a decision about certain features to include and others to exclude due to time constraints. This appendix will briefly cover some of the often-requested features for OneNote as well as provide some speculation as to where the product might be going in the future.

If any of the features discussed in this appendix interest you, or if you have additional feature requests you'd like to see in future versions of OneNote, send an email to mswish@microsoft.com. Use a subject line of OneNote. This is the proper email address for all feature requests for Microsoft software. The emails are read and categorized and your suggestion will be read.

Pocket PC Integration

Pocket PCs are everywhere these days. Whether for business, school, or personal use, they are steadily gaining popularity. Many handheld users take notes during classes or meetings with their Pocket PC. An often-requested addition to OneNote is the ability to take OneNote notes on a Pocket PC device.

XML and SmartTags

All other Microsoft Office programs (including Outlook and PowerPoint) now support XML and SmartTags. The first version of OneNote does not provide support for either technology. It's possible that future versions of OneNote will provide this functionality.

Linking One OneNote Item to Another

In Word, you can create links to other Word documents or Excel files. You can also create a link to a specific bookmark within another Word file. The only linking you can do within OneNote is to link one section to another through the use of a hyperlink. As you can see from Figure D.1, you can insert a hyperlink to the General section from the Doodles section. However, if the General section contains more than one page, clicking the hyperlink will take you to the last viewed page within the General section. There's no way to link to a particular page or particular note container within the General section.

FIGURE D.1

You can link to one section from another.

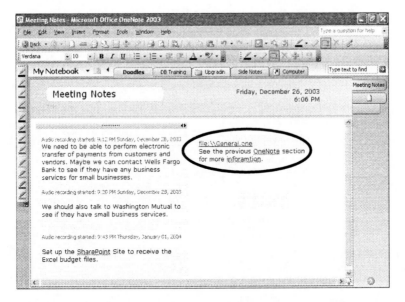

Integrating Other Programs with OneNote

Many users are content to use some or all of the Microsoft Office programs in isolation. They never export from Outlook to Excel or perform mail merges in Word. However, if you like to make multiple Office programs work together, you're probably wondering why you can't do much with OneNote and other Office applications. Well, the answer is because OneNote doesn't integrate well with other programs.

There is some integration with Microsoft Outlook, but that's about all the integration you can perform with OneNote. It's likely that future versions will have the ability to easily insert an embedded Office object such as an Excel spreadsheet control or PowerPoint slide. Other enhancements include additional Outlook integration. It's possible that you'll eventually be able to create Calendar or Journal items directly from OneNote.

Adding a OneNote Object Model

From a programmer's viewpoint, OneNote is missing a critical feature—an object model. An object model is much like a dictionary for a program. It contains all of the objects, properties, and methods you can use to manipulate a program. If OneNote had an object model exposed to other applications, developers would be able to control much of the operation of OneNote from other applications such as Word, Excel, or Visual Basic.

One of the advantages of exposing an object model to developers is that users no longer have to wait for Microsoft to add every little feature to the program. Third-party developers can write programs that integrate with the Microsoft program to accomplish certain tasks. For example, in Word, there are a variety of add-ins available that take advantage of Word's object model to perform various tasks. If you buy stamps online, use an address lookup service, or even ship via UPS, you can add functionality to Microsoft Word to save time and reduce hassle.

OneNote Customization

Many of the other popular feature requests fall under the category of customization. For example, you can't create your own rule lines in OneNote. Some of the other customization requests are

- Changing background color on individual note containers
- Automatically inserting a date and time stamp whenever you begin a new note container
- Adding more Note Flags
- A fully functional Print Preview
- More ink colors and weights

Let Your Voice Be Heard

Every user of OneNote will have their own feature requests based on their usage of the program. If you have specific features you'd like to see in future versions of OneNote, be sure to email mswish@microsoft.com with a subject line of OneNote.

Index

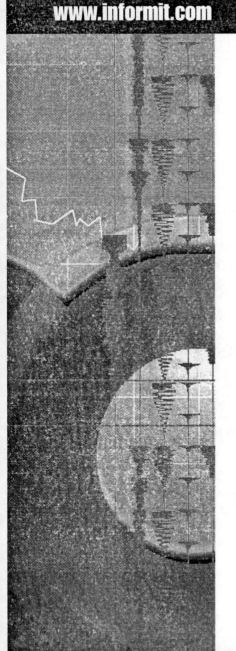